SUCCESSFUL WRITING

Second Edition

SUCCESSFUL WRITING

Second Edition

MAXINE C. HAIRSTON
The University of Texas at Austin

W. W. NORTON & COMPANY
New York   London

The text of this book is composed in Sabon, with display type set in Avant Garde Gothic. Composition by New England Typographic Service. Manufacturing by Murray Printing Company. Book design by Nancy Dale Muldoon.

Passage from A SENSE OF WHERE YOU ARE by John McPhee. Copyright © 1965, 1978 by John McPhee. Passage from LEVELS OF THE GAME by John McPhee. Copyright © 1969 by John McPhee. Reprinted by permission of Farrar, Straus and Giroux, Inc. Both passages originally appeared in *The New Yorker.*

ISBN 0-393-95416-1

W. W. Norton & Company, Inc., 500 Fifth Avenue, New York, N. Y. 10110
W. W. Norton & Company Ltd., 37 Great Russell Street, London WC1B 3NU

2 3 4 5 6 7 8 9 0

Library of Congress Cataloging-in-Publication Data
Hairston, Maxine.
    Successful writing.

    1. English language—Rhetoric.   I. Title.
PE1408.H297   1986   808'.042   86-714

CONTENTS

5 ◇ GETTING STARTED 67

6 ◇ HOLDING YOUR READER 87

7 ◇ WRITING CLEARLY   107

8 ◇ CRAFTING PARAGRAPHS 141

9 ◇ REVISING 157

Preface

From its first edition in 1981, *Successful Writing* has been an innovative text, one of the first in the field to be written specifically for writers who have mastered the basic elements of the writing process. The text assumes students who have a reasonably good command of usage and mechanics and can construct adequate sentences and paragraphs. Now they are ready to improve those writing skills and move on to learning how to adapt their writing to various audiences and purposes. They are also ready to learn more about the writing process: how to generate ideas, develop those ideas into well-crafted prose, and revise, polish, and edit that prose.

Such writers may be in second-semester or honors freshman courses or in sophomore or upper-division courses in or out of English departments. Whatever their classification or their major, in many colleges and universities they now find they are having to write more and more in all their courses, and they are also aware that they will have to continue to write when they leave college. Consequently they are motivated to try to become effective writers in their college courses, knowing that learning to write well in college will help them later in their professions.

In order to respond to this new student awareness about writing, and to meet the needs of the increasing number of professors who require writing in their courses, the second edition of *Successful Writing* has been rearranged, partially rewritten, and expanded in some sections and streamlined in others. The opening chapter is now titled "Writing in College"; it opens with a section that explains why writing is an important way of learning and it suggests strategies and guidelines students can use in order to adapt their writing to varied academic assignments. Chapter 2 explains and illustrates the elements that must be present in good writing, trying to give students a clear idea of the qualities readers expect in good prose. Chapter 3 introduces a fresh approach to understanding the writing process, pointing out that there are at least three kinds of writing and suggesting that writers may use significantly different processes in doing different kinds of writing. It also shows how those processes work and analyzes and illustrates the steps most writers go through when they compose.

Chapters 4 and 5 stress the importance of students' thinking about their readers and about their purposes every time they write and show them how to analyze each occasion for writing. They also suggest effective ways to begin different kinds of papers and point out options for exploring and developing ideas. Chapter 6, "Holding Your Reader," stresses coherence, unity, and specific ways to organize writing effectively. Chapter 7 emphasizes criteria for good word choice, ways to eliminate jargon, and organizational patterns that help the reader. It also contains a full section on sexist language: why it should be avoided and how to do so. Chapter 8 now combines material on sentences and paragraphs.

Chapter 9 on revising, a special feature of this text, stresses the difference between *global* and *local* revising and shows which strategies are appropriate for different stages of writing. It now ties the revision process to the kind of writing that a student is doing and suggests priorities for revising. New to this chapter is a student paper carried through three drafts with comments on each version. The chapter also now contains a special section about peer group revision, a section that contains guidelines for both teacher and students.

Chapter 10, "The Research Paper," has been completely rewritten and expanded to increase its value for upper-division students whose research projects may take them beyond traditional library sources. It has also been updated to include the new MLA documentation style and to explain APA documentation.

The last chapter of the book, "Writing on the Job," gives students useful pointers that they may use in some academic writing situations and later on the job when they need to write case studies, grant proposals, abstracts, and other functional documents. This chapter ends by documenting the kinds of mechanical errors and lapses in usage that business and professional people find the most offensive in the writing they must read. This pragmatic feature is unique to this text.

The second edition of *Successful Writing* retains those distinctive features that make it especially suitable for advanced writing courses of all kinds:

- All student writing examples come from the papers of students in advanced courses.
- Writing activities and writing assignments focus on believable, real-life writing situations.
- Illustrative examples come from a variety of academic and nonacademic sources.

- Special guidelines are furnished to help students to develop drafts, evaluate them, and work with their peers in and out of class.
- Advice about usage and conventions is based on and supported by the results of a questionnaire asking business and professional people what kinds of lapses from standard usage bothered them the most. Results of that survey are summarized for the students.

The underlying premises of the second edition of *Successful Writing* remain unchanged from the first: writing is a dynamic process that can be taught and can be learned, and people evolve as writers by learning to draft, revise, and polish their writing in varied situations for varied readers. I believe these principles and the methods that grow out of them work for all kinds of expository writing.

Maxine Hairston

Acknowledgments

I received encouragement, support, and valuable advice on this book from a number of colleagues and friends, but I want to express my special appreciation to Professor Michael Keene of the University of Tennessee. His contribution to the book is major. He has been a perceptive and conscientious critic for every chapter in the book and has given me invaluable help on the sections on process, logic, and revision. I owe him a great deal. I wish to thank Mary Trachsel for her assistance in rewriting the chapter on research papers.

I also want to express my thanks to the following people who made useful and enlightening suggestions at all stages of manuscript preparation: Douglas Atkins (University of Kansas), Linda Cades (University of Maryland), Edward P. J. Corbett (Ohio State University), Toby Fulwiler (University of Vermont), Richard Gebhart (Findlay College), William Harmon (University of North Carolina), E. D. Hirsch, Jr. (University of Virginia), Paula Johnson (University of Wyoming), Andrea Lunsford (University of British Columbia), Donald P. McNeilly (University of Maryland), Susan Miller (University of Utah), Amy Richards (Wayne State University), Robert Rudolf (University of Toledo), Joseph Trimmer (Ball State University), Steven J. Vander Weele (Calvin College), and John Walter (University of Texas).

1 ◇ Writing in College

WRITING AS A WAY OF LEARNING

College students are often surprised at the number of papers they have to write for their courses; in fact, sometimes it seems that the further they advance in a field of study, the more they have to write. Many find that puzzling. They can understand why professors would require writing in an English course, but why should students also write in an astronomy course or an art history course? Couldn't professors test what they have learned just as well with multiple choice or short-answer exams?

Perhaps they could, but the *students* in a class get direct benefits from writing papers, keeping a notebook, or keeping a journal or log. Here are some of those benefits:

◇ Writing helps us to discover what we know. Writing about a topic stimulates our thinking on that topic and helps us to probe knowledge and experiences we have stored in our subconscious minds.

◇ Writing generates new ideas. The very act of writing stimulates our minds to make connections, see relationships, and draw analogies that would not have occurred to us if we had not started to write.

◇ Writing helps us to organize our ideas and put them in explicit form. Often we can clarify vague or elusive concepts for ourselves by writing about them.

◇ Writing makes our thoughts available for us to look at and evaluate; we can distance ourselves from our ideas and see them more objectively when we write them down.

◇ Writing helps us to absorb and master new information; we understand material better and retain it longer when we write about it.

◇ Writing helps us to solve problems by clarifying their elements and putting them into a visual context where they can be examined.

◇ Writing about a topic makes us active learners rather than passive receivers of information.

In short, writing is a powerful tool for learning, one that plays a critical role in our education. It is for this reason that so many professors continue to insist that students write papers or keep journals even in courses that are not traditionally thought of as writing courses.

In spite of the power that writing has to make us better learners, many students remain reluctant writers because they believe that they do not have the skills they need to write the good papers that their professors expect. The purpose of this book is to help you develop those skills and make you a confident and competent writer in college and in writing situations outside and after college.

STRATEGIES FOR WRITING PAPERS IN COLLEGE COURSES

Some kinds of college writing tasks are highly specialized and you may need to take a course in scientific or technical writing in order to do them well, but in most courses in the liberal arts or social sciences you will get off to a good start on your papers if you follow some general guidelines for planning and roughing out a first draft. Then you can consult other chapters in the book to learn more about developing and refining your paper.

ANALYZING YOUR WRITING SITUATION

Before you start to write, give yourself a little time to think about your paper and analyze the total writing situation in which you are going to be working. Begin by asking these questions about the elements that will control your paper:

◇ What is my purpose in writing this paper? What specific issue or problem am I going to discuss?

◇ Who is my audience and what assumptions can I made about them? Why are they reading the paper and what do they expect to learn from it?

⋄ What are the limitations I am working under? What are my resources (information, library facilities, and so on)? How much time and energy do I have to invest? When is the paper due, and how long is it supposed to be?

Answering these questions will serve two purposes. First, it will help you to focus your paper and keep it under control by reminding you from the start about what you *can't* do. For instance, for most short papers in college courses, you don't have time to do extensive research; therefore you should remind yourself not to choose a topic that would require such research in order to cover it adequately. You usually are also limited to a certain number of pages; therefore don't choose a topic so broad that it is impossible to say anything significant about it in a few pages. More about that shortly.

Second, writing out the answers to these questions will act as a stimulus to help you begin to collect ideas for your paper. This preliminary writing is like brainstorming or preparatory note taking. You can keep cards or a legal pad beside you as you work, to jot down ideas as they come.

Here is an example of how one might go about answering these questions and establishing the context for a specific paper.

MODEL TOPIC

THE COURSE: Upper-division course in the history of science

THE ASSIGNMENT: Write a four- to six-page paper about some scientist whose work had a major impact on science in the sixteenth or seventeenth century. Describe the person's major work in his field, outline the way in which he arrived at his important discoveries, and discuss the impact of that work on the field.

TOPIC CHOSEN: Johannes Kepler and his discoveries that changed astronomical history

WORKING TITLE: "Kepler: Man of Vision"

QUESTION 1: Paper is for a history of science course. Professor wants me to show that I can identify a major scientific figure, describe his contribution to science, and show how that contribution affected the history of science. I'm going to show that although Kepler's vision of the universe was wrong, in one way it worked because it caused him to accidentally stumble across the great discoveries that changed the history of astronomy. [Notice that the writer states his purpose so specifically that it reminds him of the main points he wants to make—a loose and general statement of purpose is usually not much help.]

QUESTION 2: My professor is my audience. I don't have to explain to him what had been going on in mathematics and astronomy before Kepler's time. He mainly wants to know what Kepler's vision was and why it was important to the history of astronomy.

QUESTION 3: First, the paper is due in two weeks so I don't have time to do much research—I will only try to get one good source to supplement the textbook. Second, paper can be only four to six pages so I can't go into too much detail about Kepler's life or explain everything he did. I have to focus on just his theories and how they led to his three laws of planetary motion. Third, I have another paper to write and an exam coming up next week in Constitutional Law so I can only put a limited amount of time into this paper. I need to narrow the topic so I can handle it in the amount of time I have.

GUIDELINES FOR LIMITING A PAPER TOPIC

Some of the worst problems in college papers come about because students choose topics that are too broad for them to deal with responsibly in a paper of the assigned length or in the time available. If you choose a topic such as "Blood Guilt in Faulkner's Novels" or "Henry VIII's Conflict with the Catholic Church" and try to write about it in a short paper, you will inevitably resort to broad general statements. You cannot focus the paper sharply enough to give it substance or include enough details to make it interesting. A paper that just skims the surface has little value for either you or your professor.

The decision about how much one can expect to handle responsibly in a paper is a tough one, even for experienced writers, but these rough guidelines may help.

4–6-page paper: A short paper, probably one of several for the course. Your thesis should be a narrow one in which you make only one or two important points but support those points with specific examples. For example: "Joe Christmas's obsession with moral guilt in *Light in August* goes back to his fundamentalist religious upbringing." Or this: "For good reason, the British government disputes the Greeks' claim that the Parthenon Marbles rightly belong to them." Although an expert might write at length on either topic, each can also be handled responsibly with specifics in a short paper.

10–12-page paper: A paper in which you can treat a limited topic in some detail, giving examples and quoting from sources. This length is too short to let you write about a broad topic such as Art in the Renaissance, or a major philosophical movement such as Existentialism, without being superficial, but you could write on some subtopic within the larger topic, such as "The Influence of Van Dyke as Court Painter for Charles I" or "The Existentialist Hero in Camus's novel *The Plague*." Other topics that one could cover adequately in ten to twelve pages:

Plato's Treatment of Poets in *The Republic*

The Role of the Grand Jury in the County Judicial Process

18–20-pages: A paper that gives you enough space to treat a limited but complex topic in detail. Usually the professor who assigns a twenty-page paper expects you to do some research for it because he or she wants material from outside sources and wants you to evaluate that material and draw conclusions. You still need to be careful not to pick a topic so broad that it would require a master's thesis to do it credit. Some topics of the kind that might be suitable for a twenty-page paper:

Three Recent Supreme Court Decisions That Have Affected Freedom of the Press in the United States

The Impact on Small Banks of New Regulations for Savings and Loan Institutions

The general principles that underlie choosing a manageable topic for academic papers are these:

◦ Write more about less. Focus on a sharply limited topic and write about it in some depth and detail rather than skimming the surface of a broad topic.

◦ Avoid writing about a subject that covers a large time span such as the Middle Ages or the Golden Age of Greece. For short papers, avoid writing even about a specific time period such as the Roaring Twenties unless you focus sharply on some narrow portion.

◦ Avoid writing about a broad movement or major event such as the French Revolution or the Protestant Reformation unless you take only one or two figures or incidents and relate them to the larger context.

◦ Avoid writing about major psychological, philosophical, economic, or religious theories such as Keynesian economics or Utilitarianism unless you pick only a narrow aspect of the theory.

◦ Choose a topic on which you can find specific information, naming actual events, discoveries, examples, and individuals. (More on writing specifically in Chapter 7.)

FINDING YOUR PURPOSE

Whatever their length, most expository papers or essay exams for general college courses fall into one of these categories: informative, explanatory, critical, or argumentative. For example, you may write an informative case study, an explanatory account of an experiment, a critique of an essay, or an argument for or against a theory. Sometimes the categories overlap, but usually one will dominate, and it's important to know which one you want to focus on. (See Chapter 4 for more on determining and stating your purpose.)

Whatever your purpose in writing, here are some general cautions to keep in mind as you write papers for college courses:

◦ Organize your points so that they are easy to follow and mark them clearly: *First, second,* and so on.

◦ Document your sources. You don't necessarily have to use formal footnotes or attach a bibliography, but you should let your reader know where your information came from. You can write, "According to———" or "Koestler suggests that . . . ." Try to anticipate the places at which your reader might ask, "How do you know that?" and never let that question go unanswered for more than a few sentences. Such references strengthen your paper and show that you've done your homework.

◦ In most cases, use neutral language and avoid inserting judgments such as "tragically" or "luckily." The facts should speak for themselves. When you are writing an argumentative paper judgments are legitimate, but they should be supported with evidence, not emotional statements. The section on Toulmin logic in Chapter 5 can help you set up your case.

Chapters 3 and 5 will give tips on gathering material for your papers and on several methods of organization. Chapter 5 will suggest ways to get started writing and make some specific recommendations about opening paragraphs for academic papers.

CRITERIA BY WHICH PROFESSORS JUDGE COLLEGE PAPERS

Professors are quite clear about the features and qualities they want to see in student papers. They are these:

◦ The topic should be one on which the writer can say something significant, not one on which so much has already been written that there is little new to say. (See Chapter 2, p. 13.) While professors don't necessarily expect students to have original ideas in a subject area in which the students are not experts, they do like a fresh approach and always hope to learn from their students.

- The scope of the paper should be narrow enough so that the topic can be covered adequately within the page limit.
- A paper should have an accurate title that reflects the content of the paper.
- The paper should have a clear pattern of organization. (See Chapter 5 for possibilities.) Links between paragraphs and sections should be clealy marked with signals and transitions.
- Generalizations should be supported with specific evidence and reasoning.
- The language of the paper should be simple and direct. Contrary to popular misconceptions, most professors want to be able to understand their students' papers easily. They also want papers to be concise, not wordy. It's worth remembering that any teacher likes writing that is colorful and graceful as well as clear and informative; the suggestions on revising in Chapter 9 could help you achieve that style.
- Grammar, spelling, and sentence structure are important; mistakes distract and annoy professors.

The student paper that follows is a good example of a paper that meets these criteria and is fresh and gracefully written as well.

KEPLER: MAN OF VISION

There are few instances in which a flash of false insight has led to an important discovery, but for Johannes Kepler, an unheralded math professor in the small Austrian town of Graz, a misguided vision would lead to monumental discoveries. Kepler's vision and his pursuit of this vision would cause him to stumble unintentionally across some of the greatest discoveries in the Scientific Revolution.

According to Kepler, the universe was built around five symmetrical or perfect solids which form its invisible skeleton. These five solids, of which all faces are identical, supposedly fit in between the orbits of the six known planets of the day which were Mercury, Venus, Earth, Mars, Saturn, and Jupiter. These solids were: (1) the tetrahedron or pyramid; (2) the cube; (3) the octahedron (eight equilateral triangles); (4) the dodecahedron (twelve pentagons); and (5) the icosahedron (twenty equilateral triangles).[1] In defense of his invisible skeleton, Kepler reasoned that "God could only create a perfect world, and since only five symmetrical (perfect) solids existed, they were obviously meant to be placed between the six planetary orbits where they fit perfectly."[2]

1. Arthur Koestler, *The Sleepwalkers* (New York: Grosset and Dunlap, The Universal Library, 1959), 249.
2. Koestler, p. 254.

Kepler's Five Perfect Solids

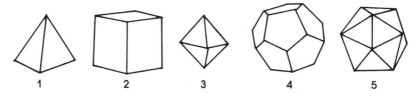

1   2   3   4   5

1. The Tetrahedron or pyramid   4. The dodecahedron
2. The cube   5. The icosahedron
3. The octahedron

In reality, the solids do not even come close to fitting and Kepler himself later admitted it. Nevertheless, the material in *The Mysterium,* the book in which this initial perfect solids theory was published, led to the birth of modern cosmology, was the first attempt to "not only describe heavenly motion in geometrical terms, and to assign them a physical cause," and was to "determine the course of Kepler's life."[3]

Although his idea that the placement of solids affected planetary position was incorrect, Kepler refused to alter his views. He still felt that there was a basic truth to his system. To get at this truth, he searched for a mathematical law to show the relationship between his solids and planetary motion. In this venture, he did research in optics, magnetism, and meteorology. When these investigations did not reveal the hidden clue, our scientific detective began to build his universe around the "musical harmonies of the Pythagorean scale."[4] The dream was the same, the methods were different. A hopeful Kepler now tried to formulate a planetary system in which there were musical sympathies between the planets. The problem with this system was that the planets do not move at a uniform speed. They move faster when they are close to the sun, and slower when they are further away from the sun. As a result of this, the planets do not "hum" at a steady pitch, but alternate between higher and lower notes.[5] Kepler was now beginning to realize that he would never be able to construct his "harmonious" universe if he did not have the measurements of the planets and the sun. The one man, the only man, who had what Kepler needed was Tycho Brahe; Kepler's dream now lay in the hands of the man with the golden nose.

Luckily for Kepler, Tycho needed Kepler just as much as Kepler needed Tycho. Tycho had all the observational data but no insight to interpret it, while Kepler had all the insight needed for interpretation but

3. Koestler, p. 258.
4. Koestler, p. 277.
5. Koestler, p. 277.

no data. Therefore, a symbiotic relationship developed between the men when Kepler accepted a position under Tycho Brahe. However, much to Kepler's dismay, Tycho was very stingy with his observational data. It was not until after Tycho's death that Kepler gained full access to Tycho's observational data.

Upon Tycho's death, Kepler was appointed Tycho's successor as Imperial Mathematicus in Prague. Eight years later, Kepler finally published a work based on Tycho's data. *A New Astronomy* founded the new sciences of physical and instrumental optics and contained the first two of Kepler's three planetary laws.[6] With the aid of Tycho's data, Kepler tackled the problem of planetary circulations. What he found was that planets had elliptical orbits which were nothing similar to the motions he had earlier predicted would be present. The use of Tycho's data, which he had longed for, had refuted instead of substantiated some of Kepler's early ideas. Although he did recognize his new Laws were an achievement, he was still more proud of his solids theory than of his Laws. He had stumbled over two of the greatest advances in science and neither he, nor anyone else, knew the significance of them. It took the genius of Sir Isaac Newton to discover the value of Kepler's discoveries.

Even though the findings using Tycho's data did not coincide with his earlier theories, Kepler refused to give up. He was convinced that the whole *New Astronomy* was merely a "stepping stone towards that ultimate aim, his sweating and panting pursuit of the Creator's Tracks."[7] In this pursuit, he published works on astrology, comets, shapes of snow crystals, and the true birth date of Christ. In 1610, his attention was drawn to Galileo's *Starry Messenger* and the discovery of Jupiter's moons.

To Kepler, Galileo's discovery "offered a highly important and wonderful show to astronomers and philosophers, that it invites all friends of true philosophy to contemplate matters of the highest import . . . Who could be silent in the face of such a message? Who could not feel himself overflow with love of the Divine which is so abundantly manifest here?"[8]

He then went on to offer Galileo his support in the "battle against grumpy reactionaries, who reject everything that departs from the beaten track of Aristotle as a desecration."[9] Why all this enthusiasm? One cannot be sure but many suggest that Kepler saw in Galileo's work some information that he could use to explain the placement and the movement of the planets. In his dialogue concerning the *Starry Messenger,* he did not mention elliptical orbits or either of his two Laws. Apparently, to Kepler, the discovery of elliptical orbits and his Laws were only a detour in his pursuit to establish universal harmony.

6. Koestler, p. 313.
7. Koestler, pp. 348–49.
8. Koestler, p. 372.
9. Koestler, p. 372.

The year 1610 had been a good one for him; Galileo's *Starry Messenger* served as a source of inspiration for the vision-chasing Kepler. However, his satisfaction would be short-lived because trouble was right around the corner in 1611. Kepler was still in Prague, a bad place to be in this particular year. Civil war and epidemic broke out; his source of livelihood, the King, abdicated and Kepler's wife and favorite child died.[10] Kepler was forced to leave Prague and become a Provincial Mathematicus in Linz, in Upper Austria. It was during these times in which he had to use a unique talent for transferring his torments into creative achievements in order to succeed. This was one of the hardest times in his life, and he had still not reached his goal. If he was to reach this goal, it appeared that it would have to be done under adverse conditions.

Incredibly, it was in bad times such as these that Johannes Kepler, chaser of dreams, finally caught up with his dream. *The Harmony of the World* was published "three months after the death of his daughter Katherine, and three days after the downfall of Prague."[11] In this book, Kepler attempted to "bare the ultimate secret of the universe in an all-embracing synthesis of geometry, music, astrology, astronomy and epistemology."[12] In this work, he first deals with the concept of harmony in mathematics, and then tries to apply mathematical harmony to music, astrology, and astronomy. The result was an elaborate and detailed study into harmonic ratios which are applied to practically everything. His earlier model universe which consisted of five perfect solids has now been altered to include two dimensional polygons, and he adjusts his harmonic reasoning and symbolism for their inclusion. Almost lost in this huge mass of harmony is his Third Law of planetary motion, which shows the correlation between a planet's period and its distance. This Law, which was very important in Newton's Law of Gravity, meant very little to Kepler. Once again, he did not realize the treasure that lay right before his eyes. Perhaps his most important achievements seemed to be of very little value to him because he did not have the knowledge to fully understand them.

In any event, this man of vision contributed much to science. He was responsible for a tremendous increase in the accuracy of astronomical tables, for advancements in optics, calculus, and many other things. His chief contributions, however, were his Three Laws on planetary motion. But Kepler would never have discovered these laws if it were not for his vision which caused him to walk among diamonds but believe them mere glass. I tip my hat to the vision of Johannes Kepler.

Reggie Rice

10. Koestler, p. 380.
11. Koestler, p. 388.
12. Koestler, p. 389.

2 ◇ What Is Good Writing?

Because people must write to suit the particular needs of specific readers, one cannot say that there is just one kind of good writing. Good writing can be formal or casual, elegant or plain, straightforward or subtle. Nevertheless, editors and other people whose business it is to evaluate writing almost all agree that the key element of good writing is that it communicates effectively with the readers for whom it is intended. That phrase "for whom it is intended" is crucial to the definition because effective writers never work in a vacuum. They think about their readers both before and as they write, knowing that a writing style and tone that work well with one group of readers may not work with a different group of readers in different circumstances.

CHARACTERISTICS OF GOOD WRITING

Regardless of the concessions that writers must make when writing for different audiences, most editors and critics could identify certain qualities common to good expository writing. They would say that in order for such writing to do a good job, it should be:

◇ Significant
◇ Clear
◇ Unified
◦ Economical
◇ Grammatically acceptable.

When your writing meets these standards, you can be fairly sure that your readers will be able to understand it. Writing that is excellent, however, almost always has two other important qualities:

- It is vigorous
- It has an authentic voice.

When you read, you probably already use these criteria intuitively and make judgments on the basis of them. After all, you know immediately that you enjoy reading something more and learn more from it when it's interesting, when it is clear and well organized, and when the author gets to the point without wasting your time. You appreciate writing that's *readable*.

Of course, none of us should be so arrogant or so impatient that we assume any writing we can't understand must be poorly written. Sometimes authors must deal with complex topics that are difficult to explain in simple terms, and occasionally one must be willing to read and reread a piece of writing. Sometimes a reader may not have the background information or vocabulary to understand a piece of writing and that problem is not necessarily the writer's fault. Nevertheless, if intelligent readers who are willing to work at understanding a nontechnical piece of writing have trouble, then those readers are justified in suspecting that what they are reading is badly written.

THE PROBLEM OF MODELS

Unfortunately, instead of trusting their instincts and trying to write the kind of prose they like to read, some writers pattern their writing after poor models. Intimidated by writing they can't understand, particularly if it appears in a textbook or under the name of some famous person, they assume that obscure and wordy writing must be good academic style. Here is an example by the psychologist B.F. Skinner:

> The struggle for freedom and dignity has been formulated as a defense of autonomous man rather than as a revision of the contingencies of reinforcement under which people live. A technology of behavior is available which would more successfully reduce the aversive consequences of behavior, proximate or deferred, and maximize the achievements of which the human organism is capable, but the defenders of freedom oppose its use.[1]

1. B. F. Skinner, *Beyond Freedom and Dignity* (New York: Alfred A. Knopf, 1971), 125.

One reason the average reader has trouble understanding such prose is that Skinner uses unfamiliar phrases such as "contingencies of reinforcement," but the chief problem is that the writing is colorless and abstract. The reader can't see anyone doing anything. No people seem to be involved, yet Skinner is writing to and about human beings.

Here is another example of obscure writing that might intimidate someone on first reading. Ironically, it comes from a pamphlet inviting people to submit grant proposals for ways to improve writing.

> Studies here should concentrate on the links between discourse rules and cognitive achievement through such mediating factors as social and referential understandings and the teacher's differential distribution due to the varying expectations of student abilities.[2]

Again, the reader cannot see anyone doing anything, but is dazed by a string of fuzzy phrases such as "referential understandings" and "differential distribution." This is the kind of writing that at first glance may seem scholarly and profound, but as you read it you find that your eyes glaze over and you lose interest. Your mind begins to "hydroplane" over the surface because it doesn't connect with anything on the page.

This kind of deceptive language recalls the Hans Christian Andersen fairy tale, "The Emperor's New Clothes." In that story a pair of confidence men dupe the emperor into believing that he is wearing elegant clothes when actually he is naked. None of his courtiers dare tell him that he has nothing on for fear they are the only ones who can't see the clothes that are supposed to be so grand. In the same way, intimidated readers often pretend to understand confusing writing because they are afraid that if they ask "What does it mean?" other people will think they're stupid. To expose that kind of fraud, someone finally has to become impatient enough to say, "What does this mean? I don't understand." Professors or bosses who have trouble understanding your writing are apt to say so rather quickly.

GOOD WRITING IS SIGNIFICANT

Good writing must say something of some consequence to someone; it should make a point. Otherwise it is not worth writing or reading. The reader for whom it is intended should find some element in it that is enlightening or persuasive, something that is surprising. Writing that only re-

---

2. *Basic Skills Research Grants Announcement*, The National Institute of Education (Summer 1977): 5.

peats what most of its readers already know and bores both the reader and the writer is not good writing, no matter how correct or smoothly written it may be.

College students who do much of their writing for instructors might find these standards confusing. With justification, they could point out that they really can't be expected to surprise their professors with their writing, and that at times they would find it hard to judge what professors are going to think significant. How are students supposed to know?

Those are good objections, and the only answer to them is that sometimes you don't know. You have to analyze your audience and make the best judgment you can. How you analyze your audiences and then adapt your writing to suit them is a complex process, one that we will be studying throughout the book. But as a rough test ask yourself these questions:

◦ Are the readers for whom I am writing this going to profit in some way from reading it?
◦ Will it give them new information or new insights?

If your writing is exclusively for your professor, ask yourself:

◦ Will this writing show my professor I have read and mastered the material I am writing about?

If the answer to any of these questions is No, your writing probably has little real content.

For example, here is a student paragraph that wouldn't meet the test:

> The idea that a candidate elected to public office should owe favors or special treatment to those special interests which helped to finance or support his campaign goes against the concept of representative government. Each citizen has a right to be represented, and an elected official has an obligation to represent all his constituents equally. The elected official should owe no more to special interest groups which supported his campaign than he owes to every citizen he represents. Special interests should be given no more weight than the interests of any other group, and the public interest should be paramount.

This is *canned discourse,* writing that has no real significance for anyone, either writer or reader. In the first sentence the writer gives a glib generality about representative government and in the next three sentences does no more than repeat the generality in slightly different words. He doesn't give any examples to illustrate his point nor does he explain what a candidate should do to avoid owing favors to special interests. The paragraph is a collection of pious platitudes that seems to have been generated off the top of the writer's head and gives no information and no specifics. (Tips on how to avoid this kind of writing are given in Chapter 7.)

GOOD WRITING IS CLEAR

Writing is clear when the readers *for whom it is intended* can read along at a steady pace and grasp the meaning if they put out a reasonable amount of effort. They shouldn't get confused, have to guess at meanings, or go back and reread to find out what the writer is saying. Clear writing doesn't have to be simple, although it often is, but it shouldn't be any more difficult than it has to be, given the subject and the purpose. Busy people who must read for information rank clarity above all other desirable qualities in writing. (See survey on p. 230.) If they don't find it, they will not stay with a report or letter for long.

Authors who want to write clearly employ dozens of strategies, some obvious and some subtle. For the most part, they use strategies that people who want to be good writers can learn in a comparatively short time and start putting into practice almost immediately. Much of the rest of this book will focus on those strategies.

GOOD WRITING IS UNIFIED

A piece of writing is unified (or coherent) when the reader can follow it easily because it is clearly organized according to some plan and because the parts are connected either by an underlying pattern or by transitional words or phrases. Everything fits into place and helps to develop the author's central idea; the reader doesn't get lost or distracted by irrelevant details. For example, here is a good paragraph from a student paper written for young readers. In it the writer catches the reader's interest right at the beginning and holds it by tying every sentence to his main point. He does it through a pattern of assertion and support and by repeating his key word.

What is a geyser? Where are they found? When people think about geysers they usually picture Yellowstone's Old Faithful shooting water hundreds of feet in the air. But Old Faithful is only one type of geyser. Geysers normally eject hot, cloudy water like Old Faithful, but did you know that they can also shoot out yellow, orange, and green water? Some of these spouting fountains are not large at all but very small, and they trickle out softly on the land forming steamy, crystal-clear pools of hot water. Some stand alone far from other geysers, while others cluster together in large groups that look like geyser cities. All geysers are different, and each one has its own personality. But all geysers do have something in common: they are all hot and gush from beneath the ground.

Josh Lucas

In contrast, here is a poorly organized paragraph from a student paper.

Another big chunk of the union man's wage pays for medical and dental care. The health benefits paid out to auto workers cost more than the steel used to manufacture the cars they are assembling. How dangerous can throwing cars together be when those meddling sissies from OSHA practically make it a felony to allow a man to scrape his knuckles on the assembly line? Where can the money be going? The doctors and dentists profiting from these costs understand better than anyone what a poor value these add-on costs make American products. When they go shopping for a new car, they frequently choose a Mercedes or BMW.

Even though the paragraph has many specific details, the reader has trouble following it because the writer starts by discussing the high costs of union medical benefits but then takes off in another direction and takes up two new topics. The paragraph seems to have no plan, no central idea.

GOOD WRITING IS ECONOMICAL

Good writers don't want to waste their reader's time, so they try to cut all excess words from their writing, get rid of what William Zinsser, author of *On Writing Well*, calls "clutter." As he points out,

[The average reader] is a person with an attention span of about twenty seconds. He is assailed on every side by forces competing for his time: by newspapers and magazines, by television and radio and stereo, by his wife and children and pets, by his house and his yard and all the gadgets that he has bought to keep them spruce, and by that most potent of competitors, sleep. The man snoozing in his chair with an unfinished magazine open on his lap is a man who was given too much unnecessary trouble by the writer.[3]

If you want to hold that reader's attention, you have to work constantly at keeping your writing terse and streamlined. That doesn't mean leaving out pertinent details—notice that Zinsser takes time to list specifically the

---

3. William Zinsser, "Rewriting," in *On Writing Well*, 2d edition (New York: Harper and Row, 1980).

forces that compete for a reader's attention—but it does mean trimming out many adjectives, eliminating repetitive phrases, and generally trying to do away with words that do not enhance meaning or advance your idea. You need to be particularly careful to squeeze excess words out of your writing when your main purpose is to inform, but you probably need fewer words than you think even when one of your purposes is to entertain.

For example, here is a colorful, effective, and uncluttered opening paragraph for a paper on unusual jobs for women:

> Beth Allen has a very special job. Her first role is a full-time wife and mother. But each morning at 8:45, after the breakfast bustle is over and her family has gone for the day, Beth becomes another character. Quickly she tosses her dish towel onto the counter and whips her apron over a chair. She shoves her feet into a pair of floppy yellow shoes and pops on a fuzzy orange wig. Grabbing several large bunches of helium balloons, she checks her purse for the house keys and bounds out the door. Beth the Balloon Clown has just checked in for work.
>
> Paula Johnson

It may help to remind yourself that most of the terse uncluttered writing you find in the work of authors like Russell Baker, Ellen Goodman, or Carl Sagan didn't start out that way; almost certainly those authors had to work at revising sentences and cutting out extra words. In several places in this book you will find guidelines for ways to trim your writing. Several sections of the book will suggest how a writer works toward clarity and give some specific guidelines.

GOOD WRITING IS GRAMMATICALLY ACCEPTABLE

For our purposes, I am going to define "grammatically acceptable English" as standard English usage; that is, the kind of English that most educated people in our society use and expect others to use in formal or informal communication, particularly written material. It is the kind of English you encounter in a magazine or newspaper or hear people use on news programs, in interviews, or in public speeches. For the most part, standard English conforms to the rules of usage you learned in elementary and secondary school and may have reviewed in college.

But the phrase "for the most part" is important. Anyone who has managed to learn all or most of the hundreds of rules that govern English usage and who has a sensitive ear knows that many successful and well-educated people do not always speak absolutely "correct" English. Perhaps they don't distinguish between "who" and "whom" or between "fewer" and "less," and they may occasionally be careless about pronoun reference or using subjunctive verbs in the proper places. But their mistakes are minor, and so common among even well-educated people that their audiences usually don't notice. Their grammar is *acceptable,* suitable for the situation in which they are speaking or writing.

In Chapter 11, you will find the results of a survey I made of business and professional people to find out how they ranked grammatical mistakes in writing that they read in the course of their work. If you study these results, you should get a fairly good idea of which mistakes are so serious that you should take great care to avoid them.

Anyone who wants to be an effective writer needs to master the conventions of standard English: mistakes do distract your readers from *what* you are saying to *how* you are saying it. You can't afford such distractions, so it's worth your time to do whatever it takes to write grammatically acceptable English, not necessarily in your first draft, but certainly in your finished product.

You also need to learn how to spell or find some reliable way to check your spelling. Many readers are almost irrationally irritated by bad spelling, making quick judgments that a poor speller is both incompetent and ignorant. Thus you can't afford bad spelling—it simply costs too much. If you know you are a poor speller, find some way to solve your problem.

One good way to monitor your spelling is to ask a trusted friend who *can* spell to proofread your papers for you. Another is to compose on a word processor that includes a spelling check program. Certainly such spelling programs are helpful, particularly since they will also pick up typographical errors. You should know, however, that such programs are not cure-alls for your spelling problems. If you write "affect" when you mean "effect" or if you think that "elicit" is spelled "illicit," the computer won't help you. As far as it's concerned, all those words are correct because they are in its spelling dictionary, and it cannot tell that a word has not been spelled correctly for the context in which it appears. You still need that good friend.

THOSE FINAL TOUCHES

VIGOR

You sometimes hear an author's writing described as "strong" or "vigorous," and in a tone that makes it obvious that those terms are complimentary. They are terms that are easier to illustrate than to define, but in general they mean that a writer chooses words that show the readers what is happening through active verbs and clear images, that he or she uses specific examples and striking metaphors to get ideas across, that the writing is concrete, direct, and efficient. It moves along like a person walking vigorously and confidently toward a goal. It's a quality that you can almost count on finding in the writing of first-rate journalists and essayists like Norman Cousins, William Raspberry, Nora Ephron, or Tom Wolfe, and in the oral essays of television commentators like Alistair Cooke or Walter Cronkite. Here is an example from Joan Didion:

> We have reached a certain understanding, my migraine and I. It never comes when I am in real trouble. Tell me my house is burned down, my husband has left me, there is gunfighting in the streets and panic in the banks, and I will not respond by getting a headache. It comes instead when I am fighting not an open but a guerilla war with my own life, during weeks of small household confusions, lost laundry, unhappy help, canceled appointments, on days when the telephone rings too much and I get no work done and the wind is coming up. On days like that my friend comes uninvited.[4]

Here Didion makes her writing vigorous by using simple language, concrete images, and direct and simple verbs like "comes," "rings," and "get." Contrast her writing with the turgid writing in the example from Skinner on p. 12.

For most writers, that vigorous quality doesn't just come naturally in the first draft. They have to work for it by cutting extra words, adding details that are visual and personal, getting rid of passive or dull verbs, rearranging their sentences into simpler patterns—in other words, by employing all their strategies for revising. Many sections in the rest of the text explain and illustrate such strategies.

AUTHENTIC VOICE

In good writing the reader can sense the *presence* of the writer behind what he or she is reading. The writer's character comes through the writing and makes the reader feel that a real person is trying to communicate ideas and information. The writing does not seem fake or canned or put together by formula. The reader feels that he or she is actually engaging with another person's mind. Writing that has an authentic voice gives you the feeling that only that writer could have written that particular piece—it is distinctive and original. For example, here is the opening paragraph of a student paper that projects a strong and authentic voice:

4. Joan Didion, "In Bed," in *The White Album* (New York: Simon and Schuster, 1979).

A water shortage in Texas? The very thought is difficult to imagine in a state where thousands of farmers depend on irrigation. But when a blistering heat wave struck the state in the summer of '80, Texans were flooded with news about yet another rapidly disappearing resource. No, not oil, copper, zinc, or uranium, but a resource much more important to Texas and far too often taken for granted: an unpolluted supply of water.

Writers are certainly more likely to project an authentic voice in their writing when they care about their topic, but you don't have to be passionate about your topic to sound genuine and knowledgeable. You can communicate your authentic voice by referring to your personal experience and special expertise, by using specific examples to support your generalizations, and by trying to make your writing concrete, straightforward, and personal rather than abstract and impersonal.

EXERCISES

1. Rank each of the following four paragraphs on a scale of one to ten (*one* = excellent, *ten* = terrible), using as your criteria the qualities *significance, clarity, unity, economy, acceptable usage,* and *vigor.* Give the reasons for your rankings.

   Airbags are thought by many to be a miracle device which would tend to give many drivers a false sense of security against injury. This would tend to make them less alert and therefore less competent drivers. There are today already far too many incompetent drivers on the road, and a false sense of security would tend to make the situation even worse. It is far safer to have a good driver who can avoid accidents than a bad driver who will cause accidents, but has equipment which will hopefully save him from serious injury or death. Another safety problem with airbags is that in tests, for one reason or another, they have been known to inflate when there was no collision. It is impossible to control a car with an inflated airbag in it, so this would likely cause a collision.

   student paragraph

   Ronnie Prado graduated from high school two years ago and went to work for a small construction company. His weekly paycheck of $180 seemed like a lot of money. He bought a new color television set and a stereo on credit. The monthly payments were only $65—chicken feed. With all the money he had saved during school, he bought a good used truck. Nice apartment, some new clothes—everything fell into place. In November Ronnie had an accident with his truck. He hadn't insured it against collision, so it cost him a month's pay just to get it running again. The new year brought an increase in his rent of $40 a month. His grocery bill had jumped another $20 a month in the past year. Gasoline was half again as much as it was when he bought the truck, and he often had to drive fifteen or twenty miles to a construction site. By March the Friendly Finance Company had repossessed his television and stereo. The rent was ten days past due, he had no money in the bank, and his girlfriend was talking about marriage. His credit rating was shot. So Ronnie sold the truck, married the girl, and now lives with her parents.

student paragraph

One holds the knife as one holds the bow of a cello or a tulip—by the stem. Not palmed nor gripped nor grasped, but lightly, with the tips of the fingers. The knife is not for pressing. It is for drawing across the field of skin. Like a slender fish, it waits, at the ready, then go! It darts, followed by a fine wake of red. Even now, after so many times, I still marvel at its power —cold, gleaming, silent. More, I am still struck with a kind of dread that it is I in whose hand the blade travels, that my hand is its vehicle, that yet again the terrible steel-bellied thing and I have conspired for a most unnatural purpose, the laying open of the body of a human being.

Richard Selzer[5]

Such possibilities may not redeem society, but they might help make life in society more bearable for those who see its contradictions and feel that the situation is too hopeless to warrant surrendering one's own development of dreams of revolution. The resulting possibilities might remain abstract— both in content and in their isolation from social praxis—but they are pref erable to self-delusion or to paralyzing self-consciousness. Depite their experience of the limits of discourse, the modernists have recovered the two basic values inherent in the humanities: an active sensibility able to partici- pate sympathetically in the manifold particularity that constitutes empirical reality and the possibility of realizing aspects of consciousness shared by all men and offering an enlarged sense of one's own identity. Beyond that, at their most triumphant moments, the modernists have glimpsed a vision in which the structures of consciousness and the diversity of experience seem dialectically related.

Charles Altieri[6]

2. How comparatively readable are these examples from advanced writing stu- dents' papers?

Recently the President of the University proposed to the Board of Re- gents that student counseling services be discontinued because of a lack of funds. We students, as a body, need to express our concern over this impor- tant development. Throughout our lives we have had and will have need for

---

5. Richard Selzer, "The Knife," *Mortal Lessons* (New York: Simon and Schuster, 1976), 92.
6. Charles Altieri, "Objective Image and Act of Mind in Modern Poetry," PMLA 91, 1 (Jan- uary 1976): 113.

counseling of some sort. Parents raised us as children, guidance counselors listened to us in high school, and friends will help us as we get older. College is a phase in which we have certain needs. Counseling is one of them. We must all become aware of how vital this service is for us here at school.

As more and more land is used for construction sites, no appreciable efforts are being made to acquire additional land to compensate for this loss in parking spaces. The main reason for this inactiveness is the lack of available funds. It has been suggested that we draw upon the Available University Fund. This fund, however, has been committed to vital academic projects and is already tentatively budgeted for future appropriations. Thus the university has been unable to allocate funds to alleviate this problem.

The most substantial tennis equipment investment you make should be for shoes. Don't cut corners here. If your feet don't feel comfortable when you are playing tennis, it is very difficult to get into the proper position to hit the ball. For $30 you can get a fine pair of lightweight durable tennis shoes that feel so good you'll be itching to get out on the courts. Be sure to get the kind with a basically flat, no-skid tread pattern. These will be fine for whatever surface you play on: cement, asphalt, or clay. Ridged-soled jogging shoes just won't do. You'll end up slipping to a hard fall more often than not. Check the toe for a hard rubber finish. This will come in handy if you drag your back foot on serves as many people do. By the way, there's nothing wrong with that; most professionals do it.

3. Clip a short article or newspaper column that you think is clearly written. Analyze it for the features that you think make it clear.

4. Analyze the writer's word choices in this opening paragraph from a student paper; then try to rewrite it to make it more vigorous.

The rush hour traffic is heavy. Beginning at about 6:00 P.M., the narrow lanes are crowded to capacity with an array of various individuals jockeying for position. No, this description is not of a crowded street in a business district; it is of the running path which encircles Town Lake in Austin or any of the similar public running facilities in most American cities. Competitive races like the Boston Marathon have attracted record numbers of participants each year since 1973. Austin's own race, the Capitol Ten Thousand, is now so large that the sponsors are considering limiting the field.

SUGGESTED WRITING ASSIGNMENT

Write an informative and/or persuasive paper on a topic that interests you and about which you already know at least a little. No specified length, but try to keep it at 1500 words or less (five to six double-spaced pages).

On the first page identify your audience and state in what publication they would read this essay. Write out what questions they would want to have answered by the article. Also identify your purpose in writing: why would you be writing this paper? what would you hope to accomplish? In other words, think about the *rhetorical situation* in which you are writing —the need for writing, the audience, and the constraints. Some possible topics:

1. What constitutes sexual harassment in a specific situation; for example, on the job, in the classroom, or in a professional situation such as doctor/patient or therapist/client. Discuss some measures that could be taken to correct such a situation.
2. Identify and analyze one specific aspect of our secondary school system that you believe contributes directly to today's educational problems. What might be done about this problem and by whom?
3. Try to find out and document some historical truth about a major event around which myth has grown up. For example, Custer's last battle at Little Big Horn; the battle of the Alamo; the first airplane flight of the Wright brothers; the Japanese attack on Pearl Harbor.
4. The facts about one aspect of teen-age sexuality in our culture and the forces that promote it. Is change desirable? Why?

3 ◇ What Happens When People Write?

Many people who have trouble writing believe that writing is a mysterious process that the average person cannot master. They assume that anyone who writes well does so because of a magic mixture of talent and inspiration, and that people who are not lucky enough to have those gifts can never become writers. Thus they take an "either you have it or you don't" attitude that discourages them before they even start to write.

Like most myths, this one has a grain of truth in it, but only a grain. Admittedly the best writers are people with talent just as the best musicians or athletes or chemists are people with talent. But that qualification does not mean that only talented people can write well any more than it means that only a few gifted people can become good tennis players. Tennis coaches know differently. From experience, they know any reasonably well-coordinated and healthy person can learn to play a fairly good game of tennis if he or she will learn the principles of the game and work at putting them into practice. They help people become tennis players by showing them the strategies that experts use and by giving them criticism and reinforcement as they practice those strategies. In recent years, as we have learned more about the processes of working writers, many teachers have begun to work with their writing students in the same way.

AN OVERVIEW OF THE WRITING PROCESS

HOW PROFESSIONALS WORK

To learn more about what happens when professionals write, composition specialists have been studying how writers work. In my own research, I have looked especially at the way journalists and other professionals who write nonfiction work and have come to the following conclusions. Although not all of them apply to all successful writers, most writers who have read them agree that they are valid.

⋄ Most writers don't wait for inspiration; they write whether they feel like it or not. Usually they write on a schedule, beginning at a certain time every day just as if they were reporting for a job.

⋄ Professional writers usually write in a specific place and consistently use the same tools—pencil, typewriter, or word processor. The physical details of writing are important to them—the kind of paper they use, the location of their desks, and so on. They go to considerable trouble to create a good writing environment.

⋄ Successful writers make a point of constantly observing what goes on around them and have a system for gathering material.

⋄ Successful writers count on deadlines to make them work; they make commitments that force them to write regularly and to get their work in on time.

⋄ Successful writers usually plan before they write, but they keep the plan flexible and may replan as they write.

⋄ Successful writers usually write for a specific audience, and as they work they keep in mind the constraints that audience puts on them.

⋄ Most good writers work slowly, considering 1500 words a good day's work.

⋄ Even successful writers often have trouble getting started, but they know strategies for overcoming their blocks.

⋄ Successful writers seldom know precisely what they are going to say when they begin to write, and they plan on discovering at least some of their content as they work.

⋄ Successful writers stop frequently to reread what they have written and consider such rereading an important part of the writing process.

⋄ Successful writers usually do some revising as they write and expect to do two or more drafts of their writing.

⋄ Even successful writers don't always enjoy writing. Like others, they often procrastinate and feel guilty, but ultimately they find writing satisfying and rewarding.

CREATIVE PATTERNS

This information along with data gathered by people researching the creative process in other fields—music, painting, and science, for example—

seems to indicate that successful writers' habits fit the patterns of creativity and problem solving common to other disciplines. When writers work to discover what they want to say and to organize their ideas and express them effectively, their behavior resembles the efforts scientists go through when making discoveries or solving problems, or the struggles painters go through in capturing their visions on canvas.

The general pattern of creativity has four stages: *preparation, incubation, illumination and execution,* and *verification.* In writing, these stages look roughly like this:

- ◦ Preparation: The writer gathers material and prepares to write.
- ◦ Incubation: The writer suspends work while mental activity goes on in the subconscious.
- ◦ Illumination and execution: The writer identifies his or her ideas and puts them on paper.
- ◦ Verification: The writer checks and proofreads the finished product.

Such a simple summary makes the writing process look neater than it really is. Writers seldom start with Step 1 and move straight through to Step 4; most of the time the writing process is *recursive*: writers move back and forth from one stage to another, particularly between planning and executing. They may spend several hours in preparing, then write a few pages and stop to reread and reflect. Occasionally they take time off to relax and let their thoughts incubate, and when they go back to work, they may do some new preparation before they actually start writing again. They may repeat the stages of the process several times, skipping around, replanning and revising as they go. The process is messy and dynamic, not neat and orderly, but it does correspond roughly to creative patterns in other fields.

DIFFERENT CLASSES OF WRITING

Several variables affect the method and speed with which writers work— how much time they have, how important the task is, how skilled they are, and so on. Perhaps the most important variable, however, is the kind of writing task they are doing. I think that most writing tasks can be classified in one of three categories; I call these categories the *classes* of writing.

Class 1: Routine *message* writing. This kind of writing is brief and uncomplicated although it can be important. Most literate people can do it without difficulty. Examples: Announcement of a meeting, notes to family or friends, simple inquiries.

Class 2: Extended writing that is *self-contained*; that is, the writer already knows the content or knows where to look for it, and comparatively little discovery takes place. This kind of writing may take considerable time and require concentration, but it can usually be organized according to a familiar pattern—for example, introduction, assertions and support, and conclusion—and it can be developed by traditional formulas—definition, comparison, cause and effect, and so on. Practiced and competent writers have few problems with this kind of writing. Much of the writing that students do in college fits into this category, and so does much business writing. Examples: Writing samples for the Law School Admission Test, action summaries, case studies, legal briefs, technical reports, most essay exams.

Class 3: Extended *open* writing in which the writer discovers much of his or her material during the writing process. For this class, writers may start with only a "felt sense" of what they want to say and work out both form and content as they proceed. Detailed advance plans or writing formulas

Table 1 / Hypothetical Diagram of the Writing Process

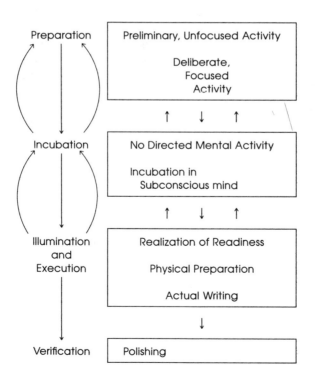

are seldom useful for Class 3 writing, and usually the writer must shape and focus the writing through several drafts. This is the most time-consuming and most complex kind of writing: it also carries the highest risk. Even experienced writers frequently have trouble when they're working on Class 3 writing. Examples: Writing in which the writer is expressing original ideas, speculative writing about theories or policies, important political speeches, and exploratory writing.

Of course, not all writing fits into these neat categories, and sometimes one might mix classes of writing in a single document, but the labels do seem to be at least broadly accurate.

Most of the writing that people do on the job or in college is Class 1 or Class 2 writing; not many of us have to work at Class 3 for long periods of time. That's just as well because it costs too much in every way—in time, in energy, in commitment. Nevertheless, I suspect it is their experiences with Class 3 writing that make people both love and hate to write. While it can be difficult and frustrating, it can also be the most satisfying kind of writing.

PREPARATION

The preparation stage for writing breaks into two parts: the first includes the writer's experiences and activity before he or she begins to write—all of the data that have been accumulating before the writer starts a specific task—and the second includes strategies for getting to those data.

STOCKING THE BANK

Before a writer begins to write, his or her mind acts like a computer, gathering and storing a variety of information from books, television, work, social gatherings, political activities, personal interactions—everything and anything. Those data go into a bank and lie there waiting to be tapped. No one should assume, however, that once the data bank is stocked it can be ignored until the writer needs it. As you draw on it for ideas and examples, you have to keep replenishing it by continually paying attention to everything that goes on around you as well as what goes on *within* you—insights, analogies, connections. Keep a notebook or cards with you all the time and try to develop an intellectual antenna or radar probe with which you continually sweep your environment and notice everything that is happening. Form the habit of looking for new experiences and new information and try to be a person on whom nothing is lost.

Hypothetical Diagram of the Writing Process: Preparation Stage

Preliminary Unfocused Activity	Travel, reading, movies, television specials, other classes, sports, hobbies, work, etc. Keeping notebook. Mental antennae are out receiving signals from whole environment. Subconscious is storing material.

↑   ↓   ↑

Discovery: Stage 1	Identification of writing task: analyzing audience and purpose. Brainstorming Narrowing the topic by subdividing it Freewriting Asking questions: Who? What? When? Where? Why? How? General Research/ Serendipity Subconscious is storing excess material

↑ | ↑
Narrowing focus and increasing intellectual energy
| ↓ |

Discovery: Stage 2	Taking specific notes Collecting material through research & interviews. Thinking of useful analogies. Finding supporting material. Choosing preliminary method of organization: outlining, list, thesis sentence and tentative title. Write trial opening paragraph.

WRITING MORE ABOUT LESS

Once you know what your specific writing task is going to be and you have chosen a topic or had one assigned, it's a good idea to start by thinking how you are going to limit that topic. As indicated earlier, trying to do too much in a paper is one of the major pitfalls of even experienced writers; therefore you need strategies for narrowing and focusing your topic. One strategy is just to start writing and generate a quantity of material which you can then sift through to find the portion on which you want to focus. But that's a slow and often inefficient process. A better way to narrow your topic is to "tree it down"; that is, write your topic at the top of the page, then divide and subdivide it into progressively smaller units until you arrive at one that interests you and seems manageable. Then you can divide that again to find specifics that will help you develop your paper.

For example, a student who wanted to write a paper for college women on poor methods of weight control treed her topic down like this (see p. 32 for a copy of her actual worksheet):

POOR METHODS OF WEIGHT CONTROL

Crash diets
   Fasting
   Water diets
   High-protein diets
   Special food diets; e.g., grapefruit
   The Hollywood Diet
   Liquid protein diets
External methods
   Passive exercise
   Body wraps
   Massage
Abnormal eating patterns
   Bingeing and purging (bulimia)
Physical effects
Psychological effects
   Anorexia

She decided to write about anorexia since she had a friend who suffered from it and could use her experiences as an example. Once she focused on anorexia, she treed it down like this and generated a rough outline for her paper:

ANOREXIA

Kinds of women affected
   Upper income/higher social classes
   High achievers/perfectionists
Causes
   Cultural pressures to be thin
   Desire for attention
   Poor self-image/need for approval
   Desire to postpone sexuality

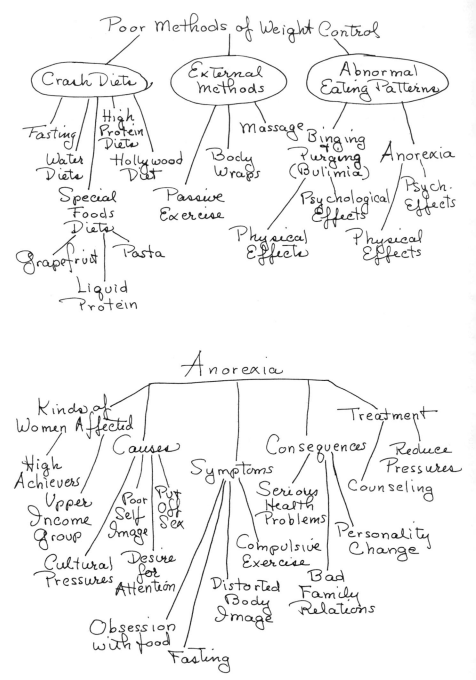

Symptoms
    Obsession with food
    Distorted image of body
    Compulsive exercise
    Fasting to the point of starvation
Consequences
    Serious health impairment, sometimes death
    Drastic personality changes
    Adverse effect on family relationships
Treatment
    Extensive counseling
    Reduce family and social pressures

Here is another example of narrowing a topic. This time the writer wanted to write a paper on computers in education. He started by subdividing like this (see p. 34 for his worksheet):

(see p. 34 for his worksheet)

COMPUTERS IN EDUCATION

College
    Computer science courses
    Tools for science courses
    Drill and practice in language courses
    Registration and record keeping
    Word processing
    Individual microcomputers for students
Secondary schools
    Promoting computer literacy among students
    Use in math and science courses
    Teaching programming
    Possible overemphasis by media and educators

Several of the subtopics looked interesting to him, but he decided to focus on whether the role of computers in schools was being overemphasized by the press and educators. He "treed" that down like this:

ARE COMPUTERS BEING OVEREMPHASIZED IN OUR SCHOOLS?

Limitations of computer use
    Drill and practice in science, math, languages
    Elementary programming
    Courses in computer science and programming
    Writing instruction
Writing-skills centers

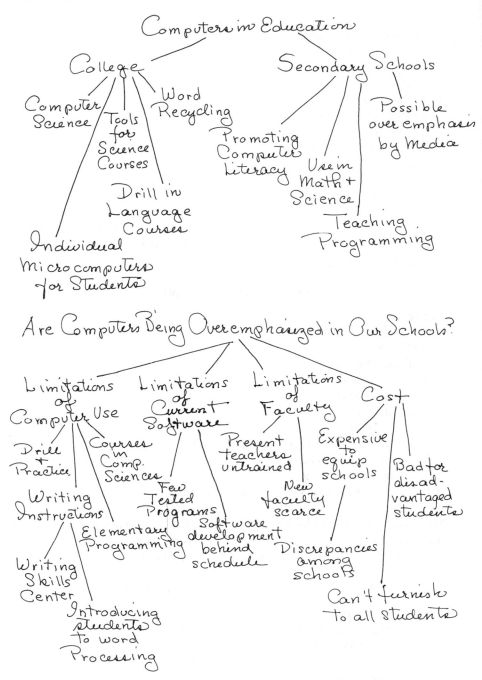

Introducing students to word processing
Limitations of current software
    Comparatively few tested programs available
    Software development far behind promised schedules
Limitations of faculty
    Present teachers untrained in computer use
    New teachers hard to get
Cost
    Expensive to equip schools adequately
    Problem of discrepancies in money among districts.
    Prohibitively expensive to provide computers for all students
    Too much emphasis puts disadvantaged students even further behind

He chose to focus on the cost of computers and their limited applications and to write a paper cautioning administrators not to let themselves be rushed into overemphasizing computers in their schools.

DISCOVERING AUDIENCE AND PURPOSE

Once you have refined your topic, you are ready to go back to those two crucial questions: *Who is my audience?* and *What is my purpose?* To complicate matters, although each is an important question that requires a separate answer, they are nevertheless so interdependent that they can't be considered separately. The answer you give to one nearly always controls the answer to the other. Let me illustrate.

Purpose	Audience
Change the test ⟶	Directors of Educational Testing Service
Persuade law schools to stop using test ⟶	Faculty and admission board of law schools
Explain performance on test ⟶	Parents or admissions board of specific law school
Inform other applicants ⟶	Pre-law students

Probably you could get some overlapping here, or an additional audience for some of the purposes; nevertheless, when you focus on a specific purpose, you should realize that you immediately sharply limit your audience. Also your writing task becomes more manageable.

If your audience is already identified, then you need to adjust your purpose to the audience. For example, if the pre-law association on campus were to ask you to speak to them about the test, you might begin by saying that you think it should be changed, but you would be wasting your time and theirs to focus primarily on that issue. That audience cannot do anything about the LSAT, and what they want from you is advice, not complaints.

Learning to keep one's audience constantly in mind may be the single most important ability any writer needs to develop. Writers' purposes sometimes change as they generate new ideas in the process of writing, but seldom can they change their audience. Good writers adapt to it and make their choices about vocabulary, tone, style, content—everything—with that audience in mind. Often the chief stumbling block for unsuccessful writers who work hard but show little improvement is that they don't seem to be able to shape their writing with someone in mind. As long as their audience is general, their writing is also apt to be general, lacking the precision, focus, and concrete details that a specific audience would require.

MODEL TOPIC: *Audience and purpose*

AUDIENCE: President and regents of the university, the people who make the decisions about what facilities the school will provide and decide how university money will be spent.

PURPOSE: To convince the regents and president that a good day-care center for the children of faculty and students would be in the best interest of the university.

STRATEGIES FOR DISCOVERY

BRAINSTORMING

Brainstorming is a quick method of generating a body of material that a writer can use for stimulus. Two principles govern brainstorming: one idea piggybacks on another, and in brainstorming there are no wrong answers.

You can brainstorm by yourself or with other people working on the same project. Often a group is more productive.

The techniques for brainstorming are simple. Using a typewriter, pencil, tape recorder, or your computer, concentrate on your topic and start writing down everything that comes into your head, no matter how extrava-

Campus day-care center

Faculty women
Peace of mind
Close to kids
    Save money
for young professors

Students
Lots of women coming
back to school

Universities & businesses have exercise
facilities so why not day care?
Just as important to employers
Would pay off
    Lower absenteeism
    Healthy children

Increased
divorce rate
single parents —

Other Countries
Israel ← get figures here
Sweden
France

Women's Lib Angle

Gives women chance
    to upgrade skills

Makes up for past
    discrimination

Objections

Cost?
Unions?
Family
interference?

Good for fathers too —
they have to worry about
    child care

What would U. admin-
istration probably say?

Not U's business —

gant or irrelevant it may seem. Don't worry about any of the niceties—just write or, if you're in a group, talk and take notes. After fifteen or twenty minutes you should have a wealth of material. You'll have to discard or store some of it, but you've begun to generate your paper.

FREEWRITING

Many writers also find *freewriting* a productive strategy for generating ideas. Start by writing out your topic on a piece of paper or your terminal screen; then start writing anything that comes into your head about that topic. Don't try to plan or organize and certainly don't stop to correct anything. Think of the process as *harvesting* the fruits of both your conscious mind and your subconscious—as you reap what your mind has generated, more will push through to the surface. The important thing is to keep writing and harvesting ideas, so don't stop to worry about details such as finding the right word. If you do, you may interrupt a potentially rich crop of ideas that you are nourishing. If you get stuck, just write down anything that comes to your mind—nonsense words if necessary. Keep your brain moving and soon it will begin to produce again.

You can freewrite for ten or fifteen minutes at a time or you can play around for an hour or more. When I am just beginning on a serious piece of writing, I will often stay at the word processor and try to freewrite as long as I can, perhaps getting up to take short breaks, but staying with it until I think I have exhausted my available resources for the time. Peter Elbow, the teacher who introduced the idea of freewriting in a book called *Writing without Teachers*, suggests that after a short session of freewriting —perhaps fifteen minutes—the writer should stop to sum up in one sentence the main point of the section just completed. Elbow calls that summary sentence "the center of gravity." Then you can start writing again, using that "center of gravity" sentence as the take-off point for your next freewriting session. You can continue this way until you think you have generated enough material.

Freewriting can be a particularly rich discovery strategy because it helps writers to take advantage of those flashes of inspiration that most of us occasionally feel when we are writing. We know that to some extent, we are going to find out what we want to say *as* we write, yet trying to write a complete paper from start to finish by relying on inspiration can produce disastrous results. With freewriting, you can reap the benefits of writing-as-discovery but avoid the risk.

ASKING THE JOURNALIST'S QUESTIONS

Another reliable discovery strategy is to ask the questions that journalists frequently rely on when they are working on an article. Those questions are,

Who?
What?
Why?
Where?
When?
How?

Writing out the answers to these questions about your topic can help you put together a framework of assertions that will outline the main points you want to make.

Notice how this question approach could work with the proposed paper on the Law School Admission Test.

WHO: Faculty and admissions board of university law school.

WHAT: Do away with the LSAT as the chief determiner of who gets into law school.

WHY: LSAT rewards a narrow, unimaginative kind of intelligence, sometimes discriminates against minorities, and cannot measure motivation or creativity.

WHEN: As soon as possible.

WHERE: University law school.

HOW: Appoint a committee to work out an admissions plan that will screen people for the qualities that characterize successful lawyers.

Although a critical reader would quickly realize that this kind of inquiry often yields oversimplified answers, the process can provide the take-off points needed for research or more focused and intensive thinking.

MODEL TOPIC: *Using reporters' questions*

Who: University president and board of regents.
What: Establish a quality day-care center on campus for children of faculty and students.
Why: Increase enrollment, attract better faculty, improve student and faculty productivity.
When: As soon as possible.
Where: Local university.
How: Appoint a director to start the center and appropriate $1.2 million to finance it.

Another way of focusing your thinking in getting started is to put your chief points in capsule form. Try imagining how the paper you are going to write would be described in a summary of fifty words or less. Theoretically, if you are clear about your proposal or argument, this capsuling should be easy to do, but you will be surprised at how tough it can be. It is an excellent intellectual exercise in forcing you to say what you mean.

MODEL TOPIC: *Capsuling*

Many young married women who want to go to college or become teachers at a college are handicapped because they have young children. The university should show its commitment to equal opportunity for women by establishing a quality, low-cost day-care center on campus for the benefit of these women.

RESEARCHING YOUR TOPIC

If you have a topic but don't know how you might focus it or what you can say about it, one good way to stimulate your thinking is to start doing research. You can begin with the traditional kind of library research (see suggestions in Chapter 10) or you can gather material by interviewing people, taking a field trip to visit an office or institution connected with your topic, watching shows or movies about the topic, going to another department in the university to find out what persons there might know, and so on. Just getting out and doing something connected with your topic will help you start to generate ideas.

CULTIVATING SERENDIPITY

In the long run, your most productive discovery strategy may be cultivating *serendipity*, the faculty of finding good things that you aren't really looking for, apparently by accident. But serendipity is more than simple luck; it is a developed ability to stay alert for unexpected opportunities and be aware of what is going on at the fringes of your consciousness so you pick up the chance remark or unexpected event. It is the habit of being places where things happen and talking to people who turn out to know something useful. It is the habit of having your intellectual antennae always tuned to pick up signals. The more mentally active you are, the more interests you have, and the more curious you are, the more likely you are to develop serendipity. And then the happy accidents that seem to happen so often to creative and productive people will begin to happen to you.

ORGANIZING MATERIAL

Most writers need to make some plans before they start to write. Writers' plans, however, are as individualistic as authors themselves, and no one should try to prescribe how anyone else should organize his or her writing. The talented writer John McPhee constructs elaborate and detailed outlines before he starts to write anything; the equally talented writer (and philosopher and teacher) Jacques Barzun says, "For my taste, outlines are useless, fettering, imbecile."[1] Some writers even seem to be able to do virtually all of their planning in their heads before they start writing. So the most a text can do is to describe some methods of organization that seem to work for many writers.

TRADITIONAL OUTLINES

One method is the traditional outline. Writers who like outlines say that they help them to marshal their thoughts and keep track of the main points they want to make. For example, John McPhee, who is an acclaimed writer for *The New Yorker,* accumulates copious notes, then cuts them up and arranges them on a bulletin board in the form of an outline before he begins to write. He says that as he does so, the ghost of his high school English teacher smiles upon him.

If you are the kind of person who likes to classify things into orderly stacks, then outlining may be for you. The only thing to keep in mind is that you can change any outline—it's not a blueprint.

MODEL TOPIC: *Traditional outline*

I. Introduction: the growing number of women faculty and women students at universities raises the issue of day-care facilities on campuses.
   A. Returning women students often cannot afford to come to school full time if they have children.
   B. Women faculty with children cannot teach and do research if they do not have good and cheap care for their children.
II. This situation is harmful to the university.
   A. It loses potential students
   B. Women students are distracted from their studies.
   C. Women faculty may leave the profession.
      1. They will have to choose between family and career.
      2. They will not get tenure if they do not have time for scholarship.
III. The university could take steps to remedy this situation.
   A. It could provide good child-care facilities at no cost to parents.
   B. It could subsidize off-campus child care for students and faculty.
IV. Conclusion: The university would improve its image and the quality of its faculty and student body by solving the problem of child care on campus.
   A. Industry has benefited from similar plans.
   B. The university would help women to achieve.

---

1. Jacques Barzun, *On Writing, Editing, and Publishing* (Chicago: University of Chicago Press, 1971), 11.

ROUGH OUTLINES

Other writers not only dislike making formal outlines, but, like Jacques Barzun, actually find them a handicap. Barzun favors instead what he calls "a memorandum listing haphazardly what belongs to a particular project." That is, he draws up a kind of chart grouping similar points together and listing main ideas in roughly the order he wants to put them down. When you make a rough outline, you are sketching yourself a kind of map. It doesn't have to be complete or elegant.

OPEN-ENDED LISTS

Another kind of working memo is the open-ended list. Such a list should include all your main categories and some of your subpoints and examples. It should, however, be open and flexible enough for you to move items around if necessary or to add new points in any category. The advantage of this kind of plan is that it provides you with a checklist to work from but is loose enough to allow for change and expansion as you write and generate new ideas.

TITLES

Often choosing a working title for your paper before you start will help you to organize and focus your writing. A title is, after all, an announcement and a prediction; it raises your readers' expectations and points them in a specific direction. If you keep that title in mind as you write, it will remind you of what you have promised to do and help you to stay on your topic. Finding an accurate title for your paper can also help you to narrow your topic to a manageable size.

THESIS SENTENCES

Finally, you may find that the old reliable device of an organizing thesis sentence works for you. A good one can provide a framework for your paper. For example, here are three sample thesis sentences that would serve as useful organizing tools:

◦ The Law School Admission Test, which puts a premium on having a good memory, knowing correct English, and being able to read quickly, does not adequately measure qualities that make a successful lawyer: perseverence, rationality, and good intuition.
◦ Astronomers are not people who observe and report on a fixed body of information; rather they are scientists who are observing and speculating

about an ongoing process in which stars are born, live complex and diverse lives, and expire, sometimes in spectacular ways.
◦ The futurist John Naisbett claims that in the United States the trend toward decentralization in industry has already begun in airlines, publishing, microcomputers, and information processing.

Working out such a sentence helps many writers to get started thinking about their topic and planning how they are going to develop it. Keep in mind that a thesis sentence doesn't have to be a part of your paper; think of it as a tool, not an introduction.

Possible Titles and Thesis Sentences for Model Topic

Titles:
   The Benefits of a Campus Day-Care Center

   Better Child Care for University Students and Faculty

   Quality Child Care for a Quality University

Thesis Sentences:
   Alternative 1: If the university were to sponsor and subsidize a high-quality, on-campus day-care center for its students and faculty, it would make it possible for more women to enroll in courses, enable them to do better work, and provide an incentive that would help to attract and keep the best young faculty in the country.

   Alternative 2: A university-sponsored and subsidized day-care center on campus would benefit the university in several ways: it would provide an incentive for young faculty to come to the university because they would be assured good care for their children; it would allow more women to enroll in courses because they would know that their children were well-cared for while they were on campus; it would create good will for the university among women's groups and provide a model facility for other organizations to emulate for other local institutions.

INCUBATION

ALLOWING IDLE TIME

Many inexperienced writers don't realize how important it is to allow themselves some idle time when they are writing—or engaging in any creative process, for that matter. After you have done all your preparation to write a paper, you may still have a hard time getting started. You may be pushing too hard and would do better to do something else for a while and let the material you have accumulated just "cook" in your subconscious.

Allowing this time for incubation is particularly important if you are at work on demanding Class 3 writing.

People who study and write about the creative process believe that when scientists, architects, engineers, artists, or other kinds of creative people seem to stop working for certain periods of time, they are not idle at all. Rather they are giving their minds and imaginations a necessary interval for gestation, a time that the subconscious mind must have in order to absorb, sift, and process its data and select what it needs.

We don't really know what happens during this stage. Apparently the creative part of the mind goes on a kind of fishing expedition into the subconscious, but the fishing has to be private and unsystematic. The conscious mind is not in charge here, and the only way it can help is to be receptive to any insight or idea that may surface. After a period of time—it could be hours or days—the subconscious seems to finish the process of sorting, organizing, and making connections, and finds the solution or starting point it has been looking for. When it does, the conscious mind can take over again and use its faculties to get on with the work.

Incubation is so important to creative work that writers should think of these spells of apparent inactivity as necessary parts of the process. Even when you are doing Class 2 writing, you'll do a better job if you plan to give yourself some time off between preparation and actual writing. For Class 3 writing, it's even more crucial that you start far enough ahead to allow yourself to schedule a substantial idle period while your subconscious does its work. For many people, physical activity seems to be the most relaxing and potentially fruitful kind of time out.

But incubation doesn't happen just once or even a few times during the writing process. Like preparation, it's an ongoing process that can happen several times while you are working on a paper or article. In fact, I find that I have both major and minor periods of incubation as I work. The major periods come after I have finished a long stint at my desk and have literally written myself out. I am exhausted, have no more ideas, seem no longer able to write acceptable sentences. Then I have to stop and let the productive juices replenish, let the well fill up again. This kind of incubation is absolutely necessary if I am to continue working.

But I also have frequent minor periods of incubation—when I get up to let the cat out, move the sprinkler, get a glass of tea, or make a quick trip to the grocery store. Those little bits of time usually prove to be fruitful interruptions; I have come to count on them for solutions to the many little blocks and frustrations that inevitably occur when one writes.

When you begin to see incubation periods as essential to the writing process and learn to trust your subconscious to work for you, you should begin to feel more relaxed about facing even a difficult writing assignment. Take it by stages and have confidence that if you feed your subconscious with material and nurture it with periods of relaxation, it will come through for you.

TWO IMPORTANT CAUTIONS

But now, having assured you that idleness is not necessarily laziness, I will add two important cautions. First, while you are relaxing from the period of preparation and waiting for the subconscious to do its work, keep some portion of your mind alert and ready to go into action when the moment of insight strikes. You can't know whether the incubation period is going to be a few hours or two or three days, and when the insight or idea surfaces you need to seize it and write it down as soon as possible. If you don't, it can vanish almost as quickly as it came. In fact, it is a good idea to keep notecards or a pad of paper close by all the time you seem not to be thinking about your topic.

Second, don't wait indefinitely for an idea to strike. If after a reasonable length of time your subconscious still stubbornly refuses to produce what you need, put your conscious mind back on the job and try to start writing. Review your notes or your outline and run through in your mind what some of your options might be for getting started. Consciously try some of the techniques for development or just try to get out two or three paragraphs even if you are not very happy with them. The chances are good that the ideas that have been germinating beneath the surface will start to emerge and you can start actually writing on your assignment.

ILLUMINATION AND EXECUTION

CREATING A WRITING ENVIRONMENT

If possible, choose a writing place that is comfortable, familiar, and relatively free from distractions, and do your writing there whenever you can. After a while, the very atmosphere of the place will encourage you to write. Try to write at a specific time and be consistent about it. People who write regularly get so they automatically think about writing at that time of day. Try to select the tools and equipment that seem to work best for you and stick with them. Most people who write regularly have their favorites—yellow pad and pencil for some, typewriter for others—and seem to think they cannot work any other way. In the last few years, many writers have changed over to writing on word processors and wonder how they ever wrote without them.

Many professional writers are compulsive about having just the right equipment and just the right environment for writing. As Jacques Barzun says,

> We know that Mark Twain liked to write lying in or on a bed; we know that Schiller needed the smell of apples rotting in his desk. Some like cubicles, others vasty halls. Writers' requisites, if a Fifth Avenue shop kept them, would astound and demoralize the laity. Historically, they have included silk dressing gowns, cats, horses, pipes, mistresses, particular knickknacks, exotic headgear, currycombs, whips, beverages and drugs, porcelain stoves, and hair shirts.[2]

Such eccentricities may seem like frivolous indulgences or displays of artistic temperament, but at the critical point when you are trying to discipline yourself into starting to write, external physical props may help. When you settle yourself in a familiar writing environment and take up your familiar tools, you give your subconscious mind the signal to start writing. The visual stimulus of the yellow paper or the hum of the typewriter—or maybe now the green characters on the terminal screen—helps to shut out distracting thoughts and put the intellectual processes in motion. Writers who are tempted to procrastinate—and that's almost any of us at times—can help overcome that temptation by creating the best possible circumstances for themselves.

I should add a caution, however. Even though most writers seem to work best if they can write on a regular schedule and in a comfortable and congenial place, at times almost every writer has to throw ritual and habit out the window and work under unfavorable circumstances in order to meet a deadline. If you have to take a child to the doctor at the time you planned to write, you then have to seize whatever time you can find to finish a paper. If you don't have access to your typewriter or word processor, you may have to do a rough draft in pencil in a notebook. Rituals and routines can be a great help, but if you depend on them too heavily, you run the danger of making their absence an excuse for not writing.

OVERCOMING BLOCKS

But even under the best circumstances, you may still have trouble getting started. For some interesting reasons, such blocks are not surprising.

First, you are having trouble starting to write because you don't have any writing already on the page to go back to for directional signals and guidance. Writing is a powerfully recursive activity in which writers con-

---

2. Barzun, *On Writing, Editing, and Publishing,* 12.

tinually read back through what they have already written, looking for clues to help them guide and control what they are going to write. That re-reading seems crucial to help writers generate ideas and provide them momentum to keep going, especially in Class 3 writing. Yet when you are just starting to write, you don't have any writing to look back at. That's why freewriting can be so important. By reading over it, you can often find sentences that will help you get started.

Second, most of us sense that beginnings are very important. As one expert puts it, what we write at the beginning of a paper lays down tracks for us to run on: once we have those tracks down, we can move much more easily, but the direction of the tracks also controls our writing.[3] Because of this we tend to take beginnings too seriously, feeling that they must be good or we'll be in trouble. But there are many good ways to begin a paper; when you're trying to get started, just get *something* down. If you can't think of anything good, lower your standards and put down something terrible. You just need some sentences to start the words flowing— later you can throw the sentences away. What matters is putting down some tracks to run on so you can work up momentum.

What you should not do is wait for inspiration to strike. If you wait until you *feel* like writing, you may never start. As the noted economist John Kenneth Galbraith has put it,

> All writers know that on some golden mornings they are touched by the wand—are on intimate terms with poetry and cosmic truth. I have experienced those moments myself. Their lesson is simple: It's a total illusion. And the danger in the illusion is that you will wait for those moments. Such is the horror of having to face the typewriter that you will spend all your time waiting. I am persuaded that most writers, like most shoemakers, are about as good one day as the next . . . , hangovers apart. The difference is the result of euphoria, alcohol, or imagination. The meaning is that one had better go to his or her typewriter every morning and stay there regardless of the seeming result. It will be much the same.[4]

If you are working on a paper over a period of days and have many interruptions, temporary paralysis is apt to set in each time you have to start over. And the longer you are away from your writing, the harder it will be to get started again. When that problem arises, try going back and rereading what you have already written or even rewrite the last page you did the previous time. Usually that kind of backtracking will get the creative juices flowing again.

---

3. James Britton, "Shaping at the Point of Utterance," in *Reinventing the Rhetorical Tradition,* ed. A. Freeman and I. Pringle (Conway, Ark.: L & S Books, 1980).
4. Galbraith, "Writing, Typing, and Economics," *Atlantic,* March 1978, 104.

FINDING YOUR PACE

Writers work at different paces, and you need to find the rhythms that suit you best. Some writers compose their first draft rapidly, spilling out a veritable torrent of words. They seem to be able to generate material almost as fast as they can think, and they are in a rush to get everything written down before they forget it. They work in spurts, writing several paragraphs very quickly, stopping occasionally to reread and think, but producing a lot of writing at one sitting. I call these writers *sprinters*. Most sprinters think of the first draft as a discovery draft. They don't stop to fuss with words or revise because they plan to write another two or three drafts.

Other writers work at a much slower pace when they are doing a first draft. They write their sentences slowly, stopping frequently to reread and to think. They change words, insert phrases, delete what they have already written, and they spend a great deal of time staring at their typewriters or terminals or chewing their pencils while they plan what they are going to say. They make major changes *as* they write. They also pace, eat, get drinks of water, and worry. I call these writers *plodders*. Plodders may take two or three hours to produce a page or two, but they usually make many fewer changes on the second draft. While the plodder doesn't usually regard the completed first draft as the finished product, he or she knows that when it is done, the hardest part of the job is over. Often this kind of draft can be revised fairly quickly because so much thought has already gone into it.

A third kind of writer is the perfectionist. These writers have to do everything right the first time—think out each phrase and each sentence completely before they write it down, and change any word they are not satisfied with. They cannot leave any blanks, and they cannot go on with a new paragraph until they are completely satisfied with the one they have just written. I call this kind of writer *bleeders*. Bleeders suffer more than other writers because they agonize so over decisions, and it takes them forever to produce a piece of writing. When they do finish, however, they don't usually plan to rewrite.

You will have to experiment to find the pace that works best for you, but I recommend that you try to start out as a sprinter. The advantage of "sprinting" is that it gets you started, you get a sense of accomplishment from seeing the paper grow, and you create a text that you can start working on. Even though you may be dissatisfied with what you have produced, writing the second version will be easier. You must, however, count on rewriting. Inspired first drafts seldom do the job.

But if you are not the sprinter type, don't worry about it. Many productive writers are plodders, and some of us just have to work slowly, think out our ideas as we work, and make substantial revisions in the first draft.

The progress may seem discouragingly slow, but in the long run plodders may not spend any more time achieving a finished product.

Don't, however, allow yourself to be a bleeder. Bleeders are the kind of writers most likely to develop a writer's block that will keep them from producing at all, and they are the ones most likely to miss their deadlines. Moreover, stopping too long to put one idea into precise form may make you lose the next idea, which can disappear while you are still fussing over the one that triggered it. And finally, at the distance of a day or two, that perfect document may seem much less perfect; then you'll regret the original agony. "Bleeding" has nothing to recommend it.

POSTPONING CORRECTIONS

Whether you are a sprinter or a plodder, put off making corrections in spelling and mechanics until you're ready to write the final copy. Although it is certainly important that you write standard English and that you punctuate your sentences and spell words correctly, don't worry about such matters while you are still composing. When you are actually writing, you have all you can handle just to get your ideas down and organize them into readable form—you shouldn't at the same time be fretting about where to put commas or whether *harass* has one or two r's. You can fix such details later. Writers who begin to focus on mechanics too soon stifle their creative energies; instead of concentrating on expressing their ideas, they spend their time trying to avoid mistakes. That's not productive. Better to write first and edit later.

But the most important reason you should try to keep getting your words down on paper (or the screen) is that *writing is a generative process.* Writers working beyond Class 1 writing almost never know exactly what they are going to say when they start writing, even though their writing assignment seems straightforward. Experienced writers count on material coming to them as they write, and so should you. The writing process is *not* linear—you can't expect to move smoothly from one stage to the next, tying up loose ends as you go and finishing by proofreading a completed document. And the more complex and demanding the writing task is, the more complex the process will be.

MAINTAINING THE CREATIVE TENSION

When you are engaged in serious writing and want to do the best job that you possibly can, it is important that you try to maintain a kind of *creative tension* as you work. That is, you have to practice a kind of juggling act with yourself.

On the one hand, you have to get on with the job. On the other hand, you shouldn't put on intellectual blinders and be so goal-directed that you ignore new ideas or unexpected insights that may be hovering at the periphery of your mind. One expert on creativity says that we should pay attention to our "fringe consciousness":

> Just as it is very difficult to see the sun's corona unless the disk is hidden by a total eclipse, so it is very difficult to observe our "fringe consciousness" at the instant of full illumination. . . . [Writers' thinking] can be only partially controlled by order and forethought. As they work, their whole nervous system may be half-consciously quivering with old memories and new associations and vague emotional intimations. They can . . . and they should acquire the habit of watching the unfocused fringe of their consciousness for any significant mental events which may appear there, without diverting their attention from their immediate task; just as the fencer watches in the periphery of his vision for significant movements without withdrawing the central focus of his field of vision from his opponent's eyes.[5]

The trick is to try to keep your mind functioning at a top level and a subsurface level at the same time. On the top level, you take a goal-directed, problem solving, pragmatic approach to writing and think primarily about getting the job done; on the subsurface level, however, let a second part of your mind take a more relaxed and playful approach and be open to random thoughts or surprises. You move ahead steadily but at the same time you try to avoid premature closure that might shut off some potentially rich vein of development. It's a delicate balance, but a creative one.

REVISION

Revising your writing involves much more than just correcting errors, resolving inconsistencies, and tidying up surface appearances. An outside editor could take care of those chores without really affecting the substance of your writing, but you are the only one who can actually *revise* your paper. You are the only person who knows what you want to do and thus the only one who can make it correspond more closely to your vision of what the paper should be.

In this sense, then, almost all writers continually revise *as* they work. Certainly professionals read and reread as they go, reflect on how their texts are developing, consider options, and make spot changes on work-in-progress. The process is an interesting one that involves one person acting almost simultaneously as a writer and a reader.

5. Graham Wallas, *The Art of Thought* (London: C. A. Watts and Co., Ltd., 1945), 52.

One writer and teacher puts it this way:

> The act of writing might be described as a conversation between two workmen muttering to each other at the workbench. The self speaks, the other self listens and responds. The self proposes, the other self considers. The self makes, the other self evaluates. The two selves collaborate: a problem is spotted, discussed, defined; solutions are proposed, rejected, suggested, attempted, tested, discarded, accepted.[6]

Both selves are important in the process: the self that is producing text has to learn to listen to the one that steps back from the text and evaluates it.

How much time you spend in this kind of internal dialogue and how much revising you do as a result of it depends mostly on whether you are a sprinter or a plodder. But regardless of which kind of writer you are, once you produce a completed draft of the piece you are working on, you need to get some distance from your work. If you possibly can, put the draft aside at least overnight to allow your mind to clear and give you a fresh outlook on what you have written.

When you do begin working on your second draft, try to start out by taking a broad, overall view of what the paper needs rather than working through it one paragraph at a time making corrections and changes as you go. If you try to revise for everything at once, you will have to keep so many concerns in mind at once that you are liable to bog down. Instead, it's a good idea to start out by making a plan for revising and deciding on your priorities. If you don't have time to make all the changes that you would like to make, what are the most important? What does the paper need most? When you have decided that, you can work on your revising in stages and get the most for the time you have to invest.

In Chapter 9 I suggest how you might go about setting such priorities and give specific suggestions for working through different stages of revision. You should probably go ahead and read that chapter now because revising really cannot be separated from the other stages of writing.

EXERCISES

1. List the various writing tasks that people in the following professions must do:

   engineering

   nursing

6. Donald Murray, "Teaching the Other Self," *College Composition and Communication* (May 1982).

banking
diplomatic service
college teaching
business management

2. List all the experiences you have had that you might find useful in writing a paper on one of the following topics. Include experiences such as seeing movies and television shows, reading books, or hearing someone speak on the subject.

   What it means to be a pre-med student
   The hazards involved in running
   The great health-club boom
   The growth of the fast-food industry

3. Explore a possible topic for a paper—for example, "The Joys of Scuba Diving" or "The Ballet Boom in the Eighties"—by asking these questions about the topic and writing out the answers:

   Who? What kind of people are participating?
   What? What is involved in the activity?
   Why? Why do they participate?
   When? When did the activity start, or when does it occur?
   Where? Where does the activity take place?
   How? How is the activity carried out, or how do the people involved act?

4. Write a 100-word summary of the main ideas you would include in a paper on one of these topics:

   Designing a personal exercise program
   The art of buying at discount
   Picking the right graduate school
   Preparing to take the Law School Admission Test

If you prefer to work from an outline instead of a summary, make an outline for the same topic.

5. Get together a group of three or four people and brainstorm for twenty minutes on one of these topics. Ask one person to be the recorder and write down every idea or suggestion that the group mentions.

   jet lag
   microwave ovens
   junk food

the Sunbelt
defensive driving
crash diets

SUGGESTED WRITING ASSIGNMENTS

1. The free magazines put out by airlines publish a wide variety of articles on almost every subject imaginable; for example, the psychology of wearing a tie, the art of tipping, part-time careers, coping with stress, and so on. They frequently feature articles about cities or resorts to which their airlines fly. An enterprising free-lance writer might be able to use a personal interest or hobby as the basis of a salable article for one of these magazines. Some topics are suggested below, but you could get additional ideas by thumbing through a magazine next time you fly. Your article should probably be no longer than 1,000 words unless you and your instructor decide ahead of time that you will need more to do a good job.

Before you begin to write the paper, write an analysis of what kind of people you think might read your article and what they would probably expect to get from it. Then write out your purpose in writing: What do you expect to do for the reader? Include a descriptive title.

TOPICS:
Eating seafood in New Orleans (or in Boston)
Shopping in London (or Hong Kong, Paris, or Honolulu)
Finding the best skiing in the West (or the East)
Tips for businesswomen who travel alone
Planning a fly-drive trip through the Pacific Northwest

2. For the student newspaper on your campus, write a guest editorial on one of the topics given below or on a similar topic based on some controversy that has recently made headlines at your school. The editorial should be no longer than 750 words, because that is the maximum that the paper will print in the guest column, and it should include information—not just passions and opinions—that will help to enlighten your audience and persuade them that your position is valid.

On the first page, specify which portion of the paper's readers you are trying to reach—faculty and administrators make up an important part of the audience for a campus newspaper—and what characteristics they have that will affect how you phrase your argument. Also write out your purpose: what do you hope to accomplish with the editorial?

POSSIBLE TOPICS:

A. Problems caused by using foreign graduate students as teaching assistants in certain departments.

B. The need for a campus writing center that would serve all students who need help with their writing.

C. A comment on the faculty proposal to revise the undergraduate degree requirements to include a three-hour course in computer science for everyone.

D. A comment on the university administration's proposal that starting next year every student be required to buy a personal computer when he or she comes to college.

3. Write a review of a book, a movie, or a television program that could be published in your local student or city newspaper. Clip from the paper the kind of review that you want to write and tape it to a sheet that you turn in with your paper.

Before you begin to write, define and analyze your audience. Who reads this kind of review, why do you think they read it, and what would they want to get from it? Then write your specific purpose. What is the main point you want to make in the review and how do you want your audience to react? Write a headline for your review.

4 ◇ What Is the Writing Situation?

When you begin any writing task, whether it's for a college course or on the job, it's useful to stop and review the individual components of the particular situation in which you are going to be writing. You need to think about *why* you are writing, to *whom* you are writing, and *what* you are writing.

THE COMMUNICATION SQUARE

I find it useful to think of any writing situation in terms of a communication square with its sides labeled *Audience, Purpose, Persona,* and *Message.*

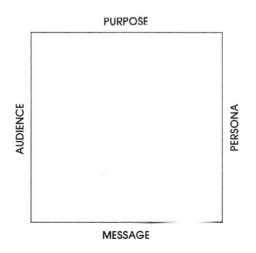

PURPOSE

AUDIENCE

PERSONA

MESSAGE

The term *persona* means an actor's mask or the character an actor is assuming. Writers also assume different roles when they write, mainly through their use of style and tone, so we speak of their different *personas*.

Drawing a communication square and writing out a descriptive label for each side can help you when you are preparing to write. First, sketch out the square and then ask yourself these questions:

◦ Who is my audience? Who do I expect to read this writing?
◦ What is my purpose? What do I hope to accomplish with this writing?
◦ What is my persona or role? How do I want my readers to picture me?
◦ What is my message? What is the chief point I want my readers to get from my writing?

As you write out the answers to these question along the sides of your communication square, remind yourself that each side affects every other side. If you change one, you need to think how the other sides may be affected.

Here is how the communication square might look for the model topic from the previous chapter.

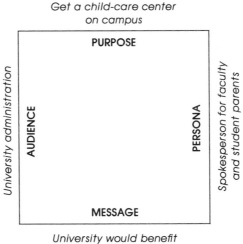

Notice that the purpose and message here are not exactly the same.

AUDIENCE

IDENTIFYING YOUR AUDIENCE

The most important advice I can give any writer is to remember your audience. Always keep in mind who is going to read your writing and why he or she is reading it. Unless you know who your readers are and what they expect to get from your writing, you cannot do a good job for them.

The advice seems obvious, yet if someone were to ask me to name the most common problems of writers in college, I would put the failure to identify and analyze audience very close to the top. Student writers have trouble realizing that part of becoming a skilled writer is learning to think beyond the immediate audience of the professors who are going to grade their papers; as a result, they don't practice thinking about what kind of impression their writing would make on a reader outside the classroom. They forget the demands that readers make on writers when they are reading primarily for information or enjoyment. And yet after college (and maybe even on your job now) you will write for readers who make just such demands. If your writing bores them, confuses them, takes up too much time, or fails to meet their expectations, they will stop reading.

If, however, you take the time to identify your readers and think about what they hope to learn from you, you are more likely to keep them reading because you meet their needs and expectations. That doesn't at all mean that you are pandering to them by telling them what you think they want to hear. It means only that if you want your readers to pay attention, you have to put yourself in their place and anticipate their needs.

ANALYZING YOUR AUDIENCE

Fortunately, all of us already know a great deal about analyzing an audience—we do it instinctively when we are writing or speaking in everyday situations. For example, if you are writing to MasterCard to report an error in the statement they have sent you, you would write a straightforward letter giving them specific information about the error. If you are leaving a note for your ten-year-old son giving him directions for cleaning the garage, you wouldn't waste time on preliminaries, and you wouldn't use formal language. When you write your parents or older friends you probably don't use the same language you use with your bowling partners. Such adjustments are intuitive when we know who our readers are and what they expect from us. In one sense, we are all communication experts: in communication situations that are personal and immediate, we adapt to our audiences automatically. Learning to analyze the needs of an unfamiliar and more distant audience is more difficult, but essentially the same strategies apply:

◦ What do I know about my audience that I need to keep in mind?

What interests or values do they have that I need to appeal to? What concerns do we share?

Are they going to be hostile, sympathetic, or neutral to my point of view?

How busy are they? How much time are they willing to invest in reading what I write?

Are they expert readers or just average?

◦ What do my readers expect from me?

Are they reading to learn or just to be entertained? Do they actually *need* to read what I'm writing? If not, what will keep them reading?

What specific questions will they have when they begin to read? Such questions might be *What is the problem? How can it be solved? Why should I care? How much will the solution cost?*

◦ How much do my readers already know about my topic?

How much do I need to explain? Do I need to give background material? Can I use specialized terminology?

What kinds of details are likely to interest my readers? Do I need to give a lot of details or would they be boring?

What experiences have they had that would help them to understand what I am writing?

◦ What attitudes are my readers likely to have toward my topic? Will they be sympathetic, hostile, or neutral?

Another, less formal way to focus on the needs and expectations of your audience is to keep asking yourself these questions as you write:

◦ Am I keeping *their* interests and concerns in mind?

◦ Am I boring them by telling them more than they want to know?

◦ Am I wasting their time by writing more than I need to?

◦ Am I intimidating them with unfamiliar terms and references or with language they don't understand?

◦ Am I threatening them by attacking their beliefs or their self-esteem?

◦ Am I patronizing them by acting superior?

◦ Am I disappointing them by not doing what I promised to do in the title or the first paragraph?

Finally, one major point to keep in mind is this: *Always assume your readers are intelligent even though they may be uninformed.*

THE PROFESSOR AS AUDIENCE

Professors dread getting what I call "teacher papers," papers not really written for any interested audience who wants to learn something, but produced only to meet the minimum requirements of an assignment. Such a paper may cover the topic adequately and earn the author a passing grade, but a "teacher paper" has no voice because the author didn't care about the topic and invested little in his or her writing. The student who wrote it was bored, and the professor who gets it will be bored. If you're going to spend several hours writing a paper, go to the trouble to find a topic or an angle that engages your interest and is worth your time. The professor is also more likely to think it's worth his or her time.

Audience analysis for day-care center paper
University administrators

Important characteristics

1. They stay informed and know there's a national crisis about day care for children. They care about the welfare and morale of faculty, staff, and students, and they want the university to run efficiently. Probably they're willing to listen to a proposal that provides services for these groups. They're very busy and won't have any patience with a proposal that wastes their time.

Hard to tell whether they'll be friendly or hostile. Need to find out whether they are mostly men and how old they are—middle-aged and older men may not like idea of subsidized child care. Women and younger men more likely to be receptive.

2. Administrators would read the proposal to get information about why the university needs a day-care center, who it would serve, how it could be set up, and operated, and what it would cost. They don't absolutely have to read the proposal, but if they think it might benefit the university, they're likely to.

3. Most of these administrators have only a general knowledge of day care centers but that's enough for now. Mainly they would want to see figures about how many faculty and students need such a center and why the university should take on such responsibility.

They know enough about the problems of working parents so that they probably don't need a lot of explanation.

PURPOSE

After you have identified your readers—or sometimes before, since it's hard to separate purpose and audience—and thought about how you can appeal to them, you need to decide what you want to do in the paper. Ask yourself

◦ What am I trying to accomplish?
◦ How do I want my readers to respond?

Your broad answer to the first question would probably be: To *inform, explain, critique,* or *argue* (see page 5). It could also be simply to entertain. For each specific writing project, however, you need to work out a narrower and more detailed statement of your goal. For example,

> I want to convince my readers to vote against the proposed bond issue.
> I want my readers to understand why computers can't translate foreign languages efficiently.
> I want my readers to understand the function of the World Bank.

While it's true that sometimes you may develop your purpose as you write or change your focus as you work and discover new content, still you need to have a fairly good idea where you are going when you start out. Writing out your purpose ahead of time can help you to avoid certain pitfalls:

◦ Writing a "cheerleader" paper, that is, a paper arguing a position that the audience already agrees with. Unless you're writing political victory speeches, there's not much point in doing this.
◦ Writing for an audience whose mind is closed on the topic. If you are advocating violence and your audience is largely Quaker, your writing is pointless. You are in a non-rhetorical situation, that is, one in which persuasion is not possible.
◦ Writing only for yourself, that is, simply writing to express an opinion for no particular reason and for no specific audience. Such writing has its function as "private" writing or sometimes as a first draft in which you are discovering what you want to say, but it doesn't work for "public writing" intended primarily for others.

Finally, finding your focus is an integral part of finding your purpose, but often a writer begins to narrow and define his or her focus more explicitly after having started to write. Therefore once again a writer needs to maintain a tension between preliminary planning and intuitive discovery. Plan ahead, know your purpose, but unless you are absolutely sure what you are going to write, don't get too committed to that purpose. As you write, you may want to sharpen the focus or change your angle, and you should feel free to do either.

Analysis of Purpose for Day-Care Center Paper

Purpose: To persuade the university administration that it should establish a low-cost, subsidized day-care center on campus. To give them enough information to show that the project is practical and would be a good investment, and to give them specific reasons why it would be a good idea.

PERSONA

CREATING A ROLE

Once you have analyzed your audience and have a clear sense of why you are writing, think about how you want to appear to that audience. Ask yourself these questions:

- What impression do I want to make on my readers?
- What role am I going to put myself in?

Each time you write (or speak) for any audience other than yourself, you create a drama in which you play a role. Using only words on a printed page, you have to get your audience's attention and win its confidence. And you have to operate without any cues or feedback from your audience; you can only imagine what kind of impression you are making.

But it is possible to develop your imagination and learn to write—or revise—keeping one part of your consciousness on how your writing is going to appear to your reader. Learn to ask yourself questions like these:

- What facts do I need to show that I've done my homework?
- Should I use contractions? How will they affect my readers?
- What effect would a personal anecdote have on my readers?
- What impression would specialized terminology have?
- How much distance do I want to establish? How can I do it?

All of these factors (and many more) affect your *persona* and influence the way your readers respond to you.

A crucial element of any persona is the author's *authentic voice* (see Chapter 2), the quality of a person's writing that makes readers feel that there is an individual behind a piece of writing who is genuinely interested in what he or she is writing. Suppose you wanted to create this kind of authentic voice in the paper written on the model topic of campus day-care centers. If you want to convince a group of intelligent but skeptical university regents that they would help the university by establishing the day-care center, you're going to have to show that you care about the center yourself. You can do that by presenting a detailed and carefully thought out proposal, not simply an emotional argument. You could also strengthen your voice by writing about your own or someone else's experience in trying to find care for her children so that she could return to college.

In a different kind of writing situation you might convey an authentic voice in a different way.

ESTABLISHING ETHICAL APPEAL

In addition to creating an authentic voice as part of his or her *persona,* an effective writer also needs to establish *ethical appeal,* the intangible quality in a piece of writing that makes readers trust and respect the writer. Writers project that quality in several ways: by showing they are well informed on an issue, that they are fair-minded, honest, and not trying to conceal anything, that they have a good record or reputation, and that they are confident. They make their readers believe in them; they show that they are qualified to write on their topic.

The strongest ethical appeal comes from a good reputation. Writers like Lewis Thomas, Barbara Tuchman, and Norman Cousins are so respected in their fields that readers who see their name on a book or article are immediately disposed to trust what they say. Unknown writers, however, have to create their ethical appeal with the style and substance of their work. They have to understand how writers make a good impression. While there is certainly no recipe that one can follow for creating such an impression, here are some useful guidelines that will help you to establish ethical appeal in most writing situations:

- ◇ Focus your topic down to manageable size. Writers lose their readers' confidence when they take on more than they can handle.
- ◇ Do your research. Use figures and examples to support your generalities. Remember the *weight of facts.* Show that you know what you are writing about by citing background information and quoting authorities.
- ◇ Acknowledge the opposition. Show that you are aware of the other side of the issue and that others may have different views. Avoid giving the impression that you have the one right answer. Don't overstate your case nor claim more than you can reasonably support. Avoid statements

using the words "never" and "always" unless you are sure they're justified. Don't oversimplify by sounding as if complex problems have easy solutions.

⋄ Show confidence. Don't denigrate yourself or say "I might be wrong, but . . ."

CONTROLLING YOUR PERSONA

A writer can control the degree to which an audience will be aware of his or her presence in the writing. At times your persona should virtually disappear. For instance, if you are writing a technical or scientific report or giving a process analysis, don't intrude yourself into the account. That restriction doesn't mean that you should never use "I," especially if avoiding the word means that you have to resort to writing "this author" or "the investigator." When you are reporting on your own discoveries "I" is quite appropriate.

In very personal writing in which you are drawing on your own experiences and expressing opinions, you may want to use "I" frequently, use contractions, and generally reduce the distance between yourself and your reader. In more formal writing in which you want to maintain some distance, avoid contractions and establish a serious tone. Whatever style you adopt, keep in mind the role you are playing and try to play it as convincingly as possible.

Analysis of Persona for the Day-Care Center Paper

Persona: Want to come across as a responsible and mature person who cares about the welfare of the university and its faculty and students. Want to appear realistic and moderate—also show that I've done my homework. I know what such a center would cost but I also have done the research that shows how great the need is and how many people would benefit from it.

MESSAGE

Before you actually begin to write, ask yourself "What is my claim? What is the point I want to make?" Your answer won't necessarily be set in concrete—you may discover part of your message as you write. Nevertheless, you should have a reasonably clear idea of what your most important point is going to be so that you can use it as a kind of anchor for your paper. You should be able to state it clearly and succinctly:

The university can increase student enrollment and attract more qualified young faculty if it establishes a low-cost, quality day-care center on campus.

The great cathedrals at Rheims and Salisbury mark the apex of medieval architecture.

Writing your message down before you start will help you to focus and control your writing as you work.

EXERCISES

1. Here is a sample showing how one might go about analyzing the audience for a specific writing situation:

   The writing situation: a young person applying to the board of elders of a church for a tuition scholarship to a college affiliated with that church.

   Audience analysis: group of mature men and women who want to spend their church's limited resources wisely. They want to be sure that the person who gets the scholarship is an active church member who has a good academic record and can demonstrate that he or she needs financial help to go to college. They would also like to know whether the applicant plans to work while in school and what career plans he or she has.

   Write a similar analysis for the audience for these writing situations:

   A. A patient complaining to the county medical society about a doctor who performed an unnecessary hysterectomy.
   B. A citizen petition to the city council for a zoning change that would prohibit apartment houses in a new subdivision that is being opened.
   C. A government pamphlet on nutrition designed especially for low-income families.
   D. A fund-raising brochure to raise $100,000 for new instruments for the college band.

2. Here is a sample showing how one might analyze a reader's reasons for reading a particular piece of writing:

   An article on buying antique clocks: The readers of this article would read it to find out where to shop for such clocks, how to tell if they were genuine, what features to look for in good antique clocks, and how much they might have to pay for the clock that they might want to buy.

   Write a similar analysis of readers' reasons for reading the following:

   A. An article on how to buy ski gear.

B. An article on reading levels of students in the city's public schools.
C. A political advertisement for a candidate for state judge.

3. Here is an example of the way one might analyze a writer's purpose in a specific writing situation.

An article on white water canoeing: The writer of this piece would probably want to let readers know what white water canoeing offers to people interested in outdoor activities, what kinds of skills it requires, where one might go to participate in the sport, and how much it costs.

Make the same kind of analysis of writer's purpose for the following writing situations:

A. An article for parents on the effects of television watching on pre-school children.
B. A report on a new brand of microwave oven for a consumer magazine.
C. A brochure on the benefits of exercise, to be distributed to company employees.

4. Here is an example showing how one might analyze the persona he or she wanted to create for a writing situation:

Driver writing to a judge to appeal a six-month suspension of a driver's license: The writer wants to communicate the image of a sober, industrious person who will no longer speed and who must be able to drive in order to keep working.

Analyze the persona a writer might want to create in these writing situations:

A. A lawyer is writing to a school board to explain why they cannot fire a teacher who has worn a bikini in a bathing beauty contest.
B. An official of a drug company is writing an article to explain to physicians the side effects of a new tranquilizer.
C. A student is writing a professor to ask for a letter of recommendation to graduate school.

SUGGESTED WRITING ASSIGNMENTS

As a part of each assignment, write a one-paragraph analysis of your audience (including a statement about where your paper would be published and what your readers would want to know), a one-paragraph analysis of your purpose in writing, and a two- or three-sentence analysis of the persona you want to project in your writing.

TOPIC 1: Write a news release to announce a seminar on one of the following issues. Include a headline. Remember that you have *two* audiences: the editor who decides whether your release is worth publishing and potential readers who have an interest in your topic and want to know what the seminar has to offer them.

ISSUES:
Survival strategies for the families of alcoholics
Guidelines for the small investor
Resumé-writing for women reentering the job market
Learning how to trace your family's roots

TOPIC 2: Some law schools ask their applicants to submit an essay responding to this question: "Why do you think your application to our law school should be looked upon with favor?" In no more than 600 words, write such an essay.

TOPIC 3: You are the owner of a small advertising agency that is just getting started. A potential client calls you saying that she has an advertising budget of $250,000 to spend in the next three months promoting a luxurious vacation condominium community in Vail, Colorado. She is planning a glossy, colorful layout and asks you to suggest three magazines that are likely to have the kind of affluent, urbane readers she wants to appeal to. She wants you to do an analysis of the readership of those three magazines and give her the information she needs on which to make a decision. She also wants to know why you think those readers would be interested in her project. Each analysis should be no more than 350 words.

On the first page of your paper, make an audience analysis of the client, including the questions she would want answered, and a purpose analysis. Then proceed inductively. Go to a magazine stand or the library and choose some possible magazines. Examine the layout, the content of the articles, the products that are advertised and the kinds of appeals the advertisements use, and so on. For the purposes of this paper you can make up circulation figures. Some possible magazines are *The Robb Report, House Beautiful, Connoisseur, The New Yorker, Town and Country,* and *Gourmet.*

5 ◊ Getting Started

Whether you are a plodder or a sprinter, think of your first draft as a draft of *discovery*. You're writing it to help organize your ideas and find out what you want to say, so turn off that self monitor that criticizes as you write and get started. Get something down that you can then begin to revise and shape into a final paper. Don't be too hard on yourself if the first draft seems dull and rambling or if you don't have enough evidence. Often a first draft is more a statement of intentions than it is an actual paper. You'll have plenty of opportunity to fix it later.

WRITER-BASED AND READER-BASED PROSE

Often it helps to think about your first draft as "writer-based" prose[1]; you are writing primarily for yourself in order to harvest your ideas before they elude you. You are in the process of finding out what you think and generating material. At this point it may not be productive to stop to ask, "How is this going to affect my reader?" or to worry about whether you're constructing a logical argument. It's more important to keep the ideas flowing.

This concept of writer-based prose can be particularly useful not only when you are writing to discover, but also when you are writing the first draft for a persuasive paper on a topic about which you feel strongly. You can be as outrageous as you like, using terms like "disgraceful" and "idiotic" and resorting to name-calling and accusations. In a writer-based draft you can get the anger out of your system and blister your opponents, not worrying whether you're being biased and irrational. Once you have vented your rage—and in the process thought of some reasons to support

1. Linda Flower, "Writer-Based Prose: A Cognitive Basis for Problems in Writing," *College English* 41 (September, 1979): 19–37.

your position—you can go back to your draft and consider how you can revise it into "reader-based" prose that would be likely to persuade rather than alienate your audience.

When you begin to revise writer-based prose into reader-based prose, you shift from focusing on your own need as an author to express yourself to thinking about the needs of your audience when they read what you have written.

Not all first drafts need to be writer-based, of course. Often you can be thinking about your readers when you start to write and not let that concern interfere with generating content. But when you are starting on a difficult paper, particularly in Class 3 writing (see Chapter 3), try to focus on expressing *your* ideas and concerns first.

SOME SUGGESTIONS ABOUT OPENINGS

Beginnings are hard—even practiced writers agree on that. That first paragraph seems terribly important, and sometimes nothing that comes to mind seems good enough. In that case, my advice is simple: lower your standards. Once you have something on paper that you can go back and reread, other paragraphs will come more easily. So for the time being, think of your first paragraph as tentative and temporary. It's like a hook that you would use to anchor your leather thongs if you were going to start braiding a halter; later you can take it out. Or it's like the motions a pilot takes a plane through when getting ready to come into the field; you're "circling to land." So on first drafts at least, don't take first paragraphs too seriously.

In Chapter 6 I will have some specific suggestions to make about how to write effective opening paragraphs, but right now I want only to mention some of the ways that professional writers frequently use to get started on an article or essay.

EXAMPLES

You might want to begin with an example that illustrates a major point you want to make. If, for instance, you were writing an article urging your legislature to take drastic measures against drunk drivers, you might begin like this:

> Last Sunday morning three teenagers returning from a regional basketball tournament in Dallas were killed when their car was struck broadside by a drunk driver careening down the wrong side of the highway at 110 miles an hour.

If you were writing an essay about why American schools should require more math and science courses, you might start out like this:

> In Russia, 90% of students graduating from high school have had four years of science and four years of math, including calculus; in the United States, only 25% of high school graduates have such preparation.

Such openings work well because they focus on specific details that are apt to be interesting to your reader, and they give the reader a strong signal about what to expect in the rest of the essay. And they give you a concrete anchor from which to start writing.

QUOTATIONS

A quotation relating directly to your topic can become a good opening for a paper. For example, a professsional journalist introduces an essay on how air conditioning has changed American society like this:

> "The greatest contribution to civilization in this century may well be air conditioning—and America leads the way." So wrote British Scholar-Politician S.F. Markham thirty-two years ago when a modern cooling system was still a luxury.[2]

If you were going to write an article about an athlete's disenchantment with playing college football, you might begin:

> The English wit Oscar Wilde once said, "There are two tragedies in life: one is not getting what you want; the other is getting it."

Starting off with a quotation immediately gives the writing a personal touch and suggests that you are well educated and alert and have good resources to draw on.

ANECDOTES

An anecdote combines the good points of examples and quotations; it catches the reader's interest with a concrete and specific incident that illustrates a point you want to make, and it strikes a personal note that most readers like. For instance, the television critic Marya Mannes begins an ar-

2. Frank Trippett, "The Great American Cooling Machine," copyright 1979, Time, Inc. Reprinted in *The Riverside Reader, Vol. II,* ed. Joseph Trimmer and Maxine Hairston (Boston: Houghton Mifflin, 1983), 337.

ticle on sexism in advertising with three anecdotes that illustrate her thesis. One of them is this:

> Eddie Albert, a successful actor turned pitchman, bestows his attention on a lady with two suitcases, which prompts him to ask her whether she has been on a journey. "No," she says, or words to that effect, as she opens the suitcases. "My two boys bring back their soiled clothes every weekend from college for me to wash." And she goes into the familiar litany of grease, chocolate, mud, coffee, and fruit juice stains, which presumably record the life of the average American man from two to fifty. Mr. Albert compliments her on this happy device to bring her boys home every week and hands her a box of Biz because "Biz is better."[3]

For an article on famous men and their mothers, the author begins with this anecdote about President Harry Truman's mother:

> Early in the evening of August 14, 1945, in the living room of her yellow clapboard house in Grandview, Missouri, a small, spry woman of 93, talking to a guest, excused herself to take a long-distance call in another room. "Hello, hello," the guest heard her begin. "Yes, I'm all right. Yes, I've been listening to the radio. . . . I heard the Englishman speak. . . . I'm glad they accepted the surrender terms. Now you come to see me if you can. All right. Goodbye."
> "That was Harry," she said, coming through the door. "Harry's a wonderful man. He has a noble disposition and he's loyal to his friends. I knew he'd call. He always calls me after something that happens is over."[4]

An opening anecdote is especially useful because it catches your readers' attention with a visual image of people doing something, and it commits you to explain why you have used it.

GENERATIVE SENTENCES

One good way to start a paper is by writing down a *generative sentence,* a statement that generates expectations in the readers' minds. For example, each of the following sentences is generative because it implies a promise that the author will generate additional statements to explain or support it:

> The new technology of gene splitting has raised several important ethical questions.

3. Marya Mannes, "TV Advertising: The Splitting Image," *Saturday Review,* 4 November 1970.
4. David McCullough, "Mama's Boys," *Psychology Today,* March 1983, 32.

If women hope to achieve economic gains in the next decade, they must adopt new tactics.

With an increasing number of lawyers being graduated every year, the legal profession faces some sobering realities.

Successful managers usually have certain distinctive personality traits.

Opening generative sentences serve both readers and writers. They signal readers that supporting details are coming and prepare them to accept those details; they also remind the writer that he or she has made a commitment to furnish additional details. Both reader and writer recognize the beginning of one of our natural thought patterns: *general to specific*. It is useful for writers to know something about such patterns as aids to organization.

COMMON PATTERNS OF ORGANIZATION

Readers expect some plan of organization when they begin to read, and they will be more comfortable with writing that falls into familiar patterns. The most common ones are these, either by themselves or in some combination:

- Inductive reasoning
- Claims and warrants
- Definition
- Cause and effect
- Comparison
- Narration
- Process

INDUCTIVE REASONING

Inductive reasoning is the process of gathering evidence about specific examples or incidents and drawing a general conclusion on the basis of that evidence. Evidence can be examples, statistics, reports, experiences, historical or empirical data, or observations. People collecting the evidence usually have a hypothesis in mind that governs and focuses their procedures. In writing up an inductive argument, two formats are possible. You can either give the evidence first and then draw a conclusion, or cite the conclusion first and then give the evidence from which it was drawn.

Inductive reasoning is the basis of what we call the "scientific method," and for that reason it can often be an especially effective form of writing for certain purposes and certain audiences—for example, if you want to make a controversial argument to skeptical readers. To make it convincing, however, you need to keep in mind the basic requirements for effective inductive reasoning: that the amount of evidence is large enough and that the evidence is randomly selected.

Any writer needs to be careful not to fall into the common fallacy of overgeneralizing from scanty evidence, but usually you can make common sense judgments about how large the sample needs to be. If you wanted to generalize about students' political beliefs at a college of 3500 students, you would need to interview at least 200 students. Citing just three examples of dishonest officials as proof of corruption throughout the state would hardly be convincing, but if those three officials were all on the city council of one town, they could indeed demonstrate corruption.

Making sure that your sample is random is probably even more important than its size. You must be careful to choose a sampling method that will give you an accurate cross section of the population you are writing about. One way is to select every tenth person or every fiftieth person from a directory or list. But that list has to be relevant to the kind of information you want. If you were trying to find out how air travelers in your city feel about the local airport facilities, calling every fiftieth name in the phone book would not give you an accurate sample since many people don't travel. Instead you would have to choose a cross section of travelers who passed through the terminal on three different kinds of traveling days —perhaps on a business day, on a Saturday, and on a holiday weekend.

When you want to get a random sample for other kinds of broader based surveys you have to be sure that your sample includes representative groups chosen according to race, sex, income, education, occupation, and age. In general, the broader and more serious your claim is, the more carefully you have to plan your sampling strategies if you want to get convincing results.

In addition to being sure that your evidence is randomly selected and represents a large enough segment of the whole, you will strengthen your use of inductive reasoning if you remember these cautions:

- Get your facts straight and present them clearly. The force of inductive reasoning comes from the *weight of facts*, so show that you have done your homework and are presenting reliable data.
- Describe the method you used to gather your data and cite your sources. Readers want to know how and where you got your information so they can judge for themselves whether your research methods were legitimate and your sources credible.

◦ Be careful not to let your initial hypothesis contaminate the way you select your evidence. If you come across a significant fact that you did not expect to find, you should include it and try to explain it. Not to do so is dishonest and risky; leaving out pertinent facts can destroy your credibility.

CLAIMS AND WARRANTS

Another thought pattern that all of us use frequently is that of *claims and warrants*. That is, we make claims or assertions and then we give warrants to justify and support them. The pattern is as common as one person saying to another, "I'm going to vote for Bill Bradley for senator because he has an excellent record on environmental issues." Such statements can be classified as *informal logic*; that is, they don't actually *prove* claims, but they give good reasons for believing them. It is the kind of logic that lawyers use to argue cases in court.

BASIC TERMS AND FORMS

The English logician Stephen Toulmin has devised a model for analyzing and constructing claims and warrants.[5] It employs five basic terms:

CLAIM: The conclusion to an argument, the statement that is advanced for the approval of others. It may be stated or implied.

DATA: The data or evidence available to support a claim.

WARRANT: A statement of general principle that establishes the validity of the claim on the basis of its relationship to the data.

SUPPORT: Any material provided . . . to make the data or warrant more credible to the audience.

QUALIFIER: A qualification placed . . . on some claims (frequently in the form of such words as *possibly, probably,* or *most likely*).[6]

In their basic form, arguments constructed on the Toulmin model use only the first three terms, and they follow this pattern:

5. Stephen Toulmin, *The Uses of Argument* (London: Cambridge University Press, 1958), 6.
6. Richard D. Reike and Malcolm O. Sillars, *Argumentation and the Decision Making Process* (New York: John Wiley and Sons, Inc., 1975), 77–78.

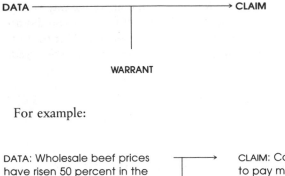

For example:

DATA: Wholesale beef prices
have risen 50 percent in the
past six months.

CLAIM: Consumers will have
to pay more for steaks in the
future.

WARRANT: An increase in wholesale prices
causes an increase in cost to consumers.

One might expand one part of the argument. For example:

DATA: Exhaust fumes cause
serious pollution problems in
cities.
DATA: Traffic congestion
causes serious problems.

CLAIM: All major cities should
ban private autos.

WARRANT: Banning private autos from cities
would reduce traffic and pollution problems.

Sometimes, however, the arguments a writer wants to make are more complex, and one or more statements need to be qualified. When that happens, the writer can add a qualification to any section. For example:

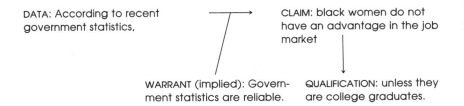

DATA: According to recent
government statistics,

CLAIM: black women do not
have an advantage in the job
market

WARRANT (implied): Government statistics are reliable.

QUALIFICATION: unless they
are college graduates.

Sometimes writers also realize that they must support one or more parts of their arguments. In such cases, another element appears in the Toulmin model for argument. For example:

DATA: on the average, pre-
school children spend 60 percent of their waking time
watching television.

↑

SUPPORT: According to the
book *The Plug-in Drug,*

CLAIM: Modern children are
conditioned to be consumers
at an early age.

WARRANT: (implied) Watching television conditions people to be consumers

Here is an example of an argument that is both qualified and supported:

DATA: the average cost of a
new house In the United
States is now $98,000.

↑

SUPPORT: According to the
1984 figures

CLAIM: In the 1980s, most
people in the U.S. will not be
able to buy a house

↓

QUALIFICATION: unless both
husband and wife are
working.

WARRANT: A person who earns the average
income of less than $25,000 cannot afford a
$98,000 house.

ADVANTAGES OF CLAIM/WARRANT ARGUMENTS

Organizing your arguments in this way has several advantages. The first is
that readers who prefer rational arguments are apt to respond positively to
the data/warrant/claim pattern because they recognize its resemblance to
courtroom procedures. They expect someone who makes a *claim* to *support* it with *data* (or evidence), and they expect him or her to give a *warrant*
(or explanation) that shows the reasoning behind the claim. Thus carefully
phrased arguments on this pattern have a legitimate ring about them.

A second advantage is that you can employ the Toulmin approach flexi-
bly, making decisions about how to develop it on the basis of the audience,
the purpose, and the writing situation. For example, sometimes you do not
need to make a warrant explicit. If you were writing to a group of coastal
property owners claiming that they should oppose the construction of an
offshore port for oversized oil tankers, probably all you would need to
point out is that having such tankers near shore greatly increases the
chance of oil spills in the area. You would not have to add that such oil
spills cause major property damage.

DATA: Bringing oil tankers
near shore increases the risk
of oil spills.

CLAIM: We should not build
offshore oil ports for oversized tankers.

WARRANT: (unstated) Oil spills do major
property damage.

If, however, you were writing to the members of the port authority commission who make recommendations about building such ports, you would need to convince them that potential property damage was a serious concern. In that case you would need to state and support your warrant.

DATA: Bringing oil tankers
near shore increases the risk
of oil spills.

CLAIM: We should not build
offshore oil ports for oversized tankers.

WARRANT: Offshore oil spills do major damage
to beaches and fishing grounds.

↑

SUPPORT: Facts about 1979 Gulf of Mexico
oil spill.

In other situations you might recognize that you needed to add qualifications to a claim, give expanded support for the data, or provide more than one warrant to clarify the relationship between the data and the claim.

A third advantage of the Toulmin method is that it allows you to arrange the parts of an argument in different ways. One might catch the audience's attention by making the claim or major assertion first, then presenting the data to support it. Virginia Woolf uses that approach in the following paragraph:

> [Claim] It is unthinkable that any woman in Shakespeare's day should have had Shakespeare's genius. [Warrant] For genius like Shakespeare's is not born among labouring, uneducated, servile people. [Data] It was not born in England among the Saxons and the Britons. It is not born today among the working classes. [Warrant restated and supported] How then, could it have been born among women whose work began . . . almost before they were out of the nursery, who were forced to it by all the power of law and custom?[7]

Woolf could also have begun her argument with the warrant, or, by rearranging her sentences slightly, she could have omitted the warrant and let

7. Virginia Woolf, *A Room of One's Own* (New York: Harcourt, Brace & World, 1929), 50.

her readers supply it. And perhaps she would have strengthened her argument by beginning with the qualifier, "*Probably* no woman in Shakespeare's time . . ."

You can decide which parts of an argument might be omitted and which parts need to be stressed only after analyzing audience and purpose. Nevertheless, the following guidelines can help you make such decisions:

- In almost every case, make both the claim and the warrant explicit.
- Include the warrant if the reader is apt to be skeptical or uninformed.
- Add a qualifier if the truth of the claim is uncertain or relative.
- Include support for major points that the reader may challenge.[8]

Notice too that Toulmin's approach to constructing arguments allows you to combine claim/warrant arguments with inductive arguments just as we do when we argue extemporaneously. We observe individual cases, make a generalization on the basis of those cases (induction), and then we present that generalization as a claim. The paragraph previously cited from Virginia Woolf illustrated the process. She investigated the origins of dozens of people of genius in England and found that none of them were uneducated or had come from the laboring classes. She then generalized that genius is not likely to come from those two groups of people. Using induction again, she examined the conditions in which women lived before the nineteenth century and realized that almost all of them were uneducated and treated like servants. From that data she generalized that they could not have become great writers.

Finally, the Toulmin model for arguments helps you generate material you can use to develop your ideas. These last two examples demonstrate how the Toulmin approach can be used to construct a chain argument in which the claim from one step of the argument can be used as the data for the next step.

Most of us find it easy enough to express our opinions, but sometimes we have trouble when we have to produce evidence (data) to back them or give explanations (warrants) for them. However, if you habitually ask yourself, "What is my warrant for this claim?" or "What supporting data can I find to strengthen my case?" you will find that such questions are tools for discovery. They force you to probe your experience and examine your store of information. Generally that is a thought-provoking process.

If you can train yourself to try the Toulmin approach when you undertake a writing task that requires you to make a claim or argue a thesis, you should find it a time-saving and productive strategy.

8. Michael Keene and Kitty Locker, "Using Toulmin Logic in Business and Technical Writing," unpublished paper, 1978, 6.

DATA: the value of the dollar   ———▶   CLAIM: More Americans
in relation to European currencies   will travel in Europe this
rose this year.   year.

QUALIFICATION: Unless air fares
from the U.S. to Europe skyrocket,

      WARRANT: People like to travel in countries
      where their money will buy a lot.

DATA: American travel in ——▶ CLAIM: tourism in the U.S. is going
Europe will increase this   to decline.
year, therefore

      QUALIFICATION: unless the U.S. tourist
      industry puts on an aggressive promotion.

   WARRANT: Americans will spend only a certain amount
   of money on travel.

DEFINITION

Another natural thought pattern that one can use to organize writing is
definition. We use definitions when we want to persuade, explain, or evaluate, and often they form the basis of essays or even whole books. The historian Barbara Tuchman, for example, wrote her book *The March of Folly*
to define "woodenheadedness" in national affairs. Plato's *Republic* is a
definition of justice.

The most common methods of defining are these:

○ Attributing characteristics:

The ideal motor fuel would be cheap, efficient, and clean.

A champion athlete must be strong, well-coordinated, competitive, and
have an overpowering desire to win.

(Comparison/contrast is a subcategory of this method.)

○ Analyzing parts (this can overlap with the method above):

The stages of the creative process are preparation, incubation, illumination and execution, and verification.

The Arab world consists of Egypt, Morocco, Algeria, Tunisia, Libya,
Jordan, Lebanon, Syria, Iraq, and Saudi Arabia and its small neighbor-
ing states.

◇ Giving examples:

Today's community colleges serve a new kind of college student: retired military personnel, wives or divorcees returning to school, underemployed workers who want to improve their status, and older people who simply enjoy learning.

Today most people buy their books not at a quaint and quiet bookstore on a side street but at one of the mass market book outlets: grocery stores, airport newsstands, drug stores, and the chain bookstores in shopping malls.

◇ Stating function:

A psychotherapist is a person trained to treat emotional problems.

A convenience store is one that serves customers who need to make small purchases quickly at early or late hours.

Definition is a particularly useful pattern of organization when you are *judging* or *evaluating*. You can use it to create a standard or yardstick for the way something ought to be, then apply that standard to an existing institution or situation and show how it should be changed. The Department of Education's 1984 report on the nation's schools, "A Nation at Risk," used this method to argue for major changes in public school education. You can also use *negative definition* in this way; that is, you can define something as having bad qualities and show that it should be changed.

Definition also plays a crucial part when you are *arguing about moral principles or ethical issues* because you must base your reasoning on what you believe is right or wrong, good or bad. For example, if you argue that women are underpaid because their pay averages 60 per cent of men's pay, you are defining such an economic discrepancy as wrong. If you want to write a paper claiming that the United States should send more food to famine-stricken countries, you are defining the government's moral obligations. This kind of approach works especially well when you can start with a definition of values that your audience will almost have to accept, such as freedom of speech, equal opportunity, and similar concerns.

CAUSE AND EFFECT

Another organizational pattern that reflects natural thought patterns is *cause and effect*. In fact, the thought process is so fundamental that it should be one of the first options you consider when you are wondering how to organize a paper. It works well for many kinds of college papers; for example, you might write a paper on Faulkner's *Light in August* speculating that Joe Christmas became a murderer because his fanatic stepfather abused him as a child. For an economics course, you might write a causal analysis of the effect of a strong dollar on the U.S. trade deficit.

You will find cause and effect a particularly useful model when you are trying to convince readers who you suspect may not share your values and who are likely to respond only to pragmatic arguments. For example, if you are arguing that Illinois should increase taxes to improve the state university, childless readers may not respond to an argument that the state needs a better university. If, however, you argue that improving the state university will bring new high-tech industries to Illinois and increase its tax base, you have a better chance of persuading those readers. In effect, cause-and-effect arguments are often problem-solving arguments and thus appeal to large numbers of people. But you should keep one caution in mind: cause-and-effect arguments can quickly go wrong when a writer oversimplifies or suggests that complex problems have simple causes and simple solutions.

CIRCUMSTANTIAL ARGUMENTS

Sometimes you may want to make a cause and effect argument in terms so compelling that your audience will almost have to agree with you. In that situation you can construct a *circumstantial argument,* one in which you claim that the chain of cause and effect is so strong that if A occurs, B is inevitable. When you want to make this kind of argument, choose language that conveys great urgency. Typical phrases are, "Under the circumstances, we have no other choice. . . ," "We are forced to take these steps. . . ," and "Given this situation, we must . . "

For example, in writing an environmental-impact statement, you could point out that if a manufacturer continues to use a local lake for cooling, the water temperature will rise enough to cause an increase in algae and pollute the lake. Or in arguing for an increase in the dues of an association you belong to, you could stress that increased costs for rent, utilities, and paper will bankrupt the organization if it does not get more income. Carefully constructed arguments from circumstance are hard to refute, so if you think your case is a particularly strong one, reach for those phrases that signal a crisis.

COMPARISON

Another good way to employ common thought patterns in your writing is to draw *comparisons.* In drawing a straight comparison, you simply show likenesses or differences that illustrate and strengthen the points you are making. For example, if you are asked to prepare an analysis of the advantages and disadvantages of instituting "flex-time" as company policy, you could cite the experiences of several other companies who have adopted "flex-time." If you were trying to persuade your readers that they should begin an exercise program, you could give figures that compare the blood pressures of exercisers and non-exercisers. Or if you wanted to argue the benefits of a free-market system as compared to controlled systems, you could compare the productivity of farmers in America to that of farmers in countries that have state-controlled farm programs.

Hard-fact comparisons like these are often convincing because readers like to know about parallel cases. Unfortunately, straight factual comparisons can also be dull. For a more illuminating and striking kind of comparison, you can use *analogy,* another one of our common thought patterns. Most readers like analogies because they dramatize similarities and use the familiar to explain the unfamiliar.

One mark of a good writer is the ability to draw good analogies that bring a flash of recognition to the reader: for example, Alfred Kazin's comparison of his boyhood school to a "factory over which has been imposed the facade of a castle," or David Riesman's description of an outer-directed person as one who employs radar to pick up signals from those around him. A writer trying to explain how a computer stores information might draw an analogy to storing black and white balls in numbered compartments.

Writers can develop a feeling for analogies by getting in the habit of thinking in terms of comparisons and drawing on their own experiences. For example, I have drawn analogies between my experience of taking risks in a controlled situation in a white water canoeing course and persuading students to take risks in their papers by having them write drafts that won't be graded. My students often draw analogies from their jobs or their experience in sports. One always needs to remember, however, that analogies don't *prove* an argument. They only strengthen it.

Another useful pattern of comparison is that of *a fortiori* reasoning (pronounced "ah-for-shee-or ee"). The term means "all the stronger." When we use this kind of reasoning we claim that if a person or group can do or has done a difficult thing, then it is logical to expect that same person or group can do a similar but easier thing—that is, there is "all the stronger" reason to assume they can. This kind of comparison underlies comments such as "If our university can afford to build a new $30-million dollar stadium, it should be able to spend $500,000 on minority scholarships."

The "all the stronger" approach to developing a point relies on the kind of commonsense reasoning that all of us use when we appeal to our readers' sense of what is logical and consistent. For example, one might say, "If we can spend billions on the space program, surely we can afford to send more aid to famine-stricken Africa." One has to be careful, however, not to let an *a fortiori* appeal deteriorate into oversimplification of the issues. Often apparently conflicting priorities cannot be resolved by simplistic either/or arguments because the matters are too complex. So although they can be good for capturing an audience's attention, it's not a good idea to depend totally on *a fortiori* comparisons.

NARRATION

Although we usually think of narration as storytelling, writers of nonfiction can also use it in many ways. For instance, it is the basic pattern for case studies, and it works well when a story will vividly illustrate a point. Certainly narration can enliven and strengthen much everyday, working writing. Those short tales that we call *anecdotes* or *incidents* work especially well.

An anecdote is a miniature, self-contained story that usually focuses on a person in order to illustrate a point. For instance, I often tell of my own discouraging experiences in an intensive spoken French course to explain how students with poor writing skills feel when they face a theatening writing assignment.

Incidents are also short but complete accounts that make a point, but usually they focus on an action rather than a personality. For example, in "Marrying Absurd," her ironic essay about the wedding industry in Las Vegas, Joan Didion emphasizes her feelings about the city by giving capsule narratives of two weddings she observed: in one she describes a drunk bride in an orange minidress stumbling out of the chapel and falling into the car; in the other she tells about the father of an obviously pregnant bride making ritual wedding-night jokes to the bridegroom.

Whenever you incorporate narrative into your writing, remember that good narrators use concrete, vivid language to *show* their readers what is happening. They strive for visual elements to add *presence* to their writing. More in Chapter 7 on some ways to achieve those visual effects.

PROCESS

A *process* paper is a "how-to" paper; it could range from a sheet of directions for assembling a doghouse to a book titled "365 Days to a More Beautiful You." Typically, the person doing a process paper leads the reader through a series of steps chronologically, explaining and illustrating, sometimes with diagrams.

Much of the day-to-day writing that goes on in technology, business, and the professions is process writing, and to function effectively in those fields, most people have to master the art of writing clear process papers. In some fields, such as engineering and computer science, achieving clarity is not easy, and executives in those professions often require that their people take special courses in technical or scientific writing. For the most part, however, writers who have trained themselves to write clear and direct expository prose can also become good process writers for nontechnical papers. Many of the suggestions in other chapters for organizing and developing your writing will help you with process writing.

COMBINING METHODS

Experienced writers seldom stop to think about what methods or modes of discourse they are going to use when they start to write. Rather they make their plans, decide on their lead or opening, and start writing according to their natural thought patterns. They could probably identify the patterns they are using—an argument from circumstance or an extended definition, for instance—but they're not conscious of those patterns as they work. And they seldom write according to just one pattern; usually they move from one to another as the topic seems to demand. For example, they may begin by using definition to state the problem they want to talk about, then go to cause and effect argument when they suggest solutions.

As you gain experience, however, you may help yourself get started on a writing task if you think deliberately about what kinds of patterns you could use to develop your ideas. It's one way to generate material and find structure for your writing.

EXERCISES

1. Here is an example of a generative sentence that could help you to get started writing a paper on the machine-scored examinations used to screen applicants for most professional schools:

    The admissions officers of professional schools have come to rely too heavily on machine-scored tests that are culturally biased and cannot measure motivation, perseverance, or creativity.

    Write a similar generative sentence that could help you get started writing on one of these topics:

A. A comparison of foreign-made and American-made bicycles.
B. A review of a movie or play you have seen recently.
C. An analysis of attendance at athletic events on your campus.
D. An explanation of jet lag.

2. Here is a sample list of details that a writer planning a paper on local art fairs might write down:

booths in tents
oil painting
stained glass
$10 pictures
handmade jewelry
weaving
leather goods
pottery
watercolors
on-the-spot portraits
macrame
credit-card users

Make a similar list of details for a paper on one of these topics:

A. Cheerleaders for professional football games.
B. Coping with on-the-job stress.
C. A boat and camper show.
D. Rodeo clowns.

3. Suppose that your professor of urban planning asks you to write a paper about how airline passengers in your city feel about airport facilities and what improvements they would like to see. What criteria would you establish for taking the survey on which your report would be based? Then answer these questions and explain the basis of each of your answers.

How many people to be interviewed?

What distribution of sexes? Ages? Business travelers? Pleasure travelers?

When would you conduct the interviews? More than one session?

Where would you conduct the interviews?

4. Review the section on Toulmin logic; then write out your claim, warrant, and data for arguing each of these propositions. Add a qualifier if necessary.

A. Basketball is a better spectator sport than football.
B. The top stars in the music businessmake too much money.
C. Your state should authorize no-fault automobile insurance policies.
D. People under twenty-one should not be issued credit cards.

5. Set up a cause-and-effect relationship that you could use to argue these propositions:

   A. The state should double the cost of hunting licenses for out-of-state hunters.
   B. The Federal Communications Commission should ban the advertising of junk food on television.
   C. Divorced women as well as men should be liable for child-support payments.
   D. State legislatures should appropriate more money for research in universities.

6. How could you use the following comparisons in developing a writing assignment?

   A. If we can develop the technology to put astronauts into space, we ought to be able to design a method of transportation that doesn't depend on oil.
   B. The apartment buildings in a certain part of town are like islands of affluence in a sea of poverty.
   C. Trying to enforce the 55-mile-an-hour speed limit is like trying to enforce the Prohibition amendment.
   D. The average cost of writing a business letter is now $5.41; the average cost of a three-minute out-of-state long-distance phone call between 8:00 a.m. and 5:00 p.m. is $3.32.

7. Write a short narrative about a person or incident that you could use to start a paper on one of these topics:

   A. Strengthening enforcement of penalties against drunk drivers.
   B. The growing popularity of fast-food restaurants.
   C. Sexual harassment of women in the armed services.
   D. Backpacking on the Appalachian Trail.

SUGGESTED WRITING ASSIGNMENTS

As a part of each writing assignment, write a detailed analysis of your audience. Specify characteristics they have that you need to keep in mind, problems they might present, and what they would expect to get from reading your paper. Also analyze your purpose in writing, specifying what you hope to accomplish in the paper. If appropriate, include an accurate and descriptive title for your paper.

TOPIC 1: Write a professional brochure for an agency or business, giving as much information as you can squeeze into no more than 600 words. Your writing should be clear, simple, and lively so that the audience can read the brochure quickly and enjoy it. Here are possible topics for such a brochure. You might think of a similar one suited to your own job or interests.

A basic guide for buying your first house

A fund-raising brochure for your local ballet, symphony, or community theater

A brochure on birth control for teenagers

A guide to getting around your campus for students in wheelchairs

A budget-minded student's guide to campus recreation

The smart driver's guide to seatbelts

A guide to the best teachers on campus

TOPIC 2: Write an argument for or against one of the propositions below. Identify who would want to read your paper and in what journal or paper it could be published to reach those readers. Also identify your purpose: What do you want to accomplish with your writing?

1. Congress should pass legislation prohibiting any company whose officials have been convicted of fraud, bribery, or price fixing from being awarded government contracts for three years after the conviction.

2. Your city should pass a payroll tax of one percent of the salary of all employees who commute to work in your city but do not live there. The rationale for such a tax is that those people use city services but do not pay for them.

6 ◇ Holding Your Reader

One writing teacher compares the task of a writer to that of a tour director escorting a group of sightseers who do not have to pay their fares until they arrive at their destination and get off the bus. The job of both author and tour director requires that they keep their audiences so interested in what is going on that they will stay until the end of the journey. Readers, like tourists, are capricious and impatient, and they will go off and do something else if they get confused, bored, or led off on a detour that seems pointless to them. When you write, you may find it helpful to keep this analogy in mind and from time to time ask yourself, "Are my readers liable to get off the bus here?" And writers, like tour directors, must keep their audiences oriented. If there is any way for readers to get lost, they will!

All writers need to keep this caution in mind as they write (especially their second or third drafts) and to work consciously to help their readers stay on track as they are reading. Once they stray, they are hard to recapture. For that reason, a writer needs to have some specific strategies for holding readers.

But you should also remember that the most important way of holding your readers involves a principle, not a strategy. That principle is that *most readers will stay with you as long as they are learning something*. As long as you can give them information that interests or entertains them, teach them something they didn't know before, you are likely to keep them reading.

USING AN EFFECTIVE TITLE

Titles play a crucial part in getting off to a good start with your readers. In fact, people often decide whether or not to read something primarily on the basis of the title, so it's important that it be clear, accurate, and if possible interesting.

A good title should *predict* the contents of the paper accurately enough for the reader to decide if he or she wants to read it. Titles like "Energy-Efficient Homes" or "Kayaking in the Box Canyon of the Rio Grande" are direct and accurate enough to immediately attract readers who are interested in those subjects.

An effective title should *set limits* on a topic and *focus* it for the readers; that is, narrow the topic for them and point them in the right direction. It prepares them to receive the writer's message and thus makes it more likely that they will understand. On complex issues, the writer can give the reader even more help by adding a more specific subtitle. For example, "Excellence or Elitism: Which Do Ivy League Colleges Promote?" or "The Cycle of Starvation in Africa: What Lies Ahead?"

A good title *identifies* and *categorizes* so that someone who is doing research can immediately tell whether an article or paper relates to his or her topic. Writing that is significant may be around for several years, and you want people to be able to find it. So when you choose a title, one element to think about is the cataloger or file clerk who may have to classify your paper. Will he or she be able to decide easily where it should be filed? The way to make your work easy to classify is to use key words in your title that will serve as "descriptors" for computer purposes. For example, an article on ways to start a small business while you are in college should have the words "small business" and "college" in it—perhaps "How To Work Your Way Through College by Starting a Small Business." That does everything a good title should do. If, however, you titled such an article "A Profit on Your Own Campus," would-be future readers would have no way to locate the article. In general, it's a good idea to get in the habit of testing your titles with the question, "Could this be misconstrued?" If it can be, you need to change it.

Finally, in most instances you should resist the impulse to give your writing cute, facetious, or deliberately ambiguous titles. They're tempting, particularly if you like jokes, but they're risky. You may mislead your readers or annoy them because they don't share your sense of humor, and of course such titles are the ones most likely to be misclassified. Moreover, witty or inside-joke titles can wear thin. The title that seems clever and classy today may embarrass you when you want to put it on your resume a few years from now.

MAKING AN OPENING PROMISE

If you ask editors, business executives, or public administrators how long it takes them to make a preliminary decision on the manuscripts, proposals, requests, or reports that come across their desks, most would tell you, "A minute or so. I read the first page, or two pages at the most, and I can usually tell if it's worth my time to go on." *One minute* that's how long you have to persuade any reader who is not your captive audience that what you have to say is going to be interesting, informative, or useful, and to keep that reader from tossing your article aside or dropping your communication into the wastebasket.

Given this limitation, you can see that you need to think carefully about how you handle those first few paragraphs. You don't necessarily have to come up with a startling or gimmicky opening that will snag your reader; in fact, in many kinds of writing, such openings would be so inappropriate that they would do more harm than good. What you do need to do is remember that most good openings have one element in common: *they let the reader know what to expect.* As a writer, you make a promise to your reader, either directly or by implication, and raise that reader's expectations. You make a *commitment,* obligate yourself to follow through on the promise. (More on this important concept of the writer's commitment in Chapter 8.) If your reader wants to know what you have promised to tell, he or she will keep on reading to see how you are going to follow through on that promise or commitment.

Opening promises can take several forms, but two of the most common are those that promise to *intrigue* and those that promise to *inform.* The writer who starts out by trying to intrigue the reader usually does so with an anecdote, a quotation, an analogy, or an example of some kind. For instance, in this essay about the great German composer Richard Wagner, the music critic Deems Taylor starts out this way:

> He was an undersized man with a head too big for his body—a sickly little man. His nerves were bad. He had skin trouble. It was agony for him to wear anything next to his skin coarser than silk. And he had delusions of grandeur.

The reader is intrigued by this unflattering portrait of one of our greatest composers and goes on, hoping that Taylor will tell more. And he does.

The management consultants Thomas Peters and Robert Waterman begin one of the chapters in their book *In Search of Excellence* with this quotation: " 'The Navy,' said ex-Chief of Naval Operations Elmo Zumwalt, 'assumes that everyone below the rank of commander is immature.' "

The reader is intrigued to encounter such a quotation in a book about business management and wants to know how it is relevant to the topic. The authors immediately go on and keep their implicit promise to explain.

Here is a promise-to-inform opening from a *Smithsonian* article on astronomy:

> Ever since the human mind first grasped the immensity and complexity of the Universe, Man has tried to explain how it could have come into being.

The article goes on to explain the Big Bang theory of the origin of the universe and the formation of galaxies.

Which kind of opening is better? There is no easy answer; each time you write you have to decide according to what you perceive as your readers' expectations and according to your purpose in writing. Intriguing openers can capture fickle readers and persuade them to go on reading, but they can also annoy readers if they delay too long in getting to the point. Although the straight informative opening may not seem as interesting, often it is safer, particularly for documents in business or industry, because readers there generally want to go straight to the point. You will have to decide.

THOSE CRITICAL FIRST PARAGRAPHS

You usually make your strongest commitment to your readers in your opening paragraph, giving signals and setting the tone for what will follow. As a commitment, that opening paragraph should serve three subpurposes:

◦ Engage the readers' attention.
◦ Shape the readers' expectations.
◦ Give the readers a reason to continue reading.

In other words, the opening paragraph lays down the tracks for both reader and writer.

DIFFERENT KINDS OF OPENING PARAGRAPHS

We have no clear-cut formulas for opening paragraphs, because different kinds of writing tasks call for different kinds of openings. In some cases—grant proposals or technical reports, for example—you may get specific instruction about how to begin. In others—academic papers or critical analyses—there may be traditional patterns that you can follow: review of the literature or statement of the problem, for example. If you are doing those kinds of writing, you can get hints about good openings by looking at typical models. However, in other, more diverse kinds of writing—travel articles, informative essays, book or movie reviews, political analyses, or persuasive speeches, to name a few—you may use many kinds of opening paragraphs, all of them effective. Choose your openings according to the writing situation, taking your audience and purpose into consideration.

STRAIGHTFORWARD ANNOUNCEMENT

In many instances, you will do best to begin with a direct, clear, and economical statement. Certainly this guideline applies to writing whose main purpose is to convey factual information to a busy reader; for instance, market reports, case studies, summaries of action, or requests for information. In this kind of writing, the reader wants key information as quickly as possible—no anecdotes or ceremonial preliminaries. For example:

> My object in this article is to isolate and illuminate one small part of what I take to be a continuing historiographic revolution in the study of science. The structure of scientific discovery is my particular topic, and I can best approach it by pointing out that the subject itself may well seem extraordinarily odd. Both scientists and, until quite recently, historians have ordinarily viewed discovery as the sort of event which, though it may have preconditions and surely has consequences, is itself without internal structure. Rather than being seen as a complex development extended in both space and time, discovering something has usually seemed to be a unitary event, one which, like seeing something, happens to an individual at a specifiable place and time.[1]

Direct openings that announce your thesis also work well for academic research papers. For instance, here is the opening paragraph of a paper done for a course in international business:

> Lockheed Aircraft and Gulf Oil were recently prosecuted by the federal government for giving bribes to foreign businessmen in order to make their products more attractive to those potential clients. During indictment proceedings both corporations contended that their cash payments were both necessary and common among international businesses. The question then is how common is bribery in foreign nations

---

1. Thomas Kuhn, "The Historical Structure of Scientific Discovery," in *The Essential Tension: Selected Studies in Scientific Tradition and Change* (Chicago: University of Chicago Press, 1977), 165.

and whether the United States should prevent our corporations from offering bribes even when doing so is a common and accepted practice.

Straight-to-the-point opening paragraphs also work well when you are writing a request. Although many of us are reluctant to be blunt when we have to ask people for time or money or favors, most readers prefer a straightforward request to a preliminary buildup that wastes their time. When you have a legitimate and reasonable request to make, state it quickly and clearly so you don't waste your readers' time.

OPENING PROMISES OR NARRATIVES

In other writing situations, you must find a way to entice your audience with the promise of something interesting to come. When you have only those first two minutes to catch the attention of a reader with no obligation to read what you write, you need to make that opening paragraph particularly provocative. Experienced freelance writers know a multitude of ways to meet this challenge, but one of the most common is the description or anecdote that lures the reader into the world the author is going to write about. Here are two examples:

A hundred writers have said it before and a hundred will say it again, but it is no less true for being a commonplace that the way to an understanding of Russian life lies through the ordeal of a Russian winter. *Russkaya zima*, the great depressant of spirit and waster of animation. It is not a season of the year like other seasons, not merely a longer, darker, crueler span of time than that which annually slows the countries of northern Europe and America. It is a life sentence to hardship that prowls near the center of the Russian consciousness, whatever the time of year. As a prime cause and a symbol of Russia's fate, it molds a state of mind, an attitude toward life.[2]

A young woman arrives at school balancing a bag of books and papers for the day on one shoulder, a smaller bag containing diapers, baby food, and her own lunch on the other. She holds the hand of a beautiful 13-month-old toddler with a dozen tiny braids in her hair. In a sense, she is just like any other career woman with a child, juggling her own aspirations with the obligations of her motherhood. Except that the only career she is concerned about right now is finishing high school. She is one of 18 exceptionally lucky teenage mothers participating in a special program at Bay Ridge High School, an all-girls academic school in Brooklyn, New York, that has opened an on-campus day-care center expressly for the children of student mothers.[3]

2. George Feifer, "Russian Winter," *Harper's,* February 1982, 39.
3. Paula Di Perna, "Balancing High School and Motherhood: A New Program That Breaks the Dropout Cycle," *Ms,* January 1984, 57.

These are straightforward but vivid openings that catch the readers' attention, give them strong clues about what to expect from the articles, and stimulate enough interest to make them want to go on reading.

SOLVING THE OPENING PARAGRAPH DILEMMA

Even experienced writers often find themselves caught in a dilemma about opening paragraphs. On one hand, a good opening paragraph is critically important if you are to catch your readers and get them moving in the right direction; thus a careful writer puts a lot of time and thought into the introductory paragraph. On the other hand, just knowing how important that opener is can cause a writing block. Nothing you put down seems right, yet you know you have to get those tracks down and get going.

Probably the best solution to this dilemma is to remember the advice on getting started from Chapter 5. Start freewriting, circling, or "nutshelling" to get your generative juices going. Get down something, anything that bears on your topic: a question that you intend to answer in the paper, a statement of the problem you want to solve, a sketch of a person who will figure in the paper. Even if what you write is obvious and dull, getting that first paragraph on paper where you can read it over will help. So put something down, knowing that you can certainly discard it later. When you finish, go back and take a critical look at it. If it doesn't meet those three criteria for an opening paragraph—if it does not engage, entice, or inform the reader—get rid of it and write another one. Now that you have finished with your first draft, you can almost certainly do a better job of writing the opening paragraph than you did when you started. And as a bonus, you may find that you don't need a separate introduction. The paragraph that you intended to make the second one may do very well as the first.

LINKING DEVICES

Writing that is highly readable has a quality called *linearity*; that is, the reader can move steadily through it in a straight line without having to stop to puzzle about meaning or double back to reread in order to understand the writer's ideas. Getting this quality into your writing can be difficult, especially if you're writing on a complex topic or one on which your readers need to be given specialized information, but it's an ideal worth striving for. Think about how often you have found yourself bogged down in dense and difficult writing and have had to read again and again in order to comprehend what the author was saying. If you could quit reading, you probably did. If you couldn't quit, you plowed on, but you groaned and cursed the author who was wasting so much of your time. None of us want our readers to feel that way about our writing, particularly not readers who are in a position to punish us for giving them so much trouble.

HOOKS AND NUDGES

Of course, readers lose their way or get bogged down in writing for a variety of reasons, not all of them the writer's responsibility. But it is the writer's responsibility to provide *hooks*—links that hold writing together by showing the connections between its parts—and *nudging words* that give the reader a little push from one point to the next. You need to have a stock of such terms at your fingertips to draw on: hooks such as *moreover, nevertheless, in addition, however,* and *in spite of,* and nudging terms like *this, first, then, consequently, next,* and so on. Such terms are invaluable for bridging the gaps between units of thought in your writing. For instance, here is a student paragraph with both hooks and nudging words italicized:

> Like a rat that avoids electric shock, a child avoids contact with those who *hurt* him. *So* avoiding *punishment,* except as a last resort, is advisable. *Punishment* instills hate and fear and soon becomes an "aversive stimulus." *Also,* because the only real effect of *it* is to suppress a response temporarily, no permanent weakening of the unwanted behavior takes place. *And* as soon as the effect, or the sting of the *spanking,* wears off, the child repeats *it.*

It is important to realize, however, that the best source of unity in writing comes from the *inside*, from the underlying pattern or internal structure of a piece of writing, not from transitional words tacked on from the outside. Words like *moreover* and *nevertheless* should reflect organization, not impose it, and readers are most likely to feel that a piece of writing is tight and coherent if they sense that it follows one of the common thought patterns discussed in the last chapter. For example, here is a student paragraph that is held together by its narrative pattern, not by transitional devices:

> Just before noon under imposing dark storm clouds in the southern suburbs of Beirut, lunch was being served. It was an austere, poorly lit concrete house recently rebuilt from the rubble which still covered much of the suburb of Burj Al Barajinah, then the headquarters of the Shiite Muslim militia. The wife, clothed in the traditional long black robe of the local Shiite women, served coffee, small oranges and unleavened bread to be dipped in a lentil stew. She spoke with her husband and son with a boldness which custom would not permit out of doors. Friends came and went. One stayed for lunch, a tall man in new fatigues

who laid his automatic rifle by the couch and began to eat. The young son, three or four by the looks of him, with chubby cheeks and a healthy pink glow showing through his olive skin, was exchanging playful banter with his mother. After the meal and conversation, the father's and soldier's attention turned to the boy. The father stood up, the boy hugged his father's leg playfully. The father kicked the boy to the ground, and as he was falling the playful smile turned to fear and tears of pain. After the boy stopped crying, the father turned to the visitor with a smile of pride and said, "He too will learn to fight."

DIRECTIONAL SIGNALS

Often you need to add words that will act as *directional signals* to help your reader follow the thought pattern you are setting up. Some words and phrases act as *pointers* that tell the reader to keep moving forward. Typical pointers are *it follows that, then, another, for example,* and so on. (Notice that the categories of pointing words and nudging words often overlap.) Other kinds of pointing words signal causality: for example, *as a result, therefore, consequently,* and so on. All of them also move the reader forward.

Other kinds of transitional words and phrases, however, act as strong SLOW or CAUTION signals to readers, warning them to slow down because they are going to run into some qualification or exception to an idea that has just been stated. Typical signals of this kind are *however, but, nevertheless, in spite of, on the other hand,* and so on. They warn readers to expect a contrasting example and prepare them to adjust their thinking to handle that example; thus it is very important that when you use this kind of word, called an *adversative,* you really do follow it with a contrasting point. Otherwise you will confuse your readers and perhaps lose them.

REPEATING WORDS

Repeating key words, phrases, or stylistic patterns in a piece of writing can help to focus your readers' attention on points you want to emphasize. A repeated word can also serve as an effective hook between paragraphs or between sections, providing the link that keeps readers from feeling a gap as they move from one section to another. This student paragraph furnishes a good example of using repetition as links within a paragraph. (I have added italics in all of the following selections.)

If you are inclined to value your brain and/or the shape of your head, you will need a *helmet.* While Texas law does not require you to wear a *helmet* if you are over 17, most experienced riders do so—that is one reason they got to be older riders. *Helmets* come in a wide range of prices, from $10 to $125 or more. Plan to spend an amount roughly equivalent to the value of your head, e.g., $10 for a $10 head, etc. There are two basic styles in *helmets*: full-face and open-face. The full-face style gives more absolute protection and costs more, but it tends to give some people claustrophobia and it is warmer. The open-face style will not protect your face from injury and is generally less expensive. The color of the *helmet* is important too: white is probably best, because it has high visibility, both night and day, and does not bake your brains in the hot summer sun as a black *helmet* will.

Repeated pronouns can give the same effect. Here a student writer repeats the word *his* as one way to hold a paragraph together:

Stein was disillusioned not only with *his* brief stay in politics, but with the whole lifestyle and stifling educational-bureaucratic structure of the East Coast. *His* years at Yale were nothing but drudgery. *His* bosses at the FTC didn't want him to work on any more cases than any of the other lawyers. He realized that he had lived *his* life to please others. So Stein moved to Los Angeles and began living by *his* own standards and for *his* own approval and happiness.

Here is a passage in which one word, purposefully repeated in a parallel pattern, repeats the writer's central thesis:

We believe public radio and public television *can* lead the way. Intelligently organized and adequately funded public broadcasting *can* help the creative spirit to flourish. It *can* reveal how we are different and what we share in common. It *can* illuminate the dark corners of the world and the dark corners of the mind. It *can* offer forums to a multitude of voices. It *can* reveal wisdom and understanding—and foolishness too. It *can* delight us. It *can* entertain us. It *can* inform us. Above all, it *can* add to our understanding of our own inner workings and of one another.

In the conviction that it *can* be so, we make these recommendations.[4]

All of these writers value repetition as a simple and useful way of keeping their readers on the track.

---

4. From the report of the Carnegie Commission on the Future of Public Broadcasting, in the *Chronicle of Higher Education*, 5 February 1979, 9.

USING CONJUNCTIONS AT THE BEGINNING OF SENTENCES

The prejudice that many writers have against beginning a sentence with
and or *but* seems to have grown out of the notion that because these
words are called "conjunctions," they must always appear between two
other words. Not necessarily. They are also strong signal words that tell
readers what to expect next. For that reason they work particularly well
when you want to stress the relationship of a sentence to the previous one.
Notice how the following writers have used *and* and *but* for this purpose.
(Again, italics have been added.)

> *Harvard Business Review* subscribers . . . recently rated "the ability to
> communicate" as the prime requisite of a promotable executive. *And,* of
> all the aspects of communication, the written form is the most trouble-
> some.[5]

> If we hear a well-constructed, grammatical sentence, the ideas fall eas-
> ily and quickly into the slots of our consciousness. *But,* if we hear a con-
> glomerate, ungrammatical hodge-podge, we have to sort it out at an
> expenditure of time and effort.[6]

But works especially well as the opening word of a paragraph that you
want to highlight because it states an important qualification or contrast to
the content of the previous paragraph. Notice the effect in the examples:

> . . . For the most part, readers are assumed to be ideal readers, fully
> prepared to relate to the fiction or poetry on the author's terms. This
> expectation is as it should be; it is appropriate for what we regard as cre-
> ative writing.
> *But* a different expectation exists in business and technical writing
> where readers are busy executives who want the important findings up
> front, or are privates last-class who need information at a level they can
> understand, or somewhere in the bewildering range between.[7]

> . . . As my students argue when I correct them . . . : "You got the
> meaning, didn't you?" Yes, I did, and so do we all get the meaning when
> a newspaper, a magazine, a set of directions stammers out its message.

5. John S. Fielden, "What Do You Mean I Can't Write?" in *The Practical Craft,* ed. Keith
   Sparrow and Donald Cunningham (Boston: Houghton Mifflin, 1978), 47. This article originally appeared in the *Harvard Business Review,* May–June 1964.
6. Everett C. Smith, "Industry Views the Teaching of English," in *English Journal,* March
   1956. Reprinted in Sparrow and Cunningham, *Practical Craft.*
7. Sparrow and Cunningham, "What Are Some Important Writing Strategies?" *Practical
   Craft,* 114.

And I suppose, too, we could travel by ox-cart, or dress in burlap, or drive around with rattling fenders, and still get through a day.

But technical writing in this age can no more afford widespread sloppiness of expression, confusion of meaning, rattle-trap construction than a supersonic missile can afford to be made of the wrong materials, or be put together haphazardly with screws jutting out here and there, or have wiring circuits that may go off any way at all. . . .[8]

These examples, deliberately selected from a collection of articles on business and technical writing, should convince you that it is not a sin, or even a grammatical lapse, to start a sentence with *and* or *but*. If you need additional proof, check the articles in any widely read magazine. You will find an abundance of corroborating evidence.

OTHER AIDS TO THE READER

FREQUENT CLOSURE WITHIN SENTENCES

By giving readers links and signals to keep them moving in the right direction, you meet one of an expository writer's main responsibilities: helping his or her audience to process information as quickly and efficiently as possible. You are trying to keep them from having to reread all or part of what you have written in order to get your meaning.

One way to help your readers is not to make them wait too long to discover meaning. If you can construct your sentences out of phrases and clauses that make sense by themselves, your readers can process meaning as they read rather than having to hold all the content in their minds until they get to the end of a sentence. For instance, here is a confusing sentence from a student paper:

> Furthermore, *that the United States has the best medical technology in the world, yet ranks sixteenth among countries in successful births per pregnancy* results because impossible medical costs force many people to go through childbirth at home.

The strung-out twenty-two-word subject in this sentence keeps readers in suspense for so long that they miss the verb, "results," on the first reading. If the writer had rearranged his ideas into manageable units, readers would not get lost. Here is a rewritten version with the units of thought marked off:

8. Morris Freedman, "The Seven Sins of Technical Writing," in Sparrow and Cunningham, *Practical Craft*, 82. This article originally appeared in *College Composition and Communication*, February 1958.

Even though the United States has the best medical technology in the world, / it ranks below fifteen other countries in successful births per pregnancy / because impossible medical costs force many people to have their children at home.

The revised sentence is easier to read than the original because the words are arranged into segments that make sense by themselves. When we read, we make *closure* when we come to the point in a sentence where our minds make sense of a group of words; at that point, we can rest for a split second before going on to process the next segment. In the revised version, we can pause twice; in the original, we cannot pause at all until we get to the end of the sentence.

Because readers can assimilate information more efficiently when it is divided into small units, in most situations you should not let long, complicated sentences predominate. Frequently, just their appearance on the page frightens off readers. But long sentences in themselves do not necessarily cause reading problems; if closure occurs frequently, a sentence of fifty or sixty words or more can be read easily. Marking off the units of closure in this 108-word sentence from Tom Wolfe's *The Right Stuff* shows this:

A career in flying was like climbing one of those ancient Babylonian pyramids / made up of a dizzy progression of steps and ledges, / a ziggurat, / a pyramid extraordinarily high and steep, / and the idea was to prove at every foot of the way up that pyramid / that you were one of the elected and anointed ones who had *the right stuff* / and could move higher and higher and even / —ultimately, God willing, one day— / that you might be able to join that special few at the very top, / that elite who had the capacity to bring tears to men's eyes, / the very Brotherhood of the Right Stuff itself.[9]

CHUNKING TO AVOID READER OVERLOAD

Another way of segmenting your writing to make it easier for your readers to follow is called *chunking;* that is, breaking up long units of writing into parts so that they will be easier to process. If you include too much information in one sentence or one paragraph, you risk overloading the mental circuits by which readers process information, and your readers either give up or have to go back to reread the material two or three times to absorb it.

Chunking is the principle behind dividing telephone numbers into

9. Tom Wolfe, *The Right Stuff* (New York: Farrar, Straus, & Giroux, 1979), 24.

groups. You would have trouble remembering ten numbers in a sequence if they were written like this:

7045164883

If, however, the numbers are split into chunks, they are fairly easy to remember:

704-516-4883

You process each unit separately. It also helps that you know each unit has a special meaning: area code, exchange, individual number.

Here is a sentence that is overloaded with information and so badly arranged that the reader gets mired down before ever getting to the main clause of the sentence:

> With Iran's political turmoil cutting off its substantial oil imports and its announced intention to reduce imports to one-fifteenth of their former volume, Abu Dhabi and Qatar's increase in oil prices and the probable following of the other OPEC countries, and the indefinite position of Mexico concerning the availability of its oil resources, an energy crisis of some magnitude seems imminent.

However, if we divide the sentence and rearrange it into manageable chunks, adding pointers for the reader, it becomes easy to follow:

> For at least three reasons, an energy crisis seems imminent: Iran's political turmoil has cut off its substantial imports and it has announced its intention to reduce exports to one-fifteenth of its former volume; Abu Dhabi and Qatar have increased oil prices and other OPEC nations will probably follow; and Mexico has taken an indefinite position about the availability of its oil resources.

You can also chunk information by reorganizing the components of a sentence. For example, this sentence is hard to read:

> The factors that keep individuals interested in their jobs are interesting responsibilities, wide range of responsibilities, challenge, stimulation, recognition, impact on the organization, status, relationship with others, being one's own boss, freedom to act, quality of the organization, and compensation.

There's just too much information jammed together here. Notice that if you break up the content into two sentences and add verbs that help to show relationships, the content becomes much easier to understand:

The factors that keep individuals interested in their jobs are having interesting and varied responsibilities, receiving challenges and stimulations, and getting recognition and the sense that they're having an impact on the organization. They're also concerned about status and having a good relationship with others, about whether they will have freedom to act and be their own bosses, and about their compensation and the quality of the organization.

BREAKING YOUR TEXT WITH HEADINGS

The principal way to draw your readers' attention to the design or pattern of a piece of writing is to divide it into parts: sections, chapters, divisions, and subdivisions. The way you decide to divide your writing, how often you do it, and your method of labeling your divisions will strongly affect how well you are able to hold your readers' attention and keep them moving along.

To some extent, you should base your decisions about headings and subheadings on the kind of writing you are doing. Different professions follow different conventions about format, and if you are writing a proposal or report, it's a good idea to look at a model of typical writing for that genre. There may be a standard format. But if there is not, or you are writing a piece for which you have no model, here are some guidelines. It is particularly important to break up your writing and label the divisions:

◊ When a piece of writing is long—ten pages or more.

◊ When you are writing about complex matters and using difficult or specialized vocabulary.

◊ When you think that some of your readers may have poor reading skills —for example, individuals in the audience for a brochure on Social Security benefits.

In general, if you are in doubt about whether to divide and label, you should probably do so in order to give your readers as much help as possible. As one expert puts it:

> "One might say that [by headings] the reader of a report is provided with road signs; in the headings he has a way of making his way through the report without getting lost and with the assurance that he will reach his destination safely."[10]

---

10. J. Raleigh Nelson, "Sectional Headings as Evidence of Design," in Sparrow and Cunningham, *Practical Craft,* 270.

AVOID ANTAGONIZING YOUR READERS

Finally, remember that you will probably lose your readers if you make them uncomfortable or angry. Most people are not willing to read or listen to someone who is attacking them or criticizing their beliefs; if you really want a person to read what you are writing, you need to think about their emotions as well as their strictly intellectual interests.

To avoid threatening your readers, keep these points in mind:

◦ Respect your audience. From the beginning, assume that your readers are intelligent and rational people of good will and that they will respond to reason. Rather than attacking their positions, try to discover what common interests or common goals you may have and work from there. Give your readers the same kind of treatment you like to get when you read.

◦ Use objective language. Strong, biased words such as "disgraceful," "vicious," and "intolerable" are likely to trigger defensive reactions from readers who do not already agree with you. Their first response will be to argue rather than to pay attention to your point of view. If, however, you state your ideas in neutral langauge, they are likely to continue reading to learn more.

◦ Learn to write provisionally, not dogmatically. Learn to use the *subjunctive mood,* a much neglected but extremely useful verb form that allows you to speculate, hypothesize, or wish, and to express a courteous and inquiring attitude in your writing. Although fewer and fewer people seem to bother with using the subjunctive form of verbs in their writing, careful writers should at least know what the subjunctive forms are and when they should be used. They are used when one wants to express a point conditionally or to express wishes. For example:

If Castle *were* in charge, he *would handle* the protesters well.

I wish I *were* not *involved* in that proposal.

If that *should* happen, the admiral *would want* us to know.

You *would be* a great help if you *were to join* us.

Occasionally *had* is combined with a subjunctive verb to talk about events that didn't take place. For example:

Had I thought of it, I *would have written.*

Had he *known* what he was getting into, he *would have been appalled.*

The subjunctive form of a verb should be used in clauses beginning with *that* when the main verb expresses desires, orders, or suggestions. For example:

> The lawyer requested that her client *be given* a new trial.

> We suggest that there *be* a recount of the votes.

If you use these words in phrases like "If I were," "It might be that," and "We could consider," you create an atmosphere of cooperation and courtesy in which your readers can pay attention to what you are proposing because they are not forced to defend themselves.

EXERCISES

1. Here are some titles chosen from the table of contents of an essay anthology. How useful do you find them as forecasters of what the reader would find in the essay? Which titles do you think are the most informative? Which are the least informative?

The Fear of Being Alone
Business As Usual
Bag Man
The Full Circle: In Praise of the Bicycle
The Truth about Cinderella
The New Illiteracy
Work in an Alienated Society
Lessons of the Street
The Lesson of the Mask
Techno-Politics

2. Try to think of titles that would accurately reflect the content of a paper you might write on these topics:

A. Exercise as one of the major components of a good health program.
B. Credit cards as a contributing cause to the inflationary spiral.
C. An argument for or against instituting a payroll tax in your city. Such a tax would be levied on everyone who worked in but did not live in the city.
D. A review of a major art show in which all the artists were American women.

3. Evaluate these opening paragraphs taken from papers by advanced student writers. Do they pull you on to want to read the paper? Do you get lost in any of them?

If you're feeling confused, depressed, and totally void of self-confidence, you could be experiencing the common state of "college stress syndrome." At one time or another students go through this unpleasant phase. Stress refers to the way in which your body reacts to a mentally or emotionally disturbing influence. This anxiety enters our lives in many different forms. According to Dr. Richard Nemic, director of the psychiatric section of the Student Health Services Center, there are three basic sources of student stress: procrastination, career choice, and exams.

Every year, our highways needlessly slaughter many thousands of people. And every year, people are reminded that wearing their protective safety belts would dramatically increase their chances for survival. And yet people continue to ignore such advice and suffer the consequences. In an attempt to solve this problem, this country has gone as far as to install systems that virtaully force occupants of automobiles to wear protective safety belts. What happened? People resisted to such a degree that the legislation was finally repealed. So, obviously, another solution is needed if the population is to reap the benefits of being protected from their cars. Air bags are such a solution.

Humans often complicate simple situations by not using the basic abilities that are unique to our species. Sounds like another way of saying humans don't think. But not really. I think it is more accurate to say that humans are so busy thinking about big problems that we neglect small problems. Confusing? Let me try again. Remember the straw that broke the camel's back? It was the straw that did it. No one ever mentions the tree that fell on the poor animal, only the straw. To me, airports are good examples of how a straw can have the impact of a tree. If you allow yourself plenty of time, read the direction signs, and carry an assortment of change, you will probably have no problem getting where you are going.

4. Write an opening paragraph for one of the topics given in the second exercise above. Before you begin to write, think about what information you should include in order to get your readers started off in the direction you want them to go.

5. Rewrite these paragraphs with transition devices that will help to keep the reader on the right track:

You will develop a sales approach as you become more acquainted with your job. Every individual prefers to handle customers in his own way.

Keep in mind, however, three basic rules: be assertive, be helpful, and be pleasant at all costs. Remember serving the customer is the number one priority. You must keep busy. There is always something to be done: cleaning, dusting, displays, shifting stock, and setting up windows. You will be expected to perform these duties and others on a daily basis. Working in the stockroom and performance on the floor are equally important.

Mandatory installation of air bags is definitely a good idea. It will save many lives and prevent many people from being crippled or maimed. It will also save many thousands of dollars in hospital and treatment costs. The big question is whether or not it will get the support it needs to stay mandatory. Let us hope the citizens of the United States have more control over the government than do the automobile manufacturers.

6. Here are two long but fairly readable sentences from professional writers. Mark each of them off into units of closure that reveal how the content is organized.

Once that fact is recognized, it may be possible to think again about the proper building blocks of a meritocracy—measures that do not seal fate at an early age, that emphasize performance in specific areas, that expand the pool of talent in more than a hit-or-miss way, and whose limits are always visible to us, so that we are not again deluded into thinking we have found a scientific basis for the order of lords, vassals, and serfs.[11]

I yield to no one in deploring prejudice against the young, but I found it unsettling to learn that Mr. Schroeder, five years out of the University of Michigan, and four other young men of approximately the same experience constitute the entire legal staff of the FTC's Bureau of Consumer Protection, the body that now proposes to reform one of the nation's venerable technical institutions.[12]

SUGGESTED WRITING ASSIGNMENTS

As a part of each writing assignment, write a detailed analysis of your audience that specifies characteristics they have which you need to keep in mind as you write, problems that such an audience might present, and what the audience would expect to get from your paper. Also analyze your purpose in writing, specifying what you hope to accomplish in the paper. If appropriate, include an accurate and descriptive title for your paper.

11. James Fallows, "The Tests and the Brightest," *The Atlantic,* February 1980, 48.
12. Samuel C. Florman, "Standards of Value," *Harper's* Magazine, February 1980, 67.

TOPIC 1: Imagine that you write for the entertainment section of a local newspaper or magazine. One of your weekly jobs is to eat at one of the major restaurants in the city and write a 300- to 500-word review of your experience there for the Saturday paper. Although all the better restaurants advertise in the paper or magazine, your editor wants an honest review that will let potential customers know what they can expect if they eat there. You are gradually building a reputation as a fair and reliable judge of restaurants and so you should keep that in mind as you write. Don't forget to mention prices.

TOPIC 2: The regents of your college or university are having hearings to determine whether they should tear down the low-rent student housing that was built thirty-five years ago from second-hand army surplus buildings. The housing is unsightly and needs repairs; some of the regents have said that they think it is unsafe. If it is torn down, however, the apartments that would replace it would rent for almost twice as much as the present units, and the campus would be without any low-rent housing for at least two years.

Prepare a ten-minute talk (no more than 1000 words) against tearing down the buildings to be delivered at the meeting that the regents are going to hold. You will be the spokesperson for the married students who now live in the university housing.

TOPIC 3: Write a letter to the vice-president for marketing of a major firm such as General Foods or Johnson & Johnson trying to persuade him or her that the firm should no longer run a particular television commercial that you find offensive. Specify what you find offensive and why, and try to give the vice-president a good reason for dropping the commercial.

7 ◊ Writing Clearly

Professional people who must read a great deal in the course of their work —and that category certainly includes professors— agree that a prime requirement for good writing is that it has to be clear. They get annoyed and impatient when writers use obscure language or write sentences that are difficult to understand; frequently they simply quit reading a piece of writing that is muddled or riddled with ambiguity. If you care about communicating your ideas, you need to do everything you can to write as clearly as possible, given the limitations imposed by your subject matter.

WORKING TO ACHIEVE CLARITY

Writers who want to write clearly have to work at it constantly, trimming excess fat from their writing and revising out all those words and phrases that cloud meaning, confuse the reader, or just make their writing harder to understand than it needs to be. For the ingredients of bad writing tend to cluster. Writers who get in the habit of using abstract sentence subjects and *nominalizations* (see p. 117) and writing on a high level of generality also tend to use passive verbs and extended verb phrases and to forget to put people in their writing. They are also the ones who don't use metaphors. They produce prose like this:

> To serve the requirements of written language, all of the information relevant to the communication of intention must be present in the text. Further, if the text is to permit or sustain certain conclusions, . . . then it must become an autonomous representation of meaning. But for this purpose the meanings of the terms and the logical relations holding between them must be brought to a much higher degree of conventionalization. Words must be defined in terms of other words in the linguistic

system, and rules of grammar must be specialized to make them suitable indications of the text's underlying logical structure. Once this degree of conventionalization is achieved, children or adults have sufficient basis for constructing the meaning explicitly represented by the text.[1]

The passage is clogged and hard to read, and no wonder. It illustrates at least half a dozen features of bad writing that I will discuss in this chapter: heavy nominalization, abstract sentence subjects, lots of "to be" verbs, few agent/action sentences, passive verbs, and no visual elements.

On the other hand, here is a lucid paragraph on a rather abstruse concept:

> We build computers and programs for many reasons. We build them to serve society and as tools for carrying out the economic tasks of society. But as basic scientists we build machines and programs as a way of discovering new phenomena and analyzing phenomena we already know about. Society often becomes confused about this, believing that computers and programs are to be constructed only for the economic use that can be made of them. It needs to understand that the phenomena surrounding computers are deep and obscure, requiring much experimentation to assess their nature. It needs to understand that, as in any science, the gains that accrue from such experimentation and understanding pay off in the permanent acquisition of new techniques; and it is these techniques that will create the new instruments to help society in achieving its goals.[2]

These authors use some nominalizations—"experimentation" and "acquisition"—and their writing is not particularly visual, but they make it clear by writing agent/action sentences, *downshifting* (see p. 113) from their first general statement, using mostly one-word, active verbs, bringing people into their writing, and constructing their sentences in chunks that are easy for the reader to process.

WRITING CONCRETELY AND SPECIFICALLY

Usually your readers will understand your writing more easily if you use concrete and specific language to help clarify and give substance to abstract and general language. *Abstract language* consists of words that refer to intangible qualities, concepts, ideas, or attitudes. We cannot grasp the

1. David R. Olson, "From Utterance to Text: The Bias of Language in Speech and Writing," *Harvard Educational Review,* 47.3 (1977), 257.
2. Allan Newell and Herbert Simon, "Computer Science as Empirical Inquiry," in *Mind Design,* ed. John Haugeland (Cambridge, Mass.: MIT Press, 1981), 36.

abstract through our senses; we can only *conceive* of it mentally. Words like *loyalty, intelligence, philosophy, value,* and *evil* are abstract.

Concrete language consists of words that refer to tangible physical objects or qualities that we can know through our senses; we *perceive* the concrete. Words like *bottle, hot, kitten, car,* and *computer* are concrete.

But most words do not fall so neatly into these either/or categories. Instead we have to classify them according to a scale, place them somewhere on what semanticists call the *ladder of abstraction.* It is from that metaphorical ladder that we derive the term *level of abstraction;* we are also referring to that ladder when we talk about *high level* or *low level* abstractions. Here is how the ladder works:

8. ideologies
7. religions
6. western religions
5. Christianity
4. Protestantism
3. Baptists
2. Southern Baptist Convention
1. First Baptist Church of Memphis, Tennessee

None of these terms refers to anything tangible—"Church" on Level 1 refers to a community of worshipers, not a building—but "First Baptist Church of Memphis" is much narrower and thus much less abstract than "ideologies."

You should also learn to distinguish between the general and the specific. *General language* consists of words and phrases that refer to large classes of people, institutions, activities, and so on, or to broad areas of study or activity. Words and phrases like *college, housing, the medical profession,* or *the American people* are general.

Specific language consists of words and phrases that refer to individual instances or persons or to particular details and examples. Words like *Queen Elizabeth, chocolate chip ice cream,* and *Masterpiece Theatre* are specific. When someone says "Use specific details," that person is asking for individual, concrete examples.

We also have different levels of generality. For example:

7. mass media
6. television
5. public broadcasting channels
4. educational programs
3. science programs
2. "Nova"
1. "Spaceship Earth"

At the lowest level we have a single, specific program, and at the highest level we have a classification so broad that we have trouble thinking of all that it includes. Someone who says "He talked at a high level of generality" means that the speaker talked in broad and general terms, giving few specific examples.

At times, all writers have to generalize and use abstract language. If we didn't, we could never get beyond citing examples (specific acts of violence, say, such as the assassination of an ambassador) to arrive at a generalization about the larger problem (terrorism). But if you want to help readers grasp your ideas quickly, learn how to use the personal, the concrete, and the specific to illustrate your points. For example, the astronomy writer who wanted to help his readers understand the abstract idea of black holes used the concrete analogy of watching streams of traffic pour into a domed stadium (see p. 122). A writer who is writing about horror movies can illustrate the general class with the specific film *The Texas Chain Saw Massacre*.

As a writer you clarify and strengthen your writing in several ways when you work at making it specific and concrete. For one thing, you add the *weight of facts* to your writing and anchor it to reality. A theory about nuclear accidents takes on greater force when you illustrate it with reference to the Three Mile Island disaster, and an admonition to teenagers to finish high school makes more of an impression when it is buttressed by statistics about the comparative earnings of graduates and dropouts.

Second, concrete examples and specific details add interest to writing because they increase the chances of your readers' learning something. A paper that generalizes about child abuse may do no more than repeat information that is commonly known and therefore hardly worth reading. If, however, you describe cases of child abuse and cite statistics about it, you are likely to give readers fresh information that will stimulate their interest in the topic.

Third, reinforcing general statements with specific instances enhances your credibility. You show your readers that you have done your homework, gone to the trouble to look up cases and facts that give special force to your claims. Most of us who keep up with current events can make broad statements about such topics as tax reform, racial discrimination, public school education, or waste in government, and we can generate a series of high-level generalities on the topic with little effort. The trouble is that an informed audience doesn't take such generalities seriously—they're just platitudes or pious wishes until they're supported with facts and specific examples.

To be sure, being specific and concrete also involves risks. When you give an example to illustrate a general statement, you run the risk of having your readers disagree with that example. For instance, if you claim that we must increase teachers' salaries to improve public school education, you're probably safe, but if you go on to claim that the experienced teacher who makes $24,000 a year is underpaid, a reader may challenge that statement. If you claim that in order to reduce the budget deficit, we must have tax reform, your readers will probably agree. That's a safe generality. If, however, you propose a national sales tax as the best solution, some readers will immediately disagree. But those are the chances you must take if you are going to move beyond generalities to gain your readers' attention and respect.

MAKING YOUR READERS *SEE* SOMETHING

When possible, give your readers a visual image. There are good reasons why writing is clearer to us when it makes us see a picture. As Arthur Koestler points out in *The Act of Creation*, "Thinking in pictures dominates the manifestations of the unconscious—the dream, the fantasy, the psychotic's hallucination. . . . Pictorial thinking is more *primitive* than mental thinking." So when you make your readers *see* things by using concrete description and specific examples, anecdotes, or analogies, you engage all your readers' learning faculties, not just their limited rational faculties.

Effective leaders and teachers seem to know these principles instinctively, and they employ them constantly by telling stories and bringing in colorful examples to illustrate their points. In a book analyzing the characteristics of America's best companies, a pair of business consultants point out that in companies like IBM and Hewlett Packard, new employees learn the values and traditions of the company by hearing what the authors call "myths and fairy tales" about the founders of the companies.[3] For example, at IBM new employees frequently hear stories about founder Thomas Watson that give specific examples of his philosophy of business. Company employees will learn that philosophy much more quickly through hearing such specific anecdotes than they would from reading an abstract statement about it.

Here is an example of non-visual writing that is hard to understand because the reader cannot *see* anything happening.

> This pragmatic approach ascribes to managers a marvelous plasticity in adapting themselves and the people in their organizations to technological change and environmental tempests, whatever happens and as

3. Thomas J. Peters and Robert H. Waterman, Jr., *In Search of Excellence* (New York: Harper and Row, 1982), 61.

often as they occur. This conviction about human malleability is, in fact, the necessary view of innate human nature required by the organizational imperative; thus it is imbedded solidly within every modern organization. This image is based on the belief that the individual is, by nature, nothing and has the potential to be made into anything. Therefore, organizations must be designed to mold individuals, since there is nothing in their nature to prevent their adapting to whatever value premises and organizational contingencies are required.[4]

At first reading, one's mind "hydroplanes" right over the surface of the paragraph because there is nothing in it to engage the senses. The reader can't find a concrete anchor anywhere, nor *perceive* anything. The words "plasticity," "malleability," "value premises," and "contingencies" do not refer to anything a reader can, at first reading, connect with people or reality. Although the content of the passage isn't particularly difficult, it's hard to process because the reader has to work at a totally abstract level.

Unfortunately, many students who encounter this kind of colorless and abstract writing assume that the harder something is to read, the more important it must be. Sometimes they even think they should be writing that way themselves, so they try to avoid language that is plain and specific and use abstract terms instead. (See discussion of models in Chapter 2.) They may also be afraid that they will be asked to write that kind of difficult and abstract style in order to get ahead in their professions. Fortunately that fear is seldom justified. My survey of business and professional people proves that. And it is still the case that in any field, most of the individuals at the top prove again and again that they value clear writing and know how to write clearly themselves. For example, here is a paragraph from a book about the beginning of the universe written by Nobel Prize-winning physicist Steven Weinberg:

> In the beginning there was an explosion. Not an explosion like those familiar on earth, starting from a definite center and spreading out to engulf more and more of the circumambient air, but an explosion which occurred simultaneously everywhere, filling all space from the beginning, with every particle of matter rushing apart from every other particle. "All space" in this context may mean either all of an infinite universe, or all of a finite universe which curves back on itself like the surface of a sphere. Neither possibility is easy to comprehend, but this will not get in our way; it matters hardly at all in the early universe whether space is finite or infinite.[5]

4. William G. Scott and David Hart, *Organizational America* (Boston: Houghton Mifflin, 1979), 57–58.
5. Steven Weinberg, *The First Three Minutes* (New York: Bantam Books, 1977), 2.

One can hardly imagine a concept more difficult to explain, but Weinberg succeeds by using clear language and giving the readers an image they can see.

DOWNSHIFTING FROM THE GENERAL TO THE SPECIFIC

Often you will want to begin a paragraph by making a broad statement that is on a high level of generality and a high level of abstraction. That can be a good way to start off, but you need to remember to shift quickly to a lower level of generality, using more specific and concrete language to clarify the broad statement. Often you can move several steps along the ladder of generality. Here is an example:

The ancestors of the mammals were a transitional form called the mammal-like reptiles. (Level 6)
    These animals were ferocious, numerous, and enormously successful. (Level 5)
        They reached their zenith about 250 million years ago, (Level 4)
        and during the next 50 million years they were the dominant form of life on land. (Level 4)
            Inspection of their fossilized remains reveals the reason for their success. (Level 3)
                The clumsy, sprawling, "push-up" posture of the original reptile was replaced in this new model by a construction in which (Level 2)
                    the arms were underslung, (Level 1)
                    the elbows tucked in, (Level 1)
                    and the body raised well off the ground at all times. (Level 1)
                    These animals had a fast running gait; (Level 1)
                    they could outrace any animal in their day. (Level 1)[6]

You see that the author has started out with a general statement and expanded on it by giving you details that get increasingly specific as he goes along. We call this process *downshifting,* and it is an important concept for you to grasp right now because it is one of the major strategies that authors use to make their writing clear. You will learn more about this useful technique in chapter 8.

6. Robert Jastrow, *The Enchanted Loom* (New York: Simon and Schuster, 1981), 32.

USING SPECIFIC AND CONCRETE SUBJECTS IN YOUR SENTENCES

If you want your sentences to be clear and easy to understand, you should try to get in the habit of frequently choosing concrete and specific words for the subjects of your sentences. You thereby give your readers an early anchor that makes the rest of the sentence easier to follow. For example, compare these two versions of the same sentence:

> The affordability of hotels is the major factor that draws tourists to Baja California.

> REVISED: Baja California attracts tourists mainly because of its cheap hotels.

The second version is easier and quicker to read because it begins with a concrete place rather than an abstract concept and uses an active verb, "attracts," rather than the uninteresting verb "is."

Here is another pair:

> An undesirable inflationary spiral would come into existence by the legislature's passing the bill.

> REVISED: If the legislature passes the bill an undesirable inflationary spiral will follow.

Readers can understand the second sentence more quickly because "legislature" is a subject they can identify immediately and "passes" is a shorter and more active verb than "would come into existence."

You should also try to avoid using abstract words as sentence subjects because such words make it harder to choose good verbs. Abstractions can't *do* anything; therefore you almost have to combine them with "is" verbs. For instance, if you begin a sentence with a subject like "desirability," you just about have to write "The desirability of the program is in question," or "Its desirability cannot be determined." Both are dull sentences because the reader can't visualize either the subject or the verb. Abstract subjects also tend to attract passive verbs. More on that problem in the section about verbs on p. 119.

USING AGENT/ACTION SENTENCE PATTERNS FREQUENTLY

You can take a positive step to reduce the number of abstract sentence subjects by trying consciously to write *agent/action* sentences, that is, sentences in which your reader can tell immediately who or what agent is acting and what action is being taken. For example, here are two versions of the same sentence:

> Consumer motivations have moved toward saving and away from debt, due to lowered price expectations and higher interest rates.

> REVISED: Consumers have started to save rather than go into debt because interest rates are going up and because they expect prices to fall.

You can understand the revised version more easily because there is an agent in it—consumers—and they are *doing* something—that is, saving. When you read the first version, on the other hand, you see no agent at all —just "consumer motivations" and "price expectations" and "interest rates." It's hard to tell who the actors are and what action is going on.

Here is another example:

> Technological expansionism and the growth of mechanization have led to more consumption of energy and more loss of availability for future generations.

> REVISED: As we have expanded technology and built more machines, we have used more energy and left less available for future generations.

Again, in the first sentence no agents appear so you can't tell who is doing what. It's hard to tell that the phrases "technological expansionism" and "growth of mechanization" refer to somebody doing something. But when you identify the agent in the sentence as "we" and link it with the action verbs "expanded" and "built," the sentence becomes much clearer.

CLARIFYING YOUR SENTENCES BY ADDING PEOPLE

Whenever you can, write about people. In fact, adding people to your sentences may do more to make them clear than any other writing habit you could develop. For example, notice the difference in the first and second versions of the sentences in each of these pairs:

> The necessity of understanding and alleviating depression is obvious.

> REVISED: Obviously we must understand and help people who are depressed.

> Programs ought to be encouraged that explore the implications of the work experience for the curricular framework on campus.

REVISED: We should encourage programs that explore how we can use people's work experience in designing college courses.

(Notice that the first version of the sentence is completely abstract—one would never know that it is *people* who are working and taking the college courses.)

Putting people in your sentences, even if you only use pronouns such as "we," "you," "they," and "I," helps the reader to visualize what is happening and remember content more easily. You are using the same strategy that people use when they illustrate points with stories: your reader will respond more quickly to writing that has a human element in it than to writing that refers only to concepts and inanimate objects.

Notice the difference between these two versions of the same paragraph:

An important aspect of a print-based culture is its cumulative nature. It is, quite simply though crudely put, a form of expression or communication that does not go away. Whereas in oral culture one of the primary efforts is to devise methods of retaining and preserving the elusive and ephemeral spoken word, one can observe by contrast how literate culture, even pre-dating the mass production of books, gave birth to its corpus simply by failing to destroy or purge its heritage from earlier generations.[7]

REVISED: It is important that in a culture based on print, people accumulate printed material. It represents a form of communication that doesn't go away. Whereas in an oral culture, individuals must go to great effort to find ways to retain and preserve the elusive and ephemeral spoken word, in a literate culture, even before the mass production of books, people create a corpus of culture simply by not destroying what they received from earlier generations.

The revised version is clearer than the original because it conveys the idea of people communicating with each other instead of abstractions about culture and communication.

In some instances, you can add people to your writing by using the pronouns "I" and "you." Although you may be reluctant to use those pronouns because of taboos that linger from earlier writing courses, they are probably appropriate more often than you think they are. For example, Darwin uses "I" throughout his *Origin of Species;* Carl Sagan also uses "I" occasionally in his book *Cosmos.* Even banks now insert the word "you"

7. Paul E. Corcoran, *Political Language and Rhetoric* (Austin, Texas: University of Texas Press, 1979), 65.

into many loan contracts to designate the person who is borrowing money. So don't just assume that you can't use these personal pronouns. You may be able to, and if you can, it can help your readers to understand more easily.

AVOIDING TOO MANY NOMINALIZATIONS

The kind of abstract words that cause the most problems are nouns derived from verbs and adjectives. Such words are called *nominalizations*. Here are some examples:

capability	immediacy
recognition	modernity
competitivenesss	accountability
viability	inclusiveness
enhancement	utilization
marketability	continuation

By adding a suffix such as *-ity, -tion, -ness, -cy, -ing, -ance, -ment, -ism,* or *-y* to a noun or adjective to change it into a noun, you make a word that is more abstract than the original.

At times you have to use such words in order to make your point, but they are rather lifeless words and difficult for the reader's brain to absorb because they don't refer to anything specific or concrete. If you form the habit of using them frequently you will make your writing much harder to read and understand. Writing that is full of nominalizations usually strikes the reader as dense and dull. And if you look back at many of the examples of poor writing I've used in the book so far, you will find that almost all of them are overloaded with nominalizations.

Here are some more examples:

A constructive relationship between representatives of education and government requires stability and predictability of financing.

REVISED: If educators are going to work constructively with government agencies, they must be able to count on stable and predictable finances.

Since achievement generally merits acceptance and recognition in our society, failures probably receive the least amount of affection.

REVISED: Since people who achieve are generally accepted and recognized in our society, those who fail are probably accepted and liked less.

Establishment of that policy reveals the officers' conviction that the qualities of innovativeness and creativity inevitably conflict with the higher goal of corporate loyalty.

REVISED: When the officers established that policy, they revealed that they believe an innovative and creative person will have trouble being loyal to the corporation.

Notice that when you write agent/action sentences you will immediately eliminate many nominalizations.

CHOOSING VERBS FOR CLARITY

Verbs are the lifeblood of writing. They affect not only clarity, but also tone and rhythm, and certainly they affect how readable and vigorous writing is. Since they are among a writer's most important tools, here are some suggestions for choosing good ones.

RESTRICTING THE USE OF *TO BE* VERBS

Although the verb *to be* in all its forms (*is, am, was, were, will be, have been,* and so on) remains the central verb in our language, careful writers use it sparingly. Although it may seem easier to write your sentences using *is* plus an adjective or noun rather than to look for a single verb to express your idea, using *is* too often weakens your writing. For example, compare these two versions of a student paragraph:

The implications of teenage sexuality are overwhelming. Probably the least tangible one is the loss of self-esteem among the young girls involved. Lisa is an excellent example. She was sexually active at 15; at age 17 she had an abortion, and at 21 she is sleeping with several men and is contemptuous of herself.

REVISED: Teenage sexuality has overwhelming implications. Among the less tangible ones, one must count the loss of self-esteem for the young girls involved. Take Lisa, for example. Sexually active at 15, at 17 she had an abortion. Now at 21 she sleeps around and despises herself.

And notice how single-word active verbs strengthen this paragraph:

So Stein *rented* furniture, *ran* into an old girlfriend, *started doing* lots of grass, *flirted* with cocaine, and *began buying* his groceries at a store which sold every soft drink known to man. He *extended* his personality with a Mercedes 450SL and *immersed* himself in a lifestyle known as California-weird. Incredibly, he *found* a kind of happiness.

Of course, in many kinds of writing you don't need to work at choosing such colorful and active verbs—sometimes *is* and *are* work perfectly well, and I certainly don't recommend that you try to eliminate them from your writing. But try to avoid starting too many sentences with "It is. . ." or "There are. . ." and when you revise your writing, check to see if you have overused *to be* verbs.

CHOOSING ECONOMICAL VERBS

Your writing will be clearer and more effective if you make a habit of choosing one-word, direct verbs rather than strung-out verb phrases that incorporate nouns and adjectives. For example:

Wordy version	*Economical version*
be cognizant of	recognize
put the emphasis on	emphasize
is reflective of	reflects
make an attempt to	try
have an understanding of	understand
make a comparison to	compare
grant permission to	allow

Stretched-out verb forms, while not wrong, tend to make writing sound stuffy and formal. One such phrase here and there does little damage, but too many of them clog writing.

AVOIDING PASSIVE VERBS

When you can, avoid passive verb constructions. (In such constructions, the subject of the sentence is *acted upon* rather than *acting*—for instance, "John was notified that he would lose his job.") For several reasons, writers who use passive verbs make their writing a little harder to read and understand than if they had used active verbs.

First, passive verbs slow writing down not only because it takes more words to express a passive construction, but because the reader usually has to wait until the last part of the sentence to find out what is happening. Thus, "Action on the issue has been taken by the board" takes longer to read and process than "The board acted on the issue."

Second, when you write sentences with a lot of passive verbs, you are likely to decrease the number of people in the sentence and increase the nominalizations. Notice what happens in this passage, in which I have bracketed the passive verbs and italicized the nominalizations:

> In this situation, it is surprising that in recent years so little work [has been done] on the theory of philosophical *argumentation*. Indeed, the only sustained inquiry into it [has been undertaken] by the logical positivists. But this inquiry [is circumscribed] by that very *assumption* whose *doubtfulness* [has just been indicated]: the *assumption*, namely, that the principles which govern philosophical disputes [can be strictly identified] with those of hitherto established *methodologies*.

A reader has trouble understanding the paragraph because it offers nothing to focus the senses on; one cannot tell who is doing the "undertaking" or "indicating" or "identifying." The passive verbs obscure identities.

Third, passive verbs cause vagueness because they conceal the agent in a sentence. Consider sentences like these:

In many countries, bribes *are considered* a legitimate business expense.

Outside agitators *are being blamed* for the trouble.

The candidate has already *been selected.*

The reader who wants to know facts—*who* considers bribes legitimate? *who* is blaming outside agitators?—becomes impatient with such evasive statements and may react by concluding that the writer is either too lazy to find the facts or that he or she doesn't want to take responsibility for the statements.

USING PASSIVE VERBS WELL

Sometimes, however, a writer needs to use passive verbs. The two principal uses are:

◦ To focus the reader's attention on the action rather than on the agent.
◦ To express action when the agent is unknown.

For instance:

Pompeii *was buried* by a volcano 2,000 years ago.

The operation *has been duplicated* in several hospitals.

Hundred of subway passengers *were overcome* by smoke.

Writers working on technical or scientific prose often need to use the passive voice to focus their readers' attention on a process or a mechanism rather than on the persons involved. If you are doing such writing, it's a good idea to check a sample passage from a document in that field. If it uses predominantly passive verbs, you may want to follow the same pattern. But even in technical writing, some editors are encouraging writers to use the active voice occasionally.

CHOOSING OTHER WORDS FOR CLARITY

CHOOSING ADJECTIVES AND ADVERBS

In general, you should try to convey your meaning with nouns and verbs rather than relying heavily on adjectives and adverbs. Use modifiers sparingly and try to make them as precise and specific as possible.

Careful writers try to avoid adjectives that seem to become attached to other words almost automatically, such as *common* courtesy, *fundamental* difference, *paramount* importance, or *final* destination. Ask yourself if a particular adjective will sharpen your meaning; if not, get rid of it.

Adjectives like *wonderful, terrific, fabulous, incredible,* and *fantastic* are "fuzzy intensifiers." They don't really describe anything; they just reflect the writer's attitudes. Such words may work well in casual conversation, but in writing they give the impression that the writer doesn't want to take the time to search for a more precise term. It's also a good idea to prune out those routine intensifying words *very, really,* and *definitely.*

One kind of modifier, the qualifying word or phrase, raises particular problems. Terms that belong in this category are *rather, somewhat, often, probably, partly, in some cases, generally, for the most part,* and so on. There are dozens of such words that signal exceptions, limitations, or caution, and prudent writers use them frequently to temper their writing and avoid sounding dogmatic or simplistic. Asserting that "In the 1980s only people who do well on machine-scored tests are going to get into medical and law schools" makes an extravagant claim that immediately exposes you to challenge. But if you say, "By the 1980s *it may be* that only people who do well on machine-scored tests can get into medical or law school," the qualification changes the statement from a dogmatic pronouncement to an arguable hypothesis.

You can, however, easily carry this kind of caution too far and end up sounding timid and insecure rather than prudent. That can happen when

you begin sentences with phrases like, "It is somewhat the case that . . . ,"
"It rather seems as if . . . ," "It is possible that one could say . . . ," or some
equally timid statement. Weak openers like this give the impression of a
person raising an arm over the head to fend off a blow. They are not likely
to command the attention or respect of the reader.

So you need to strike a balance between brashness and timidity, between
sounding dogmatic and sounding insecure. It's a matter of controlling your
tone. In most writing situations you can create a confident but courteous
tone by making positive statements that you tone down with an occasional
mild qualifier.

ADDING METAPHORS FOR CLARITY

Metaphor, along with analogy, serves as an invaluable device for illustrating and clarifying abstract concepts because it helps readers to *see* the
writer's meaning. It explains the unfamiliar by drawing from the familiar.
Here is an example from modern astronomy:

> The domed-over stadium gives no evidence to the traveller of the
> crowd within. However, he sees the lines of traffic converging from all
> directions, becoming more and more tightly packed in traffic jams as
> they approach the center of attraction. A black hole whirling about, and
> being whirled about in orbit by, a normal star will also be the recipient
> of clouds of gas from this companion, with all the puffs and swirls that
> one can imagine from watching a factory chimney belch its clouds of
> smoke. This gas will not fall straight in. It will orbit the black hole in
> ever tighter spirals as it works its way inward, making weather on its
> way. It, like the traffic approaching the stadium, will be squeezed more
> and more.[8]

One of the bonuses of using metaphor is that you can simultaneously
enrich and condense your writing. For instance, the sociologist David
Riesman illustrated his theories of inner-directed and outer-directed per-
sonalities by writing that inner-directed people make decisions by consulting internal gyroscopes that have been pre-set by parents and society;
outer-directed people make their decisions by putting out radar-like signals
to test the attitudes of people around them. His metaphors both dramatize
his ideas by giving them a visual dimension and communicate them more
economically than he could have in a detailed, theoretical explanation. In
other words, good metaphors are a kind of shorthand.

8. John A. Wheeler, "Black Holes and New Physics," *Discovery: Research and Scholarship at
the University of Texas at Austin* (Winter 1982), 5.

AVOIDING JARGON, GOBBLEDYGOOK, AND DOUBLESPEAK

When you encounter writing that is not only flat and colorless, but hard to understand because it is wordy, heavy with abstractions and passive verbs, and padded with qualifiers and evasive language, you should suspect that you are encountering jargon. In its original sense, the word *jargon* means the specialized language of a profession or trade; lawyers, for instance, have to talk about *habeas corpus* and *writs of mandamus,* and editors have to talk about *layouts* and *galleys.* In such contexts specialists are justified in using specialized terms. But writers who use intimidating and confusing language when they are writing for an average audience, or use highly specialized and unfamiliar terminology when it is not necessary, are writing another kind of jargon, that confusing and pretentious kind of language that is sometimes also called gobbledygook, doublespeak, or bureaucratese. This kind of jargon is another form of the emperor's-new-clothes language discussed in Chapter 2.

Certain kinds of evasive or puzzling words and phrases tend to crop up in this kind of writing. The most common are euphemisms, such as *career apparel* for *uniforms,* or *quality control person* for *inspector;* vague words such as *viable, interface,* or *meaningful;* foreign words or phrases such as *modus vivendi* or *comme il faut;* or gimmicky words like *actualize* and *prioritize.* All of these terms can cause problems for readers, who may have to stop and ask themselves, "Now what is a *quality control person?*" or "What does *interface* mean?" If they don't know what *modus vivendi* means, they either have to stop to look it up or go on without understanding. And a reader who bumps into a term like *prioritize* will usually do a double take. In fact, perhaps the earliest signal a reader gets that he or she may be getting bogged down in jargon is that feeling of the mind glazing over and the words not penetrating. When that happens a reader has to backtrack and start over again.

Almost certainly people *learn* to write jargon; it does not grow out of a genuine need to communicate. Students seldom write it until the last years of high school or until they get to college. People who write it do so, I think, for several reasons. At one extreme they use euphemisms to disguise unpleasantness—*sanitary landfill* for *garbage dump*—or to alter negative connotations—*golden years* for *old age.* At the other extreme writers may use doublespeak to conceal the truth or mislead the reader. No one has described that kind of jargon better than George Orwell in his essay, "Politics and the English Language":

> Defenseless villages are bombarded from the air, the inhabitants driven out into the countryside, the huts set on fire with incendiary bullets, and this is called *pacification.* Millions of peasants are robbed of

their farms and sent trudging along the roads with no more than they can carry; this is called *rectification of frontiers*. People are imprisoned for years without trial, or shot in the back of the neck or sent to die of scurvy in Arctic prison camps; this is called *elimination of unreliable elements*. Such phraseology is needed if one wants to name things without calling up mental pictures.[9]

Students most often use jargon for reasons that fall somewhere between these extremes. They use it because they think it sounds impressive—the emperor's new clothes again; they use to to protect themselves—if the reader is not sure what they mean, he or she can't get too angry about it; or they use it because they're lazy. It is much easier to string together abstract words and fuzzy phrases than it is to write precise, clear prose.

Here is an example of authentic military jargon used as a classroom exercise by a colleague who teaches future officers to write at the U.S. Air Force Academy:

SUBJECT: Pilferage of Dining Hall Common-Use Items
To: Wing Group, Staff, Squadrons and Tenant Units

1. Every attempt is made to provide quality service to all patrons of the Dining Hall; however, the excessive pilferage of silverware, cups, glasses, plates and dispensers (salt, pepper, and sugar) has degraded service. Due to supply delays these items cannot always be replaced in a timely manner; additionally replacement of these items consumes funds that could be better utilized for improvement. The cost of these items has steadily increased, thereby requiring a greater expenditure of funds for replacements. Reduced fund allocations dictate maximum utilization of all common-use items and the cooperation of all personnel.

2. It is requested that all barracks, offices, work shops, etc. be cleaned out and these items returned to the Dining Hall.

3. All personnel should be apprised of this subject and the detrimental effect it has on service and morale.

Notice how stiff and flat this writing is, and how wordy. By writing *in a timely manner* instead of *quickly, fund allocations* instead of *funds,* and *utilization* instead of *use,* and by relying heavily on passive verbs, the faceless author projects a pompous, fussy image that will probably make no impression on the people he is trying to reach.

9. George Orwell, "Politics and the English Language," in *Shooting an Elephant and Other Essays* (New York: Harcourt, Brace & World, 1945), 88.

ELIMINATING SEXIST LANGUAGE

Finally, you need to think about making your writing as clear and accurate as possible by avoiding sexist language, that is, language that suggests sex discrimination or stereotyping. Such language is not only demeaning to one sex—nearly always women—but potentially confusing because it fails to distinguish among individuals and tends to lump them into categories.

CHARACTERISTICS OF SEXIST LANGUAGE

Sexist language has these characteristics:

⋄ It consistently uses the pronoun "he" as a *generic* pronoun—that is, an all-purpose pronoun denoting any individual whose gender is not specified. For example, "The serious runner takes time in choosing his running shoes," or "Everyone should consider his position on this issue."

⋄ It consistently uses the terms "man" and "men" as a generic term to refer to all people ("All men acquire language by a natural process") and it uses the suffix *-man* with nouns that describe occupation or function ("chairman" or "salesman").

⋄ It typically uses masculine pronouns and terminology to refer to people in professions traditionally thought of as male ("If a doctor is sued, you can be sure he is well insured") and feminine pronouns and terminology to refer to people in professions typically thought of as female ("Today's nurse earns less in real wages than her predecessor did twenty years ago").

⋄ It often suggests that certain traits, attitudes, and behavior are typically male (men are rational, independent, ambitious) and other traits, attitudes, and behavior are typically female (women are emotional, passive, and eager to please). The writer may also use cliches that reflect sexist attitudes: "chattering females," "the weaker sex," or "swaggering males."

There are other, subtler forms of sexist language. One is to refer to prominent men by their title or last name but to prominent women by their full name or married name: for instance, designating the United States president as "President Reagan" but the British prime minister as "Mrs. Thatcher" or referring to the American male writer as "Hemingway" but the American female writer as "Eudora Welty." Another is to mention specifically the appearance or marital status of women but not of men. For instance, it would be sexist to mention in a report that a woman employee is "an attractive blonde" or "a divorcee" but not indicate whether a man employee is married or divorced or whether he is attractive or homely.

Reasons to Eliminate Sexist Language

Many writers protest that they are not sexist and that the fuss about masculine pronouns or the generic term *man* is ridiculous. They claim that their readers know that the term refers to all people, and that they shouldn't have to worry about such trivial matters. They also claim that in order to get rid of all allegedly sexist references they will have to write awkward sentences. They reject "he and she" or "her/his" as ugly constructions. One can sympathize with these complaints. Getting rid of sexist innuendoes in writing takes attention and effort—it's a nuisance. Nevertheless, our language changes as our society changes, and for several reasons today's writers need to work at eliminating sexism from their writing.

The first reason is to improve clarity and accuracy. Consistently using *he* as a pronoun without considering the gender of the referent may mislead your readers. The sentence *A scholarship athlete must be able both to practice and to keep up his grades* seems to suggest that there are no women athletes on scholarship. And the writer who always uses "him" to refer to an lawyer or doctor or scientist gives the impression of not knowing that one-third of all medical students and one-half of all law students are women, and that women now get about 20 per cent of the advanced degrees in science.

The second reason is pragmatic and economic. Today more than half of all college students and more than half of the workers in the United States are women. Politically, socially, and financially, these women wield substantial power. They make up a large segment of most writers' audiences, and most of them dislike sexist language and are sensitive about being stereotyped or patronized by writers. If you want to inform or persuade an audience that is made up even partially of women you need to avoid sexist language.

A third reason is legal. Federal and state laws now stipulate that a person cannot be discriminated against because of sex when he or she applies for credit, for a job, for a scholarship, a grant, or for admission to a school or program. Thus the administrators and executives who are in charge of advertising and administering the guidelines in any of these situations must be sure that the language of all documents is completely nonsexist. Anyone who is going to be writing for a corporation, a bureau, an educational institution, or an agency needs to become conscious of sexist language and how to avoid it.

The last reason, and from my point of view the strongest, is psychological and ethical. *Language shapes thought*—linguists, anthropologists, politicians, and leaders all know that, and the writer who persists in using only masculine pronouns or suggesting that certain occupations and attitudes are male, others female, reinforces stereotypes and sexist attitudes. I think this quotation demonstrates that truth:

[The typical writer] would have a wife and one, two, or three children.
. . . The writer of forty would own his own house—probably with a big
mortgage—but there will be less than the usual number of appliances
because he has developed a high resistance to salesmanship. . . . If he
owns a television set he will explain apologetically that he got it for the
children, but now the writer and his wife have taken to watching a few
programs. Probably he is dissatisfied with his work and his mode of life.
. . . He has begun to take part in local activities. Recently his wife was
elected to the school board, and he would like to run for office himself,
but he has decided that the office, and even the campaign, would take
too much time from his writing.[10]

Only by great effort can the reader of this passage remember that not all
writers are men.

Ways to Eliminate Sexist Language

Cleaning sexist innuendoes out of one's writing takes effort and ingenuity,
but if you work at it you can finally make writing nonsexist prose as much
of a habit as spelling and punctuating correctly. Here are some suggestions
for ways to go about it:

◇ When you can, use plural nouns to avoid using the pronoun *he* or the
  phrase *he and she* (often this is the simplest remedy): "Painters who want
  to exhibit their work," rather than "A painter who wants to exhibit his
  work."

◇ Reword your sentences to eliminate reference to gender: "The average
  American drives a car three years," rather than "The average American
  drives his car three years."

◇ When you can, substitute the word *person* or *people* for *man* or *woman*:
  "A person who wants to get ahead in business" rather than "A man who
  wants to get ahead in business," and "Young people who want to become engineers," instead of "Boys who want to become engineers."

◇ When you can, substitute *one* for *he* or *she* or for specific reference to a
  man or woman: "If one plans ahead, one can retire comfortably at 55,"
  instead of "If he plans ahead, a man can retire at 55." Often you can use
  you instead of *one*. For example, "If you plan ahead, you can retire at
  55."

◇ Occasionally, when the noun to which you want to refer has to be singular, write "he or she" or "his or hers"; such phrases are inconspicuous if
  you do not use them too often. Some writers use he/she or him/her.

◇ Alternate between using *he* and *she* as pronouns. For example, write
  "An officer who makes an arrest must show her badge."

10. Malcolm Cowley, *The Literary Situation* (New York: The Viking Press, 1955), 195.

◇ Instead of identifying people by their sex, identify them by their role or function: student, applicant, consumer, voter, patient, parent, and so on. For instance, you can write "Consumers are alarmed by rising food costs," instead of "Housewives are alarmed by rising food costs." Such a sentence is also more accurate since almost 40 per cent of shoppers in grocery stores are now men.

◇ Refer to women by their given and married names such as Julia Walsh or Geraldine Ferraro rather than as Mrs. John Walsh or Mrs. Ferraro. Avoid reference to women's marital status unless that information is important to making your point.

◇ Be consistent when you are referring to people by their last names. If you write Hawthorne or Steinbeck, also write Dickinson or Porter.

◇ When you can, replace occupational terms ending in *-man* or *-woman* with another term. For instance, write *firefighter* instead of *fireman, mail carrier* instead of *mailman, salesperson* instead of *salesman* or *saleswoman,* and *janitor* instead of *cleaning woman. Waiter* can refer to either a man or a woman.

◇ Be careful not to stereotype people by professions or by supposedly sex-linked characteristics. For example, write "Young people who plan to become doctors should realize they will be in college at least ten years," rather than "The young man who wants to become a doctor should realize that he will be in college at least ten years."

◇ Don't refer to women's physical appearance unless it is relevant to your point or unless you also refer to men's physical appearance in the same context.

In order to develop a style of writing that is free of sexist overtones, you have to do three things. First, you have to become conscious of those overtones; that may be the greatest problem since many of us are so used to the traditional male-centered style that we have trouble spotting its typical characteristics. Second, you have to cultivate the habit of revising and editing to get rid of those characteristics. Gradually you can internalize the conventions for nonsexist writing just as you internalize other guidelines for style. Finally, and probably most important, you have to care about developing a neutral, nondiscriminatory style. Once you believe that it matters, the changes will come almost naturally.

CRAFTING SENTENCES FOR CLARITY

AVOIDING SENTENCE FRAGMENTS

Just as today's editors and practicing writers are relaxing their attitudes about punctuation, they are also becoming more tolerant about sentence fragments, that old bugaboo of traditional grammarians. In years past amateur writers have thought—and with good cause—that they must never violate that well-known rule, "Always write in complete sentences." A complete sentence was defined as one that had a subject and verb and expressed a complete thought.

In many writing situations, writers would still do well to abide by the familiar rule. My survey of professional people's response to lapses from standard usage (see page 230) revealed that more than 65 percent of them said that they would object strongly to finding these sentence fragments in writing that came across their desks:

> He went through a long battle. A fight against unscrupulous opponents.

> The small towns are dying. One of the problems being that young people are leaving.

Forty-four percent said they would object strongly to the following sentence fragment, and 32 percent said they would object a little:

> Cheap labor and low costs. These are two benefits enjoyed by Taiwan firms.

I think one must conclude from this evidence that most people in decision-making positions want the writing they see to conform to the rules for sentences that they learned in school.

Minor Sentences or Formal Fragments

But any person who notices sentence structure as he or she reads contemporary writing will recognize dozens of groups of words that are punctuated as sentences but don't fit the definition just given. They occur not only in advertising, where they are used for their eye-catching, emphatic effect, but in expository prose at both ends of the literary spectrum. For example:

> It's fashionable to knock TV news. Always has been. Thirty years ago, the news on television was amateurish. Not much different from newsreels. Superficial. Today, it's slick. Too many Adonises and Venuses posing as reporters. It's also too controversial. Or not controversial enough. Too liberal. Too conservative. Too heavy on foreign news. Too heavy on local news. Just headlines.[11]

> This millionaire—in real estate, antiquities, and royalties—who came out of the austere world of the early pioneers, the first child born in the

---

11. Edward Bliss, Jr., "There Is Good Journalism on TV," *TV Guide*, 15 July 1978, 39.

first kibbutz. Sullen, introverted, impatient with his fellow mortals. Too easily bored. "Charismatic" in a country in which that designation, in the eyes of many, is a compliment. Feline, artful, a notorious womanizer, yet probably without a single close friend: incapable of companionship among equals. Emotionally blocked, estranged from his sons as he himself had been from his father. A lover of power, money, good food, fast cars, and all manner of creature comforts. Acquisitive.[12]

Obviously both these passages work, and work well. They communicate their ideas clearly, economically, and forcefully, yet they employ almost no traditional sentences; the second one has none.

The puzzled student writer might well ask why these writers feel free to use sentence fragments. The answer, I think, is that the so-called fragments that these writers use are not really incomplete groups of words; rather they are what one team of modern grammarians calls "minor sentences" or "formal fragments." This new definition recognizes that when we can read a group of words and make sense out of it, we mentally process it as a sentence whether or not it has all those elements that a sentence is traditionally supposed to have. Or to put it another way, readers can sometimes reach closure at the end of a group of words even if that group does not have a subject or verb; when that happens, that group can be marked off with a period and called a "minor sentence."[13] It is a legitimate division of writing.

TRUE SENTENCE FRAGMENTS

Groups of words that really are sentence fragments—that is, incomplete pieces of a coherent whole—are those that *don't* work by themselves. There may be several reasons why they leave the reader in suspense. They may begin an idea and not carry it through, they may express only part of an idea and thus confuse the reader, or they may form a phrase or clause that does not make sense by itself and yet is not attached to anything else.

Here are some typical examples:

> There are few assertions in the article and little evidence to support them. *An example being, "It is unclear whether these intruders had anything to do with the crime."*

The italicized words here need to be attached to a base; although they are punctuated as a sentence, they make no sense by themselves.

---

12. Amos Elon, *New York Times Book Review,* 14 January 1979, 3.
13. Charles R. Kline, Jr., and W. Dean Memering, "Formal Fragments: The English Minor Sentence," *Research in the Teaching of English* (Fall 1977), 97.

Unlike doctors, lawyers are ready to practice when they get their degrees. *Although it is often necessary to take an expensive course in order to pass the bar exam.*

The italicized portion should be joined with the sentence; otherwise the "although" raises expectations that the writer does not meet.

To understand how all knowledge is related. That is the goal of a liberal education.

The writer would get a more economical sentence by starting out, "The goal of a liberal education is . . . ."

Harrison lived out a legend in his own time. *A man who came from nowhere and created a billion dollar business empire.*

The italicized portion here is really an appositive and doesn't work well standing by itself.

Probably the best guideline to keep in mind about writing sentence fragments is that if you are in doubt, don't use them. And if you do use them, be sure you are constructing minor sentences that convey a finished idea, not broken-off sentences that puzzle or annoy your audience. If you punctuate a group of words as a sentence, but realize it leaves your reader in suspense or seems not to fit with anything, then attach it to a sentence or rewrite it.

Also, when you make decisions about using minor sentences or word groups that are technically sentence fragments, think carefully about your audience and your purpose. Not only professionals, but also professors, particularly English professors, usually prefer that you write straightforward, traditional sentences that will convey your meaning efficiently and not raise any distracting usage problems. Many other audiences, such as a supervisor reading a report or an evaluation committee reading a proposal, feel the same way because, as with most educated readers, their school background has conditioned them to react against sentence fragments. The thoughtful writer knows and respects those attitudes. So if you want to be sure that a serious piece of explanatory or persuasive writing gets a careful, unprejudiced reading from a serious audience, avoid writing fragments.

If, however, you are writing descriptive prose in which you want to communicate impressions or if you are writing an informal, breezy article for a general audience, you may find that putting in an occasional minor sentence or fragment will help to create the tone and tempo that you want. If so, don't be afraid to try using them. Often they are appropriate and effective. But do know what you are doing, and in a writing class, be prepared to defend your choices.

AVOIDING COMMA SPLICES

Sometimes, working in haste and not thinking about the relationships between the statements you are putting down, you may join two groups of words that could be read as sentences with a comma instead of with a conjunction that would show the relationship between those word groups. When you do, you produce a *comma splice* (sometimes also called a *comma fault* or a *comma blunder*). That is, you join independent clauses with a punctuation mark that is so weak it cannot properly indicate the strong pause that should come in such a sentence. Here is an example of a weakly punctuated sentence:

> The first part of the book gave Jim no problem, it was the second part that stumped him.

Notice that the reader does not get a strong sense of separation between the two parts of the sentence. The emphasis would come through more clearly if it were written like this:

> The first part of the book gave Jim no problem, but the second part stumped him.

or this:

> Although the first part of the book gave Jim no problem, the second part stumped him.

Either revision correctly de-emphasizes the first part of the sentence and puts the stress on the second. In the original, the parts of the sentence appear to be equal.

For two reasons you should usually avoid comma splices. First, independent commas that "tack" clauses together indicate that you are unsure or unconcerned about the relationship between the parts of the sentences. Second, commas that join independent clauses invite misinterpretation. A comma is such a weak interrupter that the reader is liable to slip right over it.

However, if you want to join several short independent clauses with commas to increase the tempo of your writing, you can probably do so without creating any problems. For example:

> It's not smart, it's not practical, it's not legal.

AVOIDING FUSED OR RUN-ON SENTENCES

Sentences in which two independent clauses have been run together without any punctuation are confusing and distracting to readers:

The success of horror movies is not surprising some people have always enjoyed being frightened.

Without punctuation, a reader at first makes "some people" the object of "is surprising" and then has to go back and reprocess the sentence. Also, without punctuation the reader at first misses the cause and effect relationship of the clauses. This sentence could be revised to:

The success of horror movies is not surprising because some people have always enjoyed being frightened.

AVOIDING DANGLING MODIFIERS

Modifying phrases that don't fit with the word or phrase that they seem to be attached to can cause problems for readers. Usually those misfit phrases, which we call *dangling modifiers,* come at the beginning of a sentence as an introductory phrase:

After leaving Cheyenne, the cost of living became a problem.

The reader expects to find out who left Cheyenne and is frustrated.
Notice that you increase your chances of beginning a sentence with a dangling modifier when you use abstract subjects and passive verbs. If the writer of this sentence had used an acting, concrete subject, she would probably have seen her mistake immediately.

USING PARALLELISM

Practiced writers use parallel structures frequently in order to unify and tighten their writing. That is, they incorporate two or more points in a sentence by using a series of phrases or clauses that have identical structure. For instance:

Country Western fans love Willie Nelson, jazz fans love Oscar Peterson, and ballad fans love Judy Collins.

or

> Stein hit Hollywood determined to live high, hang loose, stay single, and make money.

Sentences like these work by establishing a pattern that helps the reader to anticipate what is coming. It is like seeing groups of similar figures on a test sheet: circles together, triangles together, squares together, and so on. But when people see a figure that doesn't fit—a circle among the triangles, for instance—they find the exception jarring to their sense of unity. The same thing happens when readers find phrases or clauses that don't fit the pattern of the rest of the sentence. Here is an example of faulty parallelism:

> My purpose was to show what services are available, how many people use them, and *having the audience feel the services are significant.*

The reader does a double take after the second comma because the third point is not handled in the same way as the first two.

The time to check your writing for parallel structures is probably when you are doing the second draft. As you read over your sentences, try to see what patterns you are setting up, and be sure that you don't disappoint or frustrate your reader by making sudden switches.

AVOIDING FAULTY PREDICATION

Every complete sentence must have at least two parts: a subject and verb. The verb, along with all of the parts that go with the verb to make a statement, is called the *predicate* of the sentence. Thus the portion of the sentence that completes the assertion that began with the subject of the sentence is called the *predication of a sentence.* Sometimes, however, people writing sentences try to pair up subjects and verbs, or objects and verbs, that just don't work well together. We call the problem caused by such mismatched combinations *faulty predication.* Most cases of faulty predication seem to fall into one of three categories:

1. Mismatched subject + active verb:

> The rape center will accompany the victim to court.

> Research grants want to get the best qualified applicants.

In each of these sentences the writer has predicated an action that the subject could not carry out; a "rape center" cannot "accompany" someone, and a "research grant" cannot "want." Notice that if the writers had used personal subjects instead of abstract ones for these sentences, they probably would have avoided the mistake. If you start your main clause with a personal subject, you are much less apt to join that subject with a mismatched verb.

2. Subject + linking verb + mismatched complement:

The main trait a person needs is success.

The activities available for young people are swimming pools and tennis courts.

Energy and transportation are problems for our generation.

When people write sentences like these, they seem to have forgotten that the verb *to be* and other linking verbs act as a kind of equal sign (=) in sentences in which the complement of the sentence is a noun. Thus when they use a linking verb after a subject, they should be sure that the noun complement they put after it can logically be equated with the subject. In none of the sentences above could the reader make that equation. "Success" is not a "trait," "activity" cannot be a "swimming pool," and "energy" cannot be equated with "problem."

Again, if the writers of these sentences had started out with personal subjects, they probably would not have gotten into these tangles. These sentences could be rewritten:

A person needs to be successful.

Young people can use the swimming pools and tennis courts.

Our generation faces problems with energy and transportation.

Writers who use the construction, "[Something] is when . . ." are getting tangled in the same kind of mistake:

The worst problem is when motorists ignore these signals.

Community property is when husband and wife share all earnings.

Although a reader is not likely to misunderstand these sentences, they really are substandard usage. the writers are actually saying "problem = when" and "property = when." The best way to avoid this difficulty is simply to make it a rule not to use the construction *is when*.

3. Subject + verb + mismatched object:

These theories intimidate the efforts of amateur players.

The company fired positions which had been there only six months.

In these sentences, the writers have not thought about the limitations they put on themselves when they used the verbs "intimidate" and "fired." Both verbs have to apply to people (or at least creatures). You cannot "intimidate" an "effort" or "fire" a "position." Again, notice that if they had used concrete instead of abstract words as objects, they probably would not have gotten into the problem.

One of your concerns when you read your first draft should be checking your verbs to see that you have matched them with logical subjects and complements. And although there are no rules to follow to avoid getting yourself tangled in predication knots, I can suggest one guideline for avoiding problems: Use personal and concrete subjects whenever you can, and connect your verbs to specific and concrete terms. If you do this and write agent/action sentences (see p. 114) you will eliminate most predication errors.

EXERCISES

1. Rewrite the following sentences using concrete and specific language whenever possible:

   A. The article is intended for people who are unaware of the status of housing growth in this country.
   B. The program means elimination of access to artificially produced foodstuffs.
   C. The mere indication of legislative intent would serve as an incentive to constituents.
   D. A knowledge and understanding of the law is a necessity for those who want an alteration of it.

2. Rewrite these sentences using people or a person as the subject of the sentence:

   A. The load of responsibility on the lender is great.
   B. A stringent self-evaluation is needed to remedy your problem.
   C. The anxiety that accompanies choosing a profession is a major cause of stress.
   D. Careful selection of foods containing all the various nutrients is important for maintaining health and adequate energy.

3. Rewrite these sentences with more vigorous verbs:

   A. Abortion as a method of population control is ineffective in lessening the birthrate.
   B. There are several advantages that will be achieved by this ruling.
   C. Vitamins are substances the body requires in small amounts.
   D. There are many things to examine when looking for a used car.

4. Rewrite these sentences to replace the passive verbs with active verbs:

   A. Women are faced with similar anxieties every day.
   B. Such information should be made available to the consumers in case they ask.
   C. What should be considered is the capability and suitability of an individual for the job.
   D. It is recommended by state officials that action be taken immediately.

5. Photocopy a magazine article in which the author uses metaphor or allusion and bring it to class. Analyze what the writer's reason for using allusion and metaphor seems to be. Do you think the technique is effective?

6. Interpret these jargon-laden sentences and then rewrite each of them to make it clearer:

   A. The configuration of human and technical talents to be mobilized often transcends the jurisdiction of formal educational institutions.
   B. "Once upon a time, a small person named Little Red Riding Hood initiated plans for the preparation, delivery, and transportation of foodstuffs to her grandmother, a senior citizen residing at a place of residence in a forest of indeterminate dimensions." —Russell Baker
   C. Our investments are generating a negative capability.
   D. Nelson prioritized the company's objectives in terms of viability and expense factors.

7. Rewrite the following passages to eliminate sex-biased language:

   A. A student will be judged not on how effective he will be as a practicing lawyer, but on the number of correct answers he gives on a multiple-choice test.
   B. The businessman who is trying to achieve racial and sexual balance among his employees will have to advertise in a variety of places.
   C. The nurse who wants to work in a small town often finds that she has been replaced by unlicensed nurses' aides.
   D. Hemingway, Fitzgerald, Katherine Anne Porter, Steinbeck, and Joan Didion are among the authors who have kept notebooks on their writing habits.

8. Punctuate these sentences in a way that will help the reader comprehend their meaning:

   A. At the same time the doctor urges that therapy be used as a form of punishment not imprisonment in "dangerous and miserable" conditions but punishment that will effectively rehabilitate the individual.

   B. Surely we cannot expect the U.S. and the USSR which have known nothing but fear for each other since the first World War to completely let down their defenses and enter into a trusting relationship.

   C. Inflation robs the dollar of its worth naturally causing higher prices of goods and services and affecting all sorts of investments even so-called gilt-edged securities.

9. Decide which of the italicized word groups are effective minor sentences and which are broken sentences that do not function effectively:

   A. *Low wages and cheap energy.* These are the natural resources of Brazil.
   B. You should not depend on living on your pension. *Even though it seems adequate.*
   C. He fought an exhausting battle. *A battle against corruption, indifference, and cynicism.*
   D. The candidate was nervous about voter apathy. *That being the most serious problem in her district.*
   E. Trying to prove his point, he overstated his case. *Which was not very well thought out in the first place.*

SUGGESTED WRITING ASSIGNMENTS

As a part of each writing assignment write a detailed analysis of your audience and specify the characteristics they would have that you need to keep in mind as you write, the problems such an audience might present, and what the audience would expect to get from reading your paper. Also analyze your purpose in writing, specifying what you hope to accomplish with the paper. If appropriate, include an accurate and descriptive title for your paper.

TOPIC 1: Go and observe carefully a street, neighborhood, building, or small area in your city and write an objective report on it that might be used for a paper in an urban sociology class or course on city government. Use concrete and specific but neutral language; appeal to the senses as much as possible and avoid using vague adjectives. Think about what kind of information your reader would want to get from the report and what use that information might be put to outside of class. Some possible topics for description might be the following:

A deteriorating Victorian house that would be worth renovating and preserving.

A vacant lot that could be converted into a playground.

A block close to campus that is being invaded by x-rated bookstores and porno movie houses.

The county courthouse that was built in the last century.

TOPIC 2: The generous retirement pay of people who have served twenty years or more in the armed services costs U.S. taxpayers a substantial amount of money. For example, a colonel may retire at forty-two and receive over $1,500 a month retirement pay while holding down another job; a four-star admiral may retire at the age of sixty with a pension of more than $60,000 a year. These benefits also have the advantage of being tied to the cost of living so that they increase as the price index rises.

Assume the persona of someone who defends or opposes these benefits and write an article expressing your views. Think carefully about the consequences of your argument and support your points. Direct your paper to a specific audience.

TOPIC 3: Write a short article for young people from ten to fourteen years old explaining the basic concepts of some subject on which you are well informed or in which you are very interested. Assume that your readers are bright youngsters who read well and who enjoy learning something new. Try to explain your ideas or give your information in terms they will understand, using concrete examples and analogies. Keep your focus narrow enough so that you can treat the subject in no more than 1000 words.

Here are some suggestions for topics:

A new discovery in geology, astronomy, archeology, or other science

What it takes to be a dancer, lawyer, journalist, or other professional

How weather forecasting is done

How airplanes fly or ducks swim or whales breathe

How to budget and spend a clothes allowance

How to buy one's first horse

Choosing a sport to participate in

How to take care of a dog in hot weather

Remember that your audience doesn't have to read your article and will do so only if you keep them interested. It would be a good idea to look at some children's magazines or the column for young people in magazines such as *Smithsonian* to get a feel for what kind of writing appeals to youngsters and what qualities articles for them are likely to have. *And remember not to preach.*

8 ◊ Crafting Paragraphs

Paragraphs are artificial units of text that writers and editors create as a way of dividing a piece of writing into chunks so that readers will be able to read and assimilate it easily. We don't actually *think* in paragraphs in the way we think in sentences, and that difference may account for the trouble many writers have in deciding where to break the text into paragraphs or determining how long they should be. Nevertheless, you need to develop a strong sense of when to paragraph because how you divide your writing into paragraphs and how you develop those paragraphs affect how your readers respond to your writing.

How do you develop that sense? Partly through practice and partly by intuition. The more you write, the more you will develop a "feel" for paragraphing. But there are also two principles that underlie the concept of paragraphing, and you can certainly improve your skills by consciously thinking about and trying to apply those principles. The first principle involves looking at paragraphs from the outside; the second principle involves looking at them from the inside.

THE OUTSIDE VIEW OF PARAGRAPHING

Writers and editors sometimes break writing into paragraphs for visual reasons. They are concerned about how readers will react when they first see a page of print; they know that a printed page gives off signals to its potential readers before they ever read a word. The length of paragraphs, the size of print, the width of margins, the number of headings and subheadings, and the amount of white space—all combine to give a page a distinctive physical appearance. If a page of print looks closely packed and has few divisions and narrow margins, it gives a message that says, "I am hard to read," and many readers will instinctively shy away from it. Even good readers will be put off by very long paragraphs that run to a page or more. For this reason editors and audience-conscious writers insert frequent paragraph breaks. They want their readers to feel that a piece of writing is "reader-friendly," to borrow a term from the computer business. One way to give that impression is through careful paragraphing.

Writers who are the most audience-conscious will base many of their paragraphing decisions on what they know about a specific audience. If they are writing for an audience with widely diverse educations and reading skills—say the readers of *Family Circle* or *TV Guide*—they will write shorter paragraphs than they would for a narrower audience whom they assume to be educated and skilled readers—for example, the readers of *Scientific American* or the *Atlantic*. They will also use shorter paragraphs when they are writing for young readers.

Of course, the terms "short paragraph" and "long paragraph" are necessarily relative, but in general a paragraph of from three to six sentences of about medium length (ten to fifteen words) would qualify as a short paragraph. A paragraph of seven or eight medium-sized sentences would qualify as a comparatively long paragaph. A paragraph of more than ten medium-length sentences is definitely a long paragraph, and you should think about breaking it up if you can.

GUIDELINES FOR BREAKING PARAGRAPHS

But no competent writer just chops his or her writing into blocks arbitrarily to make it look better—you need some principles, some guidelines, or you will wind up with paragraph divisions that confuse your readers more than they help them. The traditional rule-of-thumb, that you make a paragraph break when you come to a new idea, often works quite well. For example, if you are writing a paper in which you want to give several short examples, you can probably start a new paragraph for each example. Paragraphing can be easy when your paper falls into such natural divisions.

It becomes more difficult, however, when those natural divisions seem to require that you write ten or twelve rather long sentences to develop them; then you should begin to worry about how your paragraph is going to look. In such instances, you need some more flexible guidelines to help you decide when you can make a break. Here are three:

◦ You can break a paragraph when a group of sentences seems to have reached closure and the reader can make sense of them without having additional material. So one strategy is to review your sentences to see which of them seem to group together naturally.

◦ You can break a paragraph when you come to a place where you are indicating a shift in time or in space: that is, if you shift from writing about the present to writing about the past or future, or if you shift from writing about one place to writing about another.

◦ You can sometimes break a paragraph if you are introducing a contrast with phrases like "In spite of" or "On the other hand." Such signals may indicate a logical separation that you can take advantage of.

For instance, here is an example of a long paragraph that could be broken up into more manageable chunks without its unity being affected:

"People say that Arthur [Ashe] lacks the killer instinct." (Ronald Charity is commenting.) "And that is a lot of baloney. Arthur is quietly aggressive—more aggressive than people give him credit for being. You don't get to be that good without a will to win. He'll let you win the first two sets, then he'll blast you off the court." Ronald Charity, who taught Arthur Ashe to play tennis, was himself taught by no one. "I was my own protege," he says. Charity is approaching forty and is the head of an advertising and public-relations firm in Danville, Virginia. Trim, lithe, in excellent condition, he is still nationally ranked as one of the top ten players in the A.T.A. / In 1946, when he began to play tennis, as a seventeen-year-old in Richmond, there were—male and female, all ages—about twenty Negroes in the city who played the game and none of them played it well. Charity, as a college freshman, thought tennis looked interesting, and when, in a bookstore, he saw Lloyd Budge's *Tennis Made Easy* he bought a copy and began to teach himself to play. When he had absorbed what Budge had to say, he bought Alice Marble's *The Road to Wimbledon*, and, finally, William T. Tilden's *How To Play Better Tennis*. "It just happened that I could pull off a page and project into my imagination how it should be done," he says. / Blacks in Richmond could play tennis only at the Negro Y.W.C.A., where Charity developed his game, and, a little later, four hard-surface courts were built at Brook Field, a Negro playground about two miles from the heart of the city. Arthur Ashe, a Special Police Officer in charge of discipline at several Negro playgrounds, lived in a frame house in the middle of Brook Field. When Arthur Ashe, Jr. was six years old, he spent a great deal of time watching Ronald Charity play tennis, and would never forget what he felt as he watched him. "I thought he was the best in the world. He had long, fluid, graceful strokes. I could see no kinks in his game."[1]

1. John McPhee, "Levels of the Game," reprinted in *The John McPhee Reader,* ed. William Howarth (New York: Vintage Books, 1978), 178–79.

Notice that the first place I broke this paragraph (indicated by a slash) comes at a shift in time—the narrative moves from the present back to 1946. The second place where it could be broken comes at a change in space—the narrative moves from talking about tennis books to the tennis courts at the Y.W.C.A.

AVOIDING ONE-SENTENCE PARAGRAPHS

Unfortunately, some mass-market writers let their enthusiasm for short paragraphs carry them to the extreme of habitually writing a series of one- or two-sentence paragraphs that are really not paragraphs at all. They are only separated sentences. For example:

> Once upon a time there was a little girl in a small town in South Dakota who dreamed of speaking French.
> So when she grew up and went off to college, a prestigious school in the East, she was ready for her dream to come true.
> "I had a miserable French teacher—I was disappointed," recalled Ann Clark, the chef behind Austin's La Bonne Cuisine School of French cooking. "So I dropped out of school and a girlfriend and I went to France."
> There the two worked as *au pair* girls, live-in housekeepers earning some money and gaining an entry to the ethos of France that had seemed so inviting.[2]

Although writers for newspapers probably write these one-line paragraphs because the narrow columns of a newspaper make a paragraph of normal length look long and intimidating, this kind of paragraphing chops a piece of writing into arbitrary divisions that are hard to follow. The reader senses no pattern or unity to the writing.

You shouldn't, however, assume that you can never write one-sentence paragraphs. Sometimes they serve well to emphasize a major point, and sometimes they can act as transitions from one paragraph to the next. But skilled writers usually avoid writing one-sentence paragraphs because they are distracting and make writing seem choppy.

THE INSIDE VIEW OF PARAGRAPHING

The one-sentence paragraph also violates the *inside* principle of paragraphing, that a paragraph is a unit of discourse that develops an idea. From this

2. Carolyn Bobo, "France Makes Rich Life for Cook," *Austin American-Statesman*, 21 December 1978, G–1.

point of view, the essential quality of a paragraph is *unity*. A paragraph is supposed to have a central idea, and everything in the paragraph relates to and develops that idea. The reader finds no surprises, and every sentence fits with the others. Moreover, the sentences follow each other in logical order so that one could not move the sentences around at random: each one needs to be in its particular place to advance the internal development of the paragraph.

How does one go about developing these unified paragraphs? People who write a lot probably develop their paragraphs mostly by intuition. They put down a first sentence and if it seems to work, the second sentence evolves from it. And so they continue, developing their points with examples and explanations, expanding on the idea they started with. If you were to ask them to explain how they write their paragraphs, they probably couldn't tell you. The fact remains, however, that much of the time professional writers are producing paragraphs that fit certain patterns that follow natural thought processes. Apprentice writers can learn something about good paragraph development by studying those patterns and analyzing how they are developed.

COMMITMENT/RESPONSE PARAGRAPHS

One important pattern for paragraphs is that of commitment and response. That is, the first sentence of the paragraph makes a *commitment* to the reader, makes a statement that sets up certain expectations and leads the reader to expect that they will be fulfilled. In some cases, the commitment sentence could be called a topic sentence. Whatever you label it, it works by making a promise to the reader, a promise that is developed by the rest of the paragraph.

Commitments in a paragraph can take many forms, as the following examples show. (I have italicized the commitment sentence in each one.)

First, the commitment in a paragraph can be a *generative sentence*, one that suggests more details will follow. For example:

> *A revolution is under way.* Most Americans are already aware of the gee-whiz gadgetry that is emerging, in rapidly accelerating bursts, from the world's high-technology laboratories. But most of us perceive only dimly how pervasive and profound the changes of the next twenty years will be. We are at the dawn of the smart machine—an "information age" that will change forever the way an entire nation works, plays, travels and even thinks. Just as the industrial revolution dramatically expanded the strength of man's muscles and the reach of his hand, so the smart-machine revolution will magnify the power of his brain. But unlike the industrial revolution, which depended on finite resources such

as iron and oil, the new information age will be fired by a seemingly limitless resource—the inexhaustible supply of knowledge itself. Even computer scientists, who best understand the galloping technology and its potential, are wonderstruck by its implications. "It is really awesome," says L.C. Thomas of Bell Laboratories. "Every day is just as scary as the day before."[3]

The writer makes a strong commitment in the first sentence, "A revolution is under way," and uses the rest of the paragraph to explain that statement.

The commitment in a paragraph can also take the form of *a question that will be answered*. (Notice this is the pattern I have used in the second paragraph in this section.) Here is another example:

What functions do dreams serve today? One view, published in a reputable scientific paper, holds that the function of dreams is to wake us up a little, every now and then, to see if anyone is about to eat us. But dreams occupy such a relatively small part of normal sleep that this explanation does not seem very compelling. Moreover, as we have seen, the evidence points the other way: today it is the mammalian predators, not the mammalian prey, who characteristically have dream-filled sleep. Much more plausible is the computer-based explanation that dreams are a spillover from the unconscious processing of the day's experience, from the brain's decision on how much of the daily events temporarily stored in a kind of buffer to emplace in long term memory. The events of yesterday frequently run through my dreams; the events of two days ago, much more rarely. However, the buffer-dumping model seems unlikely to be the whole story, because it does not explain the disguises that are so characteristic of the symbolic language of dreams, a point first stressed by Freud. It also does not explain the powerful affect or emotions of dreams; I believe there are many people who have been far more thoroughly frightened by their dreams than by anything they have ever experienced while awake.[4]

Writers can also make an opening commitment by *beginning a narrative* in the first sentence and signaling to the reader that the rest of the story will follow. For example:

One morning I arrived early at work and went into the bank lobby where the Negro porter was mopping. I stood at a counter and picked up the Memphis *Commercial Appeal* and began my free reading of the press. I came finally to the editorial page and saw an article dealing with one H.L. Mencken. I knew by hearsay that he was the editor of the

3. Merrill Shields et al., "And Man Created the Chip," *Newsweek*, 30 June 1980, 50.
4. Carl Sagan, *The Dragons of Eden* (New York: Ballantine Books, 1977), 151–52.

American Mercury, but aside from that I knew nothing about him. The article was a furious denunciation with one, hot, short sentence: Mencken is a fool.[5]

Another good way to make an opening commitment in a paragraph is by *using a quotation.* For example:

> *"You want to fly with the eagles, you got to pay the price,"* Dick Anderegg told me on the phone. Anderegg is an Air Force major in his middle thirties, a fighter pilot so proficient that until recently he was an instructor at the Air Force's Fighter Weapons School at Nellis Air Force Base, near Las Vegas. Now he works at the Pentagon, as an aide (or "action officer," in the current phrase) to a general, and it was in that capacity that he became my chaperone for a time early this fall.[6]

And don't forget the important technique of *downshifting,* already mentioned in the last chapter. It is a particularly useful strategy for opening your paragraph with a commitment and then developing it with statements on a lower level of generality. For example:

> *The most primary source of all is unpublished material:* private letters and diaries or the reports, orders, and messages in government archives. There is an immediacy and intimacy about them that reveals character and makes circumstances come alive. I remember Secretary of State Robert Lansing's desk diary, which I used when I was working on *The Zimmerman Telegram.* The man himself seemed to step right out from his tiny neat handwriting and his precise notations of every visitor and each subject discussed. Each day's record opened and closed with the Secretary's time of arrival and departure from the office. He even entered the time of his lunch hour, which invariably lasted sixty minutes: "Left at 1:10; returned at 2:10." Once, when he was forced to record his morning arrival at 10:15, he added, with a worried eye on posterity, "Car broke down."[7]

So writers can choose several different ways to build their paragraphs around a commitment/response pattern. The important point to remember is that the sentences that follow the opening commitment must not frustrate or confuse the reader by failing to follow through.

---

5. Richard Wright, "The Library Card," in *Black Boy* (New York: Harper and Row, 1937), 214.
6. James Fallows, "I Flew With the Eagles," *Atlantic,* November 1981, 70.
7. Barbara Tuchman, "In Search of History," in *Practicing History* (New York: Alfred A. Knopf, 1981), 11.

OTHER PARAGRAPH PATTERNS

Writers also need to be familiar with some other typical paragraph patterns that can serve them well. Some of the more useful ones are those that reflect the common patterns of organization that were discussed in Chapter 5: induction, claims and warrants, definition, cause and effect, comparison, narration, and process. Here are some examples; notice that many of them are also commitment-and-response paragraphs.

INDUCTION

This is a useful pattern when you want to present your reader with a collection of data or impressions that you will then use to develop your idea. For instance:

> Outside the Ryoanji temple, the newest Japanese surfaces shine. The taxi drivers bustle, sweeping huge feather dusters over their cars, flicking specks from the bright metal. The ritual, a writer once remarked, makes them look like the chambermaids in the first act of a French farce. But it is utterly Japanese, a set piece: the drivers handle their dusters like samurai. The scene is a sort of cartoon of the busy, fastidious superego that is supposed to preside in the Japanese psyche. The drivers even wear white gloves. There is probably not a dirty taxicab in Japan.[8]

CLAIM AND WARRANT

This pattern works well when you are setting up an argument and want your readers to know immediately that you are going to give evidence for it. For example:

> You can tell a great deal about a country by observing its waiters. There is the obsequiousness of the London waiter, who thanks you every time he performs a service; there is the professionalism, and sometimes arrogance, of the Paris waiter, for whom the job is often a lifelong metier; and there is the hysterical bustling of a waiter in the Plaka district of Athens, a city perched between the First and the Third Worlds. Finally, there is the take-it-or-leave-it independence of the American waiter, who announces in his every gesture that he is as good as his customer. America is, among other things, a way of carrying a tray of food.[9]

8. Lance Morrow, "All the Hazards and Threats of Success," *Time,* 1 August 1983, 20.
9. Michael Harrington, "Does America Still Exist?" *Harper's,* March 1984, 48.

Definition

This is a useful pattern when you want to explain a term or a concept that is important to your thesis. For instance:

> Poliomyelitis is a disease caused by a viral agent that invades the body by way of the gastrointestinal tract, where it multiplies and, on rare occasions, travels via blood and/or nervous pathways to the central nervous system, where it attacks the motor neurons of the spinal cord and part of the brain. Motor neurons are destroyed. Muscle groups are weakened or destroyed. A healthy fifteen-year-old boy of 160 pounds might lose seventy or eighty pounds in a week.[10]

Cause and Effect

This is another pattern that is useful when you are presenting an argument and need to show how you have arrived at your conclusions. For example:

> The influx of backlanders into Fortaleza [Brazil], equivalent to the sudden arrival of more than two million refugees in New York City, has resulted in chaos. The area around the train station, the João Tomé bus station, and the cathedral is overrun with beggars, cripples, and families that huddle at night on dirty sidewalks. Slums have sprung up on the fringes of the city, barely pubescent girls have turned to prostitution, and crime—particularly the theft of anything that can be sold or bartered for food—has increased.[11]

Comparison

This pattern works well when you want to develop a point by showing likenesses or differences. For instance:

> The "two cultures" controversy of several decades back has quieted down some, but it is still with us, still unsettled because of the polarized views set out by C. P. Snow at one extreme and by F. R. Leavis at the other; these remain as the two sides of the argument. At one edge, the humanists are set up as knowing, and wanting to know, very little about science and even less about the human meaning of contemporary science; they are, so it goes, antiscientific in their prejudice. On the other side, the scientists are served up as a bright but illiterate lot, well-read in

---

10. Charles L. Mee, Jr., "The Summer Before Salk," *Esquire*, December 1983, 40.
11. Edwin McDowell, "Famine in the Backlands," *Atlantic*, March 1984, 22.

nothing except science, even, as Leavis said of Snow, incapable of writing good novels. The humanities are presented in the dispute as though made up of imagined unverifiable notions about human behavior, unsubstantiated stories cooked up by poets and novelists, while the sciences deal parsimoniously with lean facts, hard data, incontrovertible theories, truths established beyond doubt, the unambiguous facts of life.[12]

In developing an idea by comparison and contrast, it also works well to compare by alternating paragraphs. For instance:

> Ross [Lockridge] was an oak of prudence and industry. He rarely drank and he never smoked. He excelled at everything he did. He had married his hometown sweetheart, was proudly faithful to her and produced four fine children. After a sampling of success on both coasts, he had gone home to the Indiana of his parents and childhood friends.
>
> Tom Heggen had a taste for the low life. He had been divorced, had no children and shared bachelor quarters in New York with an ex-actor and screenwriter, Dorothy Parker's estranged husband, Alan Campbell. Tom was a drinker and a pill addict. He turned up regularly at the fashionable restaurant "21," usually bringing along a new girl, a dancer or an actress.[13]

NARRATION

A miniature story is frequently a good way to illustrate a point that you have already made or one that you want to make. It also has the virtue of adding a visual element or a personal element to your writing. For instance:

> The legend, at least, is clear: Once upon a time, a few Celtic warlords were roving over the wide Atlantic, extending themselves and their boats northward from Europe. When they spied a green headland, it occurred to them to race for the beach—the first one to touch land, it was understood, would acquire the whole place for himself and his descendents. But as one slower boat slipped slightly but inexorably behind in the churning surf, its captain, the brave O'Neill, decided on a rash act. Deliberately wielding his battleax, he chopped off his own left hand and hurled it ashore, thus claiming the territory forever.[14]

12. Lewis Thomas, "On Matters of Doubt," in *Late Night Thoughts on Listening to Mahler's Ninth Symphony* (New York: Viking, 1983), 156.
13. John Leggett, *Ross and Tom* (New York: Simon and Schuster, 1974).
14. Michael Olmert, "Hail to Heraldry, A Most Intricate and Revealing Art," *Smithsonian*, May 1984, 86.

PROCESS

This kind of paragraph is particularly useful when you have been generalizing about a theory and need to explain specifically how it works. For instance:

> When I write, I like to have an interval before me when I am not likely to be interrupted. For me, this means usually the early morning, before others are awake. I get pen and paper, take a glance out the window (often it is dark out there), and wait. It is like fishing. But I do not wait very long, for there is always a nibble—and this is where receptivity comes in. To get started I will accept anything that occurs to me. Something always occurs, of course, to any of us. We can't keep from thinking. Maybe I have to settle for an immediate impression: it's cold, or hot, or dark, or bright, or in between! Or—well, the possibilities are endless. If I put something down, that thing will help the next thing come, and I'm off. If I let the process go on, things will occur to me that were not at all in my mind when I started. These things, odd or trivial as they may be, are somehow connected. And if I let them string out, surprising things will happen.[15]

THE DILEMMA OF THE CLOSING PARAGRAPH

No matter what kind of paper or article you are writing, conclusions are hard. Any writer will tell you that. The primary purpose of the last paragraph in any piece of writing is to give the reader a *sense of closure*, a feeling that the questions that have been raised have been answered and the issues that have been introduced have been resolved—or at least fully discussed. As a writer, you want to finish what you started in the opening paragraph and leave your readers satisfied.

Unfortunately, after studying scores of concluding paragraphs in all kinds of expository writing, I have found few patterns that one can follow for writing closing paragraphs that will accomplish all those purposes. For technical and business reports, case studies, or proposals, there are traditional forms; the author summarizes findings and, if expected to do so, makes recommendations. Such endings are clearcut and predictable, not difficult to master. In other kinds of writing, such as persuasion or an expository academic paper, the writer often needs to restate main ideas or arguments at the end of the paper, particularly when that paper runs to fifteen or twenty pages, and the reader may need to be reminded of state-

15. William Stafford, "A Way of Writing," *Field,* Spring 1970.

ments made earlier. In such cases, it is a good idea to indicate to the reader that you are drawing together the threads of the argument or restating your conclusions. You can give such reminders with words or phrases such as *finally, in conclusion, in the end, then,* or *in the final analysis.* The structure for this kind of presentation is comparable to that which a trial lawyer uses to persuade a jury: make the claim, give the evidence, sum up the findings.

For other kinds of writing—book or movie reviews, biographical essays, promotion brochures, to name just a few—writers often struggle with composing a good ending. Giving the reader a sense of closure, of completion, is important, yet often there is no point in a recapitulation or a summary that would just bore the reader. The best advice I can give is to put in some signal terms and don't belabor points that have already been made. If you have led your reader to the conclusion of your ideas, it is probably best just to stop. The best conclusions, like the best transitions, grow out of the structure of your writing. They are not something you tack on at the end to achieve an effect.

EXERCISES

1. Read over these two paragraphs to see where you think you could break them without seriously interrupting the train of thought.

   A. Bradley is one of the few basketball players who have ever been appreciatively cheered by a disinterested away-from-home crowd while warming up. This curious event occurred last March, just before Princeton eliminated the Virginia Military Institute, the year's Southern Conference champion, from the NCAA championships. The game was played in Philadelphia and was the last of a tripleheader. The people there were worn out because most of them were emotionally committed to either Villanova or Temple—two local teams that had just been involved in enervating battles with Providence and Connecticut, respectively, scrambling for a chance at the rest of the country. A group of Princeton boys shooting basketballs miscellaneously in preparation for still another game hardly promised to be a high point of the evening, but Bradley, whose routine in the warmup time is a gradual crescendo of activity, is more interesting to watch before a game than most players are in play. In Philadelphia that night, what he did was, for him, anything but unusual. As he does before all games he began by shooting set shots close to the basket, gradually moving back until he was shooting long sets from twenty feet out, and nearly all of them dropped into the net with an almost mechanical rhythm of accuracy. Then he began a series of expandingly difficult jump shots, and one jumper after another went cleanly through the basket with so few exceptions that the crowd began to murmur. Then he started to perform whirling reverse moves before another cadence of almost steadily accurate jump shots, and the murmur increased. Then he began to sweep hook shots into the air. He moved in a semicircle around the court. First with his right hand, then with his left, he tried seven of these long, graceful shots the most difficult ones in the orthodoxy of basketball—and ambidextrously made them all. The game had not even begun, but the presumably unimpressible Philadelphians were applauding like an audience at an opera.[16]

B.   In outline it was a good plan, but it quite failed to take into account the mentality of buzzards. As soon as they were wired to the tree they all began to try and fly away. The wires prevented that, of course, but did not prevent them from falling off the limbs, where they dangled upside down, wings flopping, nether parts exposed. It is hard to imagine anything less likely to beguile a moviegoing audience than a tree full of dangling buzzards. Everyone agreed it was unaesthetic. The buzzards were righted, but they tried again, and with each try their humiliation deepened. Finally they abandoned their efforts to fly away and resigned themselves to life on their tree. Their resignation was so complete that when the scene was readied and the time came for them to fly, they refused. They had had enough of ignominy; better to remain on the limb indefinitely. Buzzards are not without patience. Profanity, firecrackers, and even a shotgun full of rock salt failed to move them. I'm told that, in desperation, a bird man was flown in from L.A. to teach the sulky bastards how to fly. The whole experience left everyone touchy. A day or so later, looking at the pictures again, I noticed a further provocative detail. The dead heifer that figured so prominently in the scene was quite clearly a steer. When I pointed this out to the still photographers they just shrugged. A steer was close enough; after all they were both essentially cows. "In essence, it's a cow," one said moodily. No one wanted those buzzards back again.[17]

2. From the following opening sentences, develop paragraphs of the indicated pattern:

The student who enrolls in a pre-medical program can look forward to a grueling four years. [claim and warrant]

16. John McPhee, "A Sense of Where You Are," in *The John McPhee Reader*, ed. William Howarth, 2d ed. (New York: Vintage Books, 1978), 2–3.
17. Larry McMurtry, "Here's HUD in Your Eye," in *In a Narrow Grave* (New York: Simon and Schuster, 1968), 10–11.

After the baby boom of the sixties, the birth rate in the United States began to fall steadily. [cause and effect]

When the rock star stepped on stage, he flashed a sexy smile at all the girls in the front row. [narrative]

In Israel the cost of gasoline has gone to more than $3.00 a liter. [inductive]

3. What commitment has the writer made to the reader in these opening sentences from the paragraphs of professional writers?

"Some of us who live in arid parts of the world think about water with a reverence others might find excessive."
Joan Didion

"The weeks after graduation were filled with heady activities."
Maya Angelou

"There are, it seems, three principal states of mind in human beings: waking, sleeping, and dreaming."
Carl Sagan

4. How well does the student writer meet the opening commitment in each of these paragraphs?

Utilitarians argue that punishment is justified because it promotes utility, or the best ends for society. Punishment, they say, deters crime, incapacitates the criminal, and reforms him. It should be severe enough to provide the greatest benefit to society. If Jones is caught shoplifting, for example, he should be punished *just enough* to deter further shoplifting and to reform him. This might mean five days in jail, but certainly nothing too severe (like capital punishment) because that hurts society more than it helps.

Much of the economic strength of this country is based on mobility, and I rely on mobility through my car to make my living. The lowered speed limit has tended to endanger this economic strength, while failing to achieve the goals which it was meant to. The National Drivers Association report of Fall, 1977, stated that 14 percent of all fuel is consumed by motor vehicles, and the General Accounting Office of the United States has reported that the 55-mile-per-hour speed limit has lowered consumption by 1.8 percent, which translates to a total fuel saving of only two-tenths of one percent. The National Science Foundation and the Illinois Department of Transportation have reported that only five percent of the reduction in highway deaths are attributable to lower speeds.

5. Write a paragraph starting with one of these opening sentences and down-shifting two or three levels:

The average county jail houses an astonishing variety of lawbreakers.

Divorced fathers are getting increasingly aggressive in demanding custody of their children.

A casual observer at a California beach soon realizes most people are not there to swim.

SUGGESTED WRITING ASSIGNMENTS

As a part of each writing assignment write a detailed analysis of your audience and specify the characteristics they would have that you need to keep in mind as you write, the problems that such an audience might present, and what the audience would expect to get from reading your paper. Also analyze your purpose in writing, specifying what you hope to accomplish in the paper. If appropriate, include an accurate and descriptive title for your paper.

TOPIC 1: An organization to which you belong is going to have its annual convention in your city, and you have been asked to serve as local arrangements chairman. Among other things, that means that you must write a letter of invitation to the convention that will go out with announcements of the convention. In that letter you want to convince people that they would enjoy visiting your city and to give them information that would help them to make up their minds about coming to the convention. You do not need to mention hotel rates since that information would be in the announcement. You would want to point out what special events might be going on in the city at convention time, major points of interest such as art museums or zoos, shopping areas close to the hotel, well-known restaurants, and so on. If you want to keep your letter to one page, you could add a separate sheet with specific information. Probably your letter should not run to more than 350 or 400 words. Remember that the opening paragraph is particularly important.

TOPIC 2: You are a married person with a young child and you and your spouse want to move into an apartment nearer your job. In looking for apartments, however, you have discovered that landlords in the neighborhood you want to live in do not allow children. Write a letter to the city council pointing out that such exclusion by landlords is grossly discriminatory and may be unconstitutional. Ask for an interpretation of current city law and suggest that an ordinance against such discrimination needs to be passed if it does not already exist.

TOPIC 3: As part of your duties at the county social services bureau you have the assignment of writing informative pamphlets that will be available to any clients who come into the office. Your supervisor is particularly eager to have a pamphlet that outlines the options open to young unmarried women who have problem pregnancies, because women who would not want to ask for such a pamphlet would probably pick one up if it were displayed. She asks you to write the pamphlet, specifying that it must use direct but neutral language and be simple enough for young people to understand. The brochure should not be more than 600 words.

9 ◇ Revising

Experienced writers who care about doing good work plan on revising almost everything they write. Except under unusual circumstances, they don't expect to turn out a piece of writing that they are satisfied with in one draft; rather they see revision as an essential part of any writing task that is not strictly routine. Frequently they even expect to develop a piece of writing through the process of revision; especially when they are working on a complex and important project they depend on the revising process to help them consolidate their ideas and focus their writing.

If you learn to look at revising in this way—more as a process by which you *develop* writing than one by which you *correct* it—you may find you can relax about your writing and gain new confidence. You may feel better knowing that you don't have to turn out first-rate work right from the beginning because you can count on improving your writing through revision. And it can also help to know that people who write regularly have some reliable and systematic strategies for revising, and that those strategies can be learned.

THE REVISION PROCESS

DIFFERENT KINDS OF REVISING

Before going on to discuss specific strategies for revising, it may be useful to introduce some special terms to distinguish among the different kinds of changes that writers make as they revise a piece of writing.

One kind of change can be called *local,* that is, small-scale, limited, or surface changes: deleting words and phrases and perhaps substituting others, rearranging or combining sentences, pruning wordiness or repetition, changing verb forms, adding examples, and so on. Although such changes are not unimportant—they can make a major difference in the impression the final document makes—they are essentially *stylistic* and do not alter the substance of the paper. Another way to look at this kind of revision is to call it "tinkering." Some editors call it "fine tuning."

Significantly different are what we call *global* changes, that is, broad-scale changes in purpose, content, organization, or focus. You can make global changes by narrowing your topic or by deciding to write on a different aspect of the topic; you also make global changes when you revise your writing to adjust to a different audience, shift the emphasis of your paper, or eliminate parts of the paper you decide are irrelevant. Any major change that affects the paper as a whole is a global change; it is *substantive*, not stylistic.

It is also useful to distinguish between on-the-spot, *immediate* revising that you do as you are writing and more considered, *delayed* revising that you do after stopping to reread and reflect on what you have written. Often you do on-the-spot, immediate revising before you even finish a sentence, crossing out a word and substituting another. Or you may write sentences and then delete them almost immediately. But you also employ delayed revising, postponing changes until you have written several paragraphs or pages or even a complete draft and can go back to reread it and consider what you want to change.

Probably every writer uses all of these different revision methods at one time or another and usually doesn't stop to analyze too closely what he or she is doing. I think, however, that all writers can benefit from becoming more aware of their revising methods, and in the sections to come, I am going to suggest that some revision strategies work better than others at certain stages in writing. By paying attention to what we are doing, I think most of us can become more efficient revisers.

A PLAN FOR REVISING IN STAGES

The first time you read your draft through, try to read mainly for content, organization, and focus, for the moment ignoring sentences or words you don't like and trying not to worry about usage or spelling. If you have problems in those areas, they'll have to be fixed but not yet. Right now other concerns are more important.

The second time through you can begin to look for ways to strengthen your writing and make it more readable and coherent. This is the time to add examples, cut out repetition, and think about ways to make your writing look more appealing to your readers. You may also need to do some sentence rearranging at this stage. If you suspect you are not going to have time for a third revision, you may want to make some on-the-spot, local changes in words and phrases at this stage.

In the third draft you can begin to focus primarily on local changes, particularly sentence structure and word choice. This is the time to fix sentences that are overloaded with abstractions and nominalizations and to try to make your verbs and adjectives more active and precise. During or after this last revision, you will want to edit for misspellings or faulty usage and do a clean-up proofreading.

Although this sketchy outline obviously oversimplifies the revising process and makes it sound neater and easier than it really is—I know *my* revising is much messier and more complicated than I have indicated here—using this approach can help you revise more efficiently and keep you from getting mired down in minute details. A set of questions and suggestions to help you through each stage follows, as well as a sample student paper that illustrates how one writer revised his paper through three drafts.

DEVELOPING YOUR OWN REVISING STRATEGIES

No one else can really tell you how to revise your writing—not your fellow students nor even your professor. They can point out places in your writing that seem to be causing problems and they can suggest changes; if you take such criticism thoughtfully and use it well, you can benefit greatly from others' comments. Ultimately, however, you have to make the important decisions about revising your paper because no one else really knows what you want to say. And finally only you can decide *how* to revise your writing—writers have different ways of approaching and solving their problems and someone else's system or strategies may not work for you at all.

Nevertheless, I believe there are some general strategies for revision that work well for most writers, strategies that help them revise efficiently and get maximum results for the amount of time they invest. But before I elaborate on those, here are some preliminary concerns that writers need to think about:

- Assess the level at which you are writing, decide how much revision effort it warrants, and plan accordingly. A routine memo doesn't warrant an hour of tinkering and polishing, but a paper for an English professor who is fussy about supporting evidence and smooth transitions might warrant several hours. If you have to write an original and thoughtful paper that is important to you, allow yourself time to write several drafts and plan to make global revisions on them.
- Make as few local, on-the-spot changes as you can when you are writing your first draft. They can consume a great deal of time, and if you get to tinkering too soon, you may get distracted from your main purpose. Furthermore, you may discard large sections of your paper later so it's a

waste of time to polish too early. If you are writing with a word processor, it's especially easy to fall into the trap of tinkering with premature local revisions because they are so easy to do.

◦ When you start to revise any first draft, do the big stuff first. Too often you will have neither the time nor the energy to spend as much time as you should on your paper, so you need to set priorities and concentrate on making the most important changes first.

A SAMPLE FIRST DRAFT

Exploring the Economist

AUDIENCE ANALYSIS: The audience is composed of ten- to fourteen-year old students. They are inquisitive and seeking knowledge about the world in which they live. They are questioning themselves about their future roles in society. They are looking for clarification of the profession choices that face them.

PAPER'S PURPOSE: The purpose of the paper is to inform the audience about the profession of economics. It takes one through the process of becoming an economist. It compares schooling with other professions. It states the different branches of the discipline.

On any given broadcast of the national evening news, one can usually see an economist commenting on some financial topic or current event. However, aside from those daily thirty-second exposures, the average student is not confronted with the work of economists. What do economists do? How do they come to be economists? Why do the opinions of some economists differ from those of others?

In order to understand what economists do, it is important to know what the discipline (science) of economics is. Economics is a mixture of business, mathematics, and social studies. It tries to explain the relationships of our economy: supply and demand, cost and benefit, gain and loss. Economists usually specialize in one sub-area, labor, for example, and are generally considered scholars, or even experts, in that field. This is why economists are often quoted or interviewed on the national evening news. If a network wants to do a story on, say, labor unions and their impact on the auto industry, they will usually try to find an economist who specializes in the area and get his or her opinion.

It is because of the economist's extensive training that his or her opinion is often respected and sought after. An economist usually has had eight years of education beyond the high school level: four years of college and four years at graduate school.

During the four years at the university level, the would-be economist is exposed to the branches of economics. Some of these are macroeconomics (the study of the entire economy as a unit), microeconomics (the study of the individual firm), labor economics, developmental economics, international economics and resource economics, to name a few. The would-be economist will select one of these to be an area of focus for his or her four years of graduate school.

Graduate school in economics is similar to law school or any other post-college work. It is four years of grueling study. The student spends the first two years of graduate school taking courses in the focus area. After these two years, the student must pass preliminary exams, and then goes on to write a long, detailed work on his or her focal area: the dissertation. The successful dissertation marks the economist's entry into the professional world.

The economist's place in the real world depends on the specialty area which he or she has chosen. A financial economist might work as an analyst on Wall Street, and thus be occasionally interviewed on financial news segments. A labor economist might work for a labor union; or a developmental economist might work for the World Bank, which gives loans to developing countries. Since economics is a scholarly profession, the majority of economists spend at least part of their time teaching at universities.

Economics is not an exact science, like mathematics. The current events in the economy are open to different interpretations. Some economists are traditional, free-market economists. Others believe that economics becomes more complex as our society becomes more complex. At the present time, the traditional economists are making a comeback. The point to be made is that individuality is part of economics.

For the student who likes mathematics and social studies, economics is something worth considering. It offers a wide range of choices to fit different tastes, and encourages the individual to form his or her own ideas. Seeing one's ideas influence important decisions is what makes economics a rewarding profession.

FIRST REVISION

On the first revision, concentrate primarily on making global changes that will affect the *content* and *organization* of the paper. Ask yourself these questions:

◇ Have I tried to include more in the paper than I can adequately develop?

Should I pick some part of the topic to focus on in more detail?

◦ What is my purpose in the paper? Am I clear about what I intended to do, and have I done it?

◦ Have I made a clear commitment early in the paper (see p. 89)? Is the reader going to be able to tell what it is? Do I follow through and meet that commitment?

◦ Have I thought about my audience and asked myself what specific questions they expect me to answer in the paper? Have I answered those questions?

◦ Does my writing have a pattern that the reader can follow easily?

◦ Are the proportions of the paper okay? Have I spent too much time on some parts and not enough on others?

These are the tough questions you need to ask early on about your writing, the questions that should reveal major substantive problems that can't be fixed by tinkering or local changes. Often after you have answered them and have also gotten answers from other people, you will want to make major changes in your second draft. That's why you shouldn't stop to tinker too much with local changes too early.

REVISING FOR FOCUS

Sometimes writers get carried away when they are writing a first draft and take on too much. As they write, one idea reminds them of another, and they give in to that urge that most of us have to tell everything we know. They skim over a lot of material instead of covering one part of it well. Notice that in the first draft of the sample student paper, this is exactly what has happened. In his purpose statement, the student says that he wants "to inform the audience [ten- to fourteen-year olds] about the profession of economics . . . [and the] process of becoming an economist." The topic is much too broad for a short paper, and the writer gets in trouble, first, by trying to define economics and its subspecialties in a few paragraphs. He quickly gets in over his head and bogs down in abstract explanations that are going to bore his readers. Then when he tries to explain what economists do and the differences among them, he again has more material than he can possibly explain. He doesn't have enough space to give specific examples or show his readers what economists do. Notice that an astute reader might anticipate from the writer's title that he has taken on more than he can handle; "Exploring the Economist" isn't a realistic goal for a short paper. In the second draft of the paper, the writer narrows his focus to talking only about developmental economists, a more manageable topic.

REVISING FOR PURPOSE

As you read over your first draft, ask yourself, "Exactly what am I trying to accomplish in this paper?" If you are writing in response to a specific class assignment, it is a good idea to go back and reread that assignment, and if necessary break it down into its component parts. Then read what you have written, asking yourself, "Did I do this? and this? When I get to the end, have I actually done what I started out to do?" For example, if an assignment in an archeoastronomy course asks you to identify, describe, and explain the astronomical function of two archeological structures in the ancient world, say Stonehenge and the Great Temple at Karnak in Egypt, you need to verify that you have covered all three points for each structure. That may seem like obvious advice, but any editor could tell you that it is surprising how often writers forget such basic things.

In the first draft of the student's paper on economists, one of the major problems is that the writer's purpose is vague and too broad. He says he wants "to inform the audience about the profession of economics," but when you check his audience analysis, his real purpose is to explain to youngsters what it would be like to be an economist. That's much more specific, and when he narrows his purpose in the second draft (see his sample analysis of purpose), the paper improves greatly.

REVISING FOR COMMITMENT

Review the title of your draft and read carefully the first few paragraphs. Have you made a commitment (see p. 89) and have you given your readers a clear signal about what it is? Do your readers know what to expect from your writing? When you identify your commitment, keep it in mind as you read your draft and check to see that you're meeting it. If you think you haven't met all the expectations you raised, review your commitment. It may be too broad, and you should narrow it, or you may have to add a section to the paper to follow through on what you have promised to do.

In the first draft of the sample paper on economists, the writer has committed himself to explain what economists do, how they came to be economists, and why the opinions of some economists differ from those of others. When he reviewed the draft and checked what he did do against what he had promised to do, he realized that he had only begun to meet the first commitment he made and hadn't really addressed the second two at all. In the second draft he narrows his commitment to explaining what a developmental economist is.

REVISING FOR AUDIENCE

Even when inexperienced writers work at identifying and analyzing their audiences before they start to write, often they tend to forget about them when they actually begin to write the paper. That's natural, and in fact often desirable, because sometimes when you are writing a first draft, particularly for Class 3 writing, it is mostly a discovery or exploratory draft. You are composing *writer-based prose*. But when you start revising, you need to think how you're going to make your writing *reader-based*. Now you need to keep asking yourself, "Am I keeping in mind what my readers want to know about this topic and what questions they are going to have? Am I telling them stuff that is going to be interesting to them?"

The first draft of the sample paper seems to be strongly writer-based. You can tell from the audience analysis that the writer hasn't thought specifically about his readers' needs or expectations, and in the draft he seems to be exploring the general topic of economists to find out what he wants to say about them. In the second draft, however, when he has found his topic, he has also started thinking about how he can explain that topic to his audience, and his preliminary audience analysis reflects that concern by listing specific questions his readers would have (see Chapter 4). And now in the second draft he includes concrete details and examples that will show his readers what a developmental economist does.

REVISING FOR ORGANIZATION

As you read over your draft, ask yourself what the pattern of your writing is. Does the topic seem to lend itself to a certain kind of organizational pattern, say definition, cause and effect, comparison, or process? Are there certain organizational strategies that will work well—for example, anecdote and explanation, question and answer, or assertion and support? Have you used one of those strategies, and will the reader quickly be able to discern the pattern and follow it?

The topic for the sample paper immediately suggests two organizational patterns: definition (who are economists?) and process (what do they do?). In the first draft, the writer begins by trying to define economics but immediately runs into problems because the topic is so complex and broad it defies simple definitions, and he doesn't have enough space to downshift into examples. Then he moves to a process pattern to show how economists are educated and what they do but doesn't have space to develop that either. By this time, the reader is lost. In the second draft, however, a clear pattern emerges. First he describes a developmental economist, and then he defines one by function, by qualifications, by life-style, by accomplishments, and by rewards. The reader senses an overall plan and can follow it without trouble.

REVISING FOR PROPORTION

Check to see if you have given too much space to some parts of the paper and neglected others. Writers often tend to elaborate on the early points in a paper—sometimes more than they need to—and then, because they run out of space or energy, skimp on the last sections even though those sections are just as important. Writers who can't keep themselves from making a lot of on-the-spot local revisions as they work are especially likely to have this problem. They tinker and tinker with early paragraphs to get them exactly right, then run out of time and end up with a lopsided paper. So you particularly need to review the conclusion of your first draft to see if you need to develop it or make it more specific.

A SAMPLE REVISED DRAFT

THE DEVELOPMENTAL ECONOMIST: A DIFFERENT BREED

AUDIENCE ANALYSIS: The audience, composed of students entering high school, is likely to ask the following questions:

- How is a developmental economist different?
- What do developmental economists do?
- Who employs them?
- How much money do they make?
- Where do they work? Universities? Abroad?
- What type of students would be likely to choose this as a profession?
- What type of person is the developmental economist?

PAPER'S PURPOSE: The paper sets the developmental economist apart from the conventional economist by explaining his or her motivation, environment and goals, viz., development concerns people whereas conventional economists are concerned with theories.

When we think of an economist, we usually think of an older gentleman with tousled hair, an old suit and thick glasses. In short, the typical college professor. You may have seen him on a talk show or news interview. He's usually talking about hard-to-grasp topics like inflation or interest rates. Overall, economists don't seem like very interesting people. They seem removed from the real world. However, one type of economist does not fit this mold. This is the developmental economist.

Developmental economists do not spend a lot of time lecturing in the old lecture halls. They don't come up with complicated formulas explaining, or trying to explain, why certain things happen the way they do. The developmental economist is interested in people: not just Americans, but people in the developing countries. For example, a developmental economist in Latin America is a person who has studied the Spanish language, culture and history. He or she might spend their time helping farm communities in Peru get agricultural loans, maybe studying the possibility of setting up a factory in Venezuela and obtaining the funds to start it up. They usually don't appear on talk shows or newscasts. They're out in the field working with people who are not as fortunate as ourselves to be born into a rich society with plenty of jobs and a high standard of living.

Many developmental economists work for international development organizations like the World Bank or the International Development Bank. These organizations specialize in giving out loans for development to the less privileged countries. The loans go for dams, roads, electric power plants, schools, hospitals and farm equipment. Loans of this type have played an important part in the recent growth of countries like South Korea, Mexico and Argentina.

Developmental economists, like their teaching counterparts, are professionals. They are college educated and well paid. Salaries for economists fresh out of graduate school range from $25,000 to $30,000. As good as the pay is, it is not a job for everyone.

Developmental economists spend a lot of time away from their home countries. It's their job to get a feel for their specialty country or region. In a sense, they adopt a new country. They often have an apartment or home in the developing country, or may even board with some locals. They spend their days talking to labor officials, government workers, farmers and economists from their adopted country. They have to become a native to do their job well, to know what the people want and need. At first, local officials and citizens may not receive outsiders well. The job can be lonely or frustrating in times like these. Quickly, though, the locals warm up to the visitor and many friendships can be made. Once the locals understand that the economist is one of them, sharing their aspirations, he or she has earned their trust.

Like any job which helps people, developmental economics is a rewarding profession. It goes beyond the money. The poor and suffering we see on our television sets here in America are human beings just like ourselves. Developmental economists want to help. They don't sit in an office or preach to students in lecture halls. They go out and do something about the problem.

SECOND REVISION

In the second revision, ask these questions that focus on *economy* and *readability*:

- Can I cut out words and make my writing more concise?
- Do I need to improve readability by
  using more specific and concrete language?
  rearranging some of the sentences?
  adding examples?
- Can I help my reader by making my writing more visually attractive?

CUTTING YOUR WRITING

Most of us use too many words in our first drafts. We ramble, repeat ourselves, overexplain, and search for a third item to complete a series when we need only two. But overwriting in the first draft isn't necessarily bad if you're going to have time to rewrite it. It's better to explore your topic fully and worry about economy later. However, if you're wordy at first, be prepared for ruthless pruning later. Here are some ways you can go about that pruning.

CONDENSE LONG PHRASES

Look for places where you can substitute one or two words for long phrases. For example:

The reason the forefathers understood one-man rule to be so undesirable was that it allowed that man to make the norms for society all by himself.

could be revised to:

The forefathers rejected one-man rule because it allowed that man to set social norms single-handedly.

One vigorous verb, *rejected,* does the work of seven words strung together in a flat phrase, and substituting *because* for *the reason for* emphasizes the cause-and-effect structure of the sentence.

Here is another example:

I will attempt to present a tone that will reveal that I know what I am talking about, but assume such a manner that the audience will not be offended by my argument.

could be revised to:

I will strive for an authoritative but not offensive tone.

The revision not only substitutes one word, *authoritative,* for fifteen, but it gets rid of the bunched-up, choppy phrases and clauses of the original.

Also check out the suggestions for improving verbs on p. 177.

JOIN OR COMBINE SENTENCES

Make your writing more efficient by joining or combining sentences that have overlapping content. For example, compare these two versions of the opening paragraph of a student's paper entitled "The Portrayal of Women in Advertising":

> In a shoe store window display, a female mannequin bloodied by red tempera paint hangs out of a garbage can. The message on the window says, "We'd kill for these shoes." Whatever the medium, this is advertising, a $40-billion-per-year industry. Advertising presents us with images, values, goals, and concepts which shape our attitudes and influence behavior. Among other areas, advertising has presented the public with a warped concept of women's roles. Unfortunately most consumers are ignorant of the techniques that influence their opinions.

First, notice that we can get rid of two introductory clauses that contribute little to the point of the paragraph. The writer uses "whatever the medium" as an allusion to Marshall McLuhan's statement, "The medium is the message," but the point isn't relevant here and the phrase is just clutter. The second phrase, "among other areas," is also peripheral since the subject of the paper is the portrayal of women in advertising.

We can also eliminate words without sacrificing content by condensing the last four sentences into two. A tighter version would look like this:

> In a shoe store window display, a female mannequin bloodied by red paint hangs out of a garbage can. The message on the window says,

"We'd kill for these shoes." This is advertising, a $40-billion-a-year industry that presents us with images, values, goals, and concepts which shape our attitudes and influence behavior. It gives the public a warped concept of women's roles, but unfortunately most consumers are ignorant of the techniques that influence their opinion.

Get in the habit of rereading your sentences to see if they duplicate content. When they do you can merge or "telescope" them to make fewer but stronger and more concise sentences.

ELIMINATE DOUBLING

The practice of using pairs of words that mean almost the same thing is called *doubling:*

The agency will *control* and *regulate* the dairy industry.

We must find more *efficient* and *effective* ways to meet this need.

Donovan brings remarkable *insight* and *perception* to the task.

You should *check* and *verify* each finding before you act.

In each case a single word would be more effective.

DON'T OVEREXPLAIN

Although you certainly need to illustrate generalizations with specific examples and clarify abstract ideas with concrete illustrations, try to be sure that you aren't overexplaining, telling your readers more than they need to know. If it seems likely that they can get the point quickly without much explanation, be brief.

For example, in revising this section of *Successful Writing,* I decided I had used more examples and more words than I needed in the opening paragraph of the section "Cutting Your Writing" (p. 167). The original version read:

> Most of us use too many words in our first drafts. We pad the beginnings of our sentences with useless phrases like "It is the case that . . ." or "There exists a need for. . . ," and we use long noun and verb phrases instead of plain nouns and verbs. We repeat ourselves, we overexplain, we depend on adjectives instead of a noun to convey our meaning, and we search for a third item to complete a series even if we need only two. But overwriting in the first draft is not necessarily bad. It is probably better to get everything down that comes to mind and not worry too

much about economy at first. You must, however, be ready to start pruning ruthlessly the second and third times around if you want to produce economical prose.

By cutting examples and getting rid of what seemed to be unnecessary comments I cut the paragraph from 135 to 85 words.

As a final check for wordiness, as you read your drafts ask yourself, "If I had to pay fifty cents a word to get this typed, would I still want to keep all these words?" You will probably find that you have many words and phrases that really don't advance your idea. Your reader will appreciate it if you get rid of them.

IMPROVING READABILITY

Shorten Sentences

In recent years many states have passed laws requiring that business and government documents be written in "plain English," that is, in language that the average reader can understand without the help of a specialist. Such requirements, as well as publishers' concerns about the reading level of the material they publish, have caused writing theorists to recommend certain strategies that writers can use to increase the readability of their prose. The first two are:

◦ Try to hold your average sentence length below twenty words.
◦ Use comparatively few words of more than two syllables.

Simplistic? Yes. Anyone who wants to challenge such advice could quickly think of some very short sentences that are not easy to understand. And, as pointed out in Chapter 5, the readability of a sentence often depends less on the number of words than on how they are arranged. Nevertheless, roughly speaking, long sentences are more apt to be difficult to read than short ones. Consequently, when you are reworking your prose, you should take a careful look at sentences that run to more than twenty or twenty-five words. If they are not carefully arranged, they may be difficult to understand, and perhaps you should divide or condense them. For example:

With Einstein dead, is there another figure who has taken his place as a sort of World Conscience, someone who would be willing to listen to the plight of a distressed intellectual patiently and sympathetically, who would hearten him and his family, as Einstein heartened and comforted

William Frauenglass and his family, and who would move into the public arena and put his prestige on the line to uphold principles of dissent?[1]

The sentence is not impenetrable, but a reader could follow it more easily if it were condensed and phrased in three questions instead of one:

> With Einstein dead, is there another figure who has taken his place as a sort of World Conscience? Is there someone who would be willing to listen to the plight of a distressed intellectual patiently and sympathetically and comfort and hearten him as Einstein did for William Frauenglass and his family? Is there someone who would move into the public arena and put his prestige on the line to uphold the principles of dissent?

REARRANGE SENTENCES

Remember that the word order in sentences strongly affects their readability, and that readers will be able to process sentences more quickly if they follow agent/action sentence patterns. So if you want to make your writing easier to read, consider how you have put your sentences together. If you have too many in which the subject is an abstract word or phrase, rewrite them so that the reader can spot the agent and the action immediately. Reviewing the examples on pp. 114–15 should refresh you on that point.

Of course, you don't want to write all or even most of your sentences in agent/action patterns—that would get boring for both you and your readers. Nevertheless, if your chief goal in revising is to make your writing easily accessible to a general audience, using this kind of direct sentence pattern may be the most important rewriting you do. And it's also true that agent/action sentences are likely to be more concise and vigorous than those that have abstract words or nominalizations as the subject.

When you are reviewing your sentence patterns to see if you can improve them, it's also a good idea to check your sentences for *frequent closure* (see p. 98). In some of your sentences you may be asking your readers to hold too many ideas in their heads at one time, and you would do well to rearrange and "chunk" the content so they could process it more easily.

One good way to revise material into more manageable chunks for your reader is to rearrange clusters of phrases into a series of clauses. For example, this sentence from a scientific article requires a reader to hold too much information in mind at one time while processing the main idea:

1. Lawrence Cranberg, "Intellectual Independence," *Austin American-Statesman,* 13 May 1979, C12.

When the secrets of infantile sexuality were apparently being unearthed, Freud and his disciples were still insufficiently aware of the great power of transference on the tendency of patients in the rather authoritarian setting of early analyses to please their analysts by providing them with the kind of material which the latter seemed eager to hear.[2]

Revising it with more clauses helps the reader:

When the secrets of infant sexuality were apparently being unearthed, Freud and his disciples were not sufficiently aware that because of the great power of transference, patients in the rather authoritarian setting of early analyses tended to please their analysts by providing them with the kind of material they were eager to hear.

ADDING EXAMPLES OR ILLUSTRATIONS

On the second round of revision, you should decide if you need additional specific examples to reinforce some of your claims and generalizations. For example, notice that the examples and facts in this student paper make it more readable than it would be if the writer were presenting only her own claims:

A student's score on the Law School Admission Test is only one of several criteria that should be considered in admitting students to law school; it must not be given undue weight simply because it is convenient. The L.S.A.T., taken by 128,000 students each year, is written, scored, and controlled by the Educational Testing Service. Consumer activist Ralph Nader released a scathing study of the E.T.S. last month, calling it a "private regulator of the human mind" that "serves as a formidable barrier to millions of students each year" (*Newsweek,* 18 February 1980, p. 97). He points out that the test in no way measures perseverance, motivation, and sociability. Included in Nader's report is a study on "cram coaching" for the L.S.A.T., a luxury which only more affluent students can afford. About $10 million is spent annually by 50,000 students seeking an advantage over their untutored peers.

MAKING YOUR WRITING MORE VISUALLY ATTRACTIVE

It is difficult to make final decisions about dividing and arranging your writing until you have done most of your substantive revising. But when

2. Paul Chodoff, "Feminine Psychology and Infant Sexuality," in *Psychoanalysis and Women,* ed. Jean Baker Miller (New York: Penguin Books, 1973), 196.

you are reasonably well satisfied with content, you need to think about strategies that will make your writing look attractive in its finished version. The three principal ones are *dividing, highlighting,* and *forecasting.*

DIVIDING

You make your most important decisions about dividing when you paragraph, and when you are working on the second revision, it's time to think about how your paragraphs look and how you can improve them. Look over your printed manuscript to see if it has long unbroken stretches of type running half a page or more. If so, look for places you can break up those stretches. While you don't want to sacrifice the unity of a tightly constructed paragraph just for the sake of appearance, you may be able to detect a natural break that wasn't apparent before. (See p. 142).

You can also break up overstuffed paragraphs by presenting information in list form rather than packed into consecutive sentences. For example, here is an information-packed sentence that looks so overloaded one immediately assumes that it is going to be hard to read:

> The following individuals will be honored at Harvard Commencement this year: J. P. Jones, president of the International Foundation for Human Potential; Mary Hardin Coulthard, winner of the Howson Economics Fellowship; Daniel Moorhead, professor emeritus of biology at Oxford University; and Maxwell Cannon, director of the Harvard Fund for Excellence.

A reader trying to absorb the information in this sentence could do so more easily if it were broken up like this:

> The following individuals will be honored at Harvard Commencement this year:
> J. P. Jones, president of the International Foundation for Human Potential;
> Mary Hardin Coulthard, winner of the Howson Economics Fellowship;
> Daniel Moorhead, professor emeritus of biology at Oxford University;
> Maxwell Cannon, director of the Harvard Fund for Excellence.

HIGHLIGHTING

When you are revising your writing to make it look more attractive, you may decide that you want to draw attention to specific points or set off particular words and phrases so that they will catch the readers' attention. Here are some ways you can emphasize parts of your paper even if your only tools are your typewriter, a pen, and a ruler:

⋄ Indent and use what printers call "bullets" (like the one at the beginning of this sentence). You can make them either with the asterisk sign on the typewriter or by putting in dots with a pen. For example:

Though the demographic forecasts for the traditional cohort of high school graduates is unfavorable, there are other statistics that suggest collegiate opportunities never before possible for millions of Americans. Recent data establish that:

*40 million people regard themselves at any moment in time as undergoing some form of career transition;

*65 million Americans lack basic competency skills;

*15 million American lack college degrees

*12 million professionals require regular in-service education;

*Over $17 billion in educational benefits is available, of which only a tiny fraction is being used;

*New positions are developing for science teachers and pedagogical personnel who are able to educate the handicapped.[3]

You can also add diagrams, simple drawings, or charts that help to give a visual dimension to the information you are presenting. You can set words off with markers at each end like this—<Specifications>; by underlining them—Specifications; or by printing them in boldface—**Specifications**. You can also draw boxes around words or phrases to set them off. (See the charts and diagrams of the writing process in Chapter 2 and notice the boxes around examples illustrating the model topic.)

If you want your writing to look especially attractive, concentrate on centering it carefully and leave wide margins all around. And, of course, be sure to double-space! In general, plan on leaving enough white space on a page so that your writing doesn't look crowded. Hold your finished copy at arm's length. Would you want to read it? If you don't think it looks inviting, try using wider margins and a few highlighting devices to catch the reader's eye.

FORECASTING

You can also make your writing easier to read by continually giving your readers signals that forecast what is going to come, thus focusing their attention and shaping their expectations. Remember that titles are particularly important as forecasters. (See p. 42.)

---

3. Robert Neilsen and Irwin Polishook, "Academic Morbidity," *Chronicle of Higher Education,* 21 April 1980, 9.

Other forecasting signals can take the form of headings or subheadings that mark divisions, or they can be single words or phases. These signals are especially useful when you are writing informative material such as brochures or pamphlets. For that kind of writing, you need to make your writing as visually directive as possible.

For example, a person writing a brochure for college students on how to recognize and cope with stress might use these forecasting signals to mark off divisions and help her readers:

What Causes Stress?

What Are the Effects of Stress?

How Can a Person Manage Stress?

A SAMPLE FINAL DRAFT

THE DEVELOPMENTAL ECONOMIST: A DIFFERENT BREED

Audience analysis: The audience, composed of students entering high school, is likely to ask the following questions:

- How is a developmental economist different?
- What do developmental economists do?
- Who employs them?
- Where do they work? Universities? Abroad?
- What type of students would be likely to choose this as a profession?
- What type of person is the developmental economist?
- What should I study if I want to become a developmental economist?

PAPER'S PURPOSE: The paper sets the developmental economist apart from the conventional economist by explaining his or her motivation, environment and goals, viz., development concerns people whereas conventional economists are concerned with theories.

When we think of an economist, we usually think of an older gentleman with tousled hair, an old suit and thick glasses. In short, the typical college professor. You may have seen him on a talk show or news interview. He's usually talking about hard-to-grasp topics like inflation or interest rates. Overall, economists don't seem like very interesting people. They seem removed from the real world. However, one type of economist does not fit this mold. This is the developmental economist.

Development economists do not spend a lot of time lecturing in the old lecture halls. They don't conjure up long, complicated formulas that try to explain which direction interest rates will go next year. The developmental economist is interested in people: not just Americans, but people in the developing countries. For example, a developmental economist in Latin America is a person who has studied the Spanish language, culture and history. He or she might spend their time helping farming communities in Peru get agricultural loans, or maybe studying the possibility of setting up a factory in Venezuela and obtaining the funds to start it up. They talk with people: the farmers, the factory workers, the bankers. They go to their homes, their factories, and their offices. They don't talk at them through a television set. They're out helping people who are not as fortunate as ourselves to be born into a rich society with plenty of jobs and a high standard of living.

The mission of the developmental economist is to help set up a society where there is opportunity for all. Opportunity for good health, a good education and a good job. As Americans, we take all of these things for granted. For much of the developing world, health, education and steady employment are the things which dreams are made of.

Much of the work of the developmental economist is done through international development organizations like the World Bank or the Inter-American Development Bank. These organizations give out loans for development to the less privileged countries. These loans go for a variety of projects: dams, roads, electric power plants, schools, hospitals, and farm equipment.

Suppose the Peruvian government wants to build a hydroelectric dam outside its capital city, Lima. The development economist acts as a go-between for the government and the World Bank by writing the proposal for the dam and getting the funds to the government. Think of the results! People who didn't have electric power may now experience it for the first time in their lives. Petty merchants and unemployed migrants from the countryside will now have good jobs to support their families. Hundreds of lives will be improved because the government, through one, or a few, concerned economists, has obtained funds previously unavailable to it. Think of the satisfaction felt by the developmental economists seeing people's lives improved and knowing he or she played an important part in it.

As gratifying as this may sound, it's not a job for everyone. Development economists spend a lot of time away from their home countries. In a sense, they adopt a new country. They often have an apartment or home in the developing country. This is important since they must become natives in their new country in order to know what the people want and need. The job cannot be done from a plush office in New York or Washington, D.C.

Like any job which helps people, development economics is a rewarding profession. It goes beyond the money. The poor and suffering we see on our television sets are human beings just like ourselves. Development economists are committed to helping the less fortunate people on our planet. They don't sit in an office or preach to students in lecture halls; they go out in the real world and tackle the problem.

They do not, and cannot, tackle the problem unarmed. The developmental economist must speak the native language. The only people in the developing world who speak English are the wealthy, and they don't need any help. The economist must also have studied the culture, geography, and history of the developing country. Many careers don't use these skills and they may seem useless to younger students, but they are indispensable tools to the developmental economist. The better trained the development economist is, the easier he or she can adopt a new culture, break the culture barrier, and become a servant for the people of the developing world.

THIRD REVISION

On the third revision, ask these questions that focus on *style*:

- Can I make my writing more active and direct by selecting better verbs and strengthening transitions?
- Can I make my style more concrete and less cluttered by cutting out prepositional phrases and reducing the number of nominalizations and abstract words?
- Can I improve the rhythm and flow of my writing by making better word choices, reorganizing clauses and sentences, and changing punctuation?

Most third-revision changes are local changes that may not significantly alter your meaning, but they are important nevertheless because they can make your writing easier and more pleasant to read. If you have the time to spend tinkering with your writing and fine-tuning it, the investment will often pay off both in your own satisfaction and your reader's good will. People like to read graceful, carefully polished prose.

SELECTING BETTER VERBS

REDUCE THE NUMBER OF PASSIVE VERBS

If other readers have pointed out your tendency to overuse passive verbs, go through your draft underlining or bracketing all passive verbs. If you average several to a page, look to see which ones you can change to active verbs. For more help, see p. 119.

Reduce the Number of "Is" Verb Constructions

Check to see whether your writing is overloaded with "is + adjective or noun" patterns. If so, look for one-word verbs to replace them. For example, write "Drinking causes many accidents" rather than "Drinking is the cause of many accidents"; write "The movie reflects a new concern of young women" rather than "The movie is reflective of a new concern of young women."

Watch especially for sentences that begin "There are" or "There is." If you have several of them, consider ways to substitute more concise and effective openings.

Reduce the Number of Verb Phrases

Check for strung-out verb phrases that you could replace with one-word verbs. (See p. 119.) Look for clusters like this:

> We should *give consideration to* those areas of the city that *are in need of* renovation. If we *are not in compliance* with urban renewal laws by June 1, we *will experience the loss* of federal funds. Our failure *to take action on* this matter *will result in a lowering* of standards of health care.

Notice the improvement if we substitute plain verbs for verb phrases:

> We should *consider* those city areas that *need* renovation. If we do not *comply* with urban renewal laws by June 1, we will *lose* federal funds and *lower* standards of health care.

Avoid Buried Verbs

Check long sentences to see that the main verb isn't smothered beneath a stack of qualifiers, abstract words, and prepositional phrases. If your readers miss that verb, they're going to get lost. Here is an example:

> Once politics is defined negatively as an enterprise for drawing a protective circle around the individual's sphere of self-interested action, then public concerns *are* by definition distinct from, and secondary to, private concerns. [Italics added.]

Notice that the twenty-four words that come before "are" make it so inconspicuous that the reader is likely to run right over it and have to go back to reread. (Part of the problem, however, stems from the overly abstract language of the sentence.)

Two remedies for buried verbs are to put the main verb closer to the beginning of the sentence and to use a stronger verb. For instance:

> Public concerns become distinct from and secondary to private concerns when you define politics negatively, as an enterprise for drawing a protective circle around the individual's sphere of self-interested action.

STRENGTHENING TRANSITIONS

When you are doing your third revision, it's time to check your transitions to see if you need to put in hooks and links to close up gaps between sentences or between paragraphs or tighten the structure within paragraphs. Notice, for example, how this paragraph from the third draft of the paper on developmental economists could have been improved by adding transitions.

THIRD DRAFT:

Like any job which helps people, developmental economics is a rewarding profession. It goes beyond money. The poor and suffering we see on our television sets are human beings just like ourselves. Developmental economists are committed to helping the less fortunate people on our planet. They don't sit in an office or preach to students in a lecture hall, they go out in the real world and tackle the problem.

REVISION:

Like any job which helps people, the profession of a developmental economist has rewards that go beyond money. They are committed to helping the less fortunate people on our planet, and they don't sit in an office or preach to students in a lecture hall. Instead they go out in the real world and tackle the problem.

See p. 93 for more suggestions about improving transitions.

CUTTING PREPOSITIONAL PHRASES

Chances are that if you are a wordy writer, you use too many prepositional phrases. Although they are useful, even necessary, writing that is overloaded with them drags for two reasons. First, they slow down a sentence by making it choppy, and second, they often take the place of stronger, more economical modifiers. Look at this student example:

> At *this university* there is a need *for a high-quality day-care center for the children of students and faculty.* The regents should authorize funds *for the establishment of such a facility* even though opponents claim that the university should not be *in the business of providing baby-sitters for anyone.*

Nine prepositional phrases in two sentences. Look how they can be cut:

> University faculty and students need a high-quality day care center *for their children.* The regents should authorize funds to establish such a facility even though opponents say the university should not provide baby sitters *for anyone.*

Shorter, easier to read, and it has only two prepositional phrases. Notice too that prepositional phrases tend to cluster with abstract language and nominalizations. (See next section.)

ADDING PEOPLE

As you looked for ways clear clutter out of your writing and rearranged sentences to make them more readable, you have probably already gotten rid of many nominalizations and much abstract language. They seem to diminish as one improves sentences and gets rid of verb phrases and weak verbs. But on the third revision, you should check once more for typical nominalizations, words that end with *-ity, -ness, -ance, -tion, -ment,* and so on. If you find clusters of them, see if you can prune them out and replace them with phrases or clauses that include people.

CHECKING THE RHYTHM OF YOUR PROSE

You must become sensitive to the cadences and tempo of your writing, and learn how and why certain word choices and patterns affect the rhythm of prose. You must also develop an ear for the way your writing sounds. Is it monotonous, sing-songy, clogged with hard-to-say phrases and sentences that make the reader run out of breath? Or does it flow smoothly and help the reader to move along easily? Probably the best way to develop that ear and smooth out the rhythms of late drafts is to read them aloud to yourself. If they sound plodding or draggy or choppy, review some of these key elements:

SENTENCE LENGTH

A series of long sentences slows down writing and usually forces the reader to read more deliberately in order to process information. This is particularly true of long periodic sentences, the kind that are not intelligible until one reaches the last clause. It is less true of long sentences in which there is frequent closure. An unbroken sequence of several long sentences also creates a monotonous, sing-songy effect. And an unbroken sequence of *short* sentences often creates a choppy effect. To avoid either extreme, you need to vary sentence length, occasionally breaking up a group of long sentences with a short, pithy sentence. If you read passages from the nonfiction of writers like Joan Didion, Thomas Wolfe, and John McPhee, you will notice how skillfully they manipulate sentence length.

WORD LENGTH

Comparatively long words—three syllables or more—also slow down prose rhythm. Of course, you shouldn't choose words primarily because they're either long or short. Choose the one that best conveys your meaning. But if you have a choice between a long word and a short one that means almost the same thing—for example, "difficult" or "hard"—make your choice partly on the basis of the kind of pace you want to set in your writing.

PUNCTUATION

Since a crucial function of punctuation is to divide writing into units and establish a pattern that moves the reader along, it follows that the way in which a writer uses punctuation dramatically affects rhythm. The three most important marks of punctuation—the comma, period, and semicolon—are interrupters. Where you put them and how frequently you use them partially control how quickly your writing moves, and how often your reader pauses. Furthermore, the marks affect rhythm to different degrees; the comma indicates the shortest pause, the period the longest one.

If you write a series of short sentences with few commas and frequent periods, you will create a fast-moving, sometimes staccato rhythm in your prose. If that suits your purposes, fine. If, however, your writing seems uneven, you probably need to rethink your punctuation. You may be able to join some of your sentences with conjunctions or semicolons. As you do, you will reduce the number of periods and probably smooth out your writing.

FINAL CHECK-UP

After you have revised your paper for content, economy, and style, you can put it in final form by following through with two more steps.

First, read your paper through to see that you have corrected what you know are the most common problems in your writing. Most of us know we have certain bad writing habits: for example, I have a tendency to "double," I overuse the semicolon, and I am too fond of the phrases "of course" and "a lot." So I try to watch for these lapses when I do my final corrections.

Second, proofread your paper. Look for typical usage problems such as disagreement between subject and verb, dangling modifiers, or faulty pronoun reference. Now—*before* you invest time and/or money in a clean copy—is the time to correct such lapses. Mark them in the margin with the traditional proofreader's symbols. People who expect to write extensively in their careers need to know these symbols, which you can find them in any standard dictionary.

If you are a poor speller, this final revision stage is probably also the best time for you to go through your paper systematically and flag any words you think you may have misspelled. When you know ahead of time that you will be doing that, you can stop worrying about your spelling as you write and free yourself to choose the best words you can think of, not the ones you think you can spell.

GETTING HELP WITH REVISING

If you can, you should try to get help with your revising, even on an early draft. Students in a class especially benefit from helping each other, particularly if they cooperate to form a "community of writers," that is, a group of people who are all working at their writing and who are genuinely interested in each other's progress. In this situation students can act as friendly readers for each other, offering feedback and constructive advice *while a piece of writing is still in progress.*

But working in groups can be difficult at first because students, feeling awkward about commenting on other students' writing, may go to one of two extremes, either praising every paper and making almost no suggestions for changes, or being excessively critical, picking out every surface error they can find and making their comments almost entirely negative. If the members of a group fall into either of these habits, its members won't be very helpful to each other.

To avoid these extremes, here are some suggestions and guidelines for making group conferences on writing both stimulating and productive.

First, start out by reading the paper for *content,* just as you want others to read your papers first for content. Try to ignore any problems until you have found out what the writer is trying to say.

Second, remember that a draft conference is not the place to argue with a writer about his or her ideas—the important point is to help the writer express those ideas clearly.

Third, when you are commenting on a draft, focus primarily on large issues—scope, organization, adequate development—rather than on highly specific matters such as misspelled words, poor usage, or missing punctuation. The writer is going to revise, and many of the items you comment on may not even appear in the next draft. It could be useful, however, to make a general comment about some problem you foresee as troublesome, such as spelling or sentence fragments.

Fourth, establish the ground rules that no one starts out by apologizing for his or her draft or by making excuses. By definition, drafts are work in progress, something to be improved.

Here are specific questions you should ask about each draft as you read it:

QUESTIONS FOR DRAFT CONFERENCES

- What is the chief strength of the paper? What points should the writer keep and emphasize?
- Who is the audience for this paper? Has the writer clearly established that audience and does he or she keep it in mind while writing?
- Does the author seem to have a clear idea of what he or she is trying to do in the paper? Can the audience tell what that purpose is?
- Is the writer trying to do too much in the paper, given the limitations under which he or she is working? If so, how might he or she narrow the topic to a manageable scope?
- Does the author get your interest early in the paper and hold it? If you lost interest, where did it happen and why do you think it happened?
- Does the writer give you enough information? Or does he or she tell you more than you want to know about some part of the topic?
- Is the paper too general? Where does it need to be more specific?

- Does the writer use enough concrete language and specific examples in the paper? If not, where are they needed?
- What would you pinpoint as the single most important problem in the paper?
- If you were to make one major suggestion for improving the paper, what would it be?

If you are not in a class in which you can get regular feedback from other student writers, you should try to get a friend to read over your work and answer these questions for you. Talking with other people can not only help you get a fresh viewpoint on your writing, but it sometimes will help you to generate the intellectual energy to work out your ideas. Professionals get help when they write—from editors, if no one else—and there is no reason why you shouldn't. Don't make the act of writing any lonelier than it inevitably must be.

FACTORS THAT CONTROL REVISING

Not all writing requires the same amount of revision, and how much time and effort you need to spend on revising varies a great deal according to the writing situation. Probably the most important element is the *class* of writing you are doing. (See Chapter 3.)

When you are doing routine Class 1 or *message* writing, you should not have to revise significantly unless the message is going to someone important and you are concerned about its effect. Then you may want to tinker with word choice and sentence structure. But for most day-to-day message writing you need only to be sure that your writing is clear, accurate, and brief. Most competent writers can manage that without too much trouble.

When you are doing self-contained, Class 2 writing that may be longer and more complex than Class 1, but for which you pretty well know the form and content, you will probably have to invest more time. Usually, however, you can get by with two or at the most three drafts. This kind of revision consists mostly of deleting for brevity, rearranging or joining sentences, and making word changes to improve clarity or tone. In fact, such surface changes may be all you will have time for since many Class 2 writing tasks have to be completed against tight deadlines.

If, however, you are doing more difficult and important Class 3 writing, writing in which you are working to discover and articulate ideas and to express them as clearly as possible, you should plan to spend considerable time revising. For a paper of this kind, whether it is a statement of your goals for a scholarship application, a proposal for a new program, or a major paper in your field of study, you will probably need to do several drafts, rethinking and reorganizing as you go. Major revision becomes an essential part of the process.

Other limitations on revision are how much time you have, how important the writing task is, and how much you care about your audience's reaction. Like everyone else, you have to do the best you can given the limitations under which you work, and sometimes three or four drafts are not possible. You also have to set your priorities, and some writing projects are less important than others. Writing a 500-word autobiography to accompany an application to law school surely justifies more effort than writing a 2,500-word history term paper. The first may warrant five or six drafts, the second may warrant two. The writer who does not make those distinctions is unrealistic.

You also need to be candid with yourself about your attitudes toward writing. How much do you care about doing really first-rate work? Are you willing to put in the extra eight or ten hours that may be necessary to raise the grade on a paper from a B to an A? Are you willing to write and rewrite, get advice, rewrite once more, and perhaps once more again? Is your writing so important to you that you are willing to make it your top priority?

Competent student writers who face these questions are often dismayed when they realize how much time and effort they will have to invest to turn satisfactory writing into good writing, and they settle for doing satisfactory work. Competent writers who make that decision—and sometimes the pressures of school or a job make such a decision necessary—should do so consciously, aware that they could improve their work. Most satisfactory writers *can* become good writers. Whether they have the time, energy, and *will* to do so is another matter. But if they decide they want to be really good, they are going to have to work at revising.

REVISING UNDER PRESSURE

But all of us occasionally—sometimes frequently—find that we must write under pressure, and that we don't have time to write three or four drafts and tinker with our sentence structure and word choice as we would like to. It is impossible to set a draft aside for twenty-four hours when your deadline is tomorrow. What happens to revising under such circumstances? Do you give up and resign yourself to turning in a sloppy piece of writing?

Not necessarily. First, no matter how pressed you are, you should plan on doing two drafts. You can do them separately in quick succession, or you can in effect be writing a second draft even as you compose the first one by stopping to change, delete, and add as you write. Then when you make your clean copy you can make a few more changes as time allows.

Also, before you make the final copy, check for paragraphing and spelling. That task won't take much time, and those are important concerns for the reader.

Second, try to internalize the most important criteria for clear, readable prose so that when you have no time to revise, you won't allow certain constructions to get onto the paper in the first place. Try not to use passive verbs. And when you get ready to start a sentence with an abstract subject, stop and ask yourself whether you could use a personal or concrete one instead. If so, use it. Finally, try to keep your worst writing habit in mind so you can avoid it.

Third, keep your audience in mind constantly. As you go along, ask yourself these questions:

◇ Am I telling my readers what they want to know? More than they want to know?
◇ Do I have a design that will help them follow what I'm writing?
◇ Am I using words they understand?

Fourth, unless you are going to have to turn in your very first draft, don't worry about spelling or punctuation. If you do, you may block your flow of ideas and not get through at all. Also, when you are doing the first draft, don't worry about luxury concerns such as avoiding too many prepositional phrases or derived nouns and varying sentence length. By itself, none of them is a major concern, and you can't afford to stop to think about them when you are pressed. If on the second reading they seem to be a problem, you can change them if you have time.

Finally, read through and see what you can cut. If you are like most writers, that is the revising technique that will do most to improve your writing. And have confidence in your ability to turn out good work under pressure. The more you write, the more your subconscious mind is apt to come to your rescue in an emergency. Many writers do creditable work against tight deadlines, and you can too. And remember too that the more often you do careful revision when you have time, the more skillful you will become at revising under pressure.

WHEN TO STOP REVISING

Writing teachers and writing textbooks stress the conventional wisdom that all good writing is rewriting, and for the most part they are right. Everything we know about the writing process suggests that writing is developmental and evolutionary, and that writers improve and learn to make increasingly good choices among words and patterns by writing several versions of the same passage.

For most writing tasks, however, I think one can reach a point of diminishing returns with revising. For the average writer, that point probably comes at about the fourth or fifth draft. If you have put substantial effort into those drafts, and made significant changes as you worked, I suspect that writing another two or three drafts isn't going to improve your manuscript appreciably, at least not in proportion to the time those drafts would take. Some writers would claim otherwise; Hemingway talked about rewriting one manuscript thirty-eight times, and presumably he thought each version was an improvement. But for the following reasons I would suggest that you think twice before you go on to draft five or six.

First, when you have read and reread a manuscript over a dozen times, you are liable to lose your sense of perspective about it. If there are still flaws in it, you are so familiar with them that you probably can't see them by this time. You can get bogged down in trivia and, like the blocked writer in Camus's novel *The Plague,* you could debate endlessly over whether you should call the horse "brown" or "chestnut." At some point you have to realize that minor changes don't really make a great deal of difference.

Second, you may be blocking your own growth as a writer by investing too much in one piece of writing, worrying too much over the problems that the piece presents. Instead of continuing to wrestle with something that won't come out right, you might learn more by moving on to another kind of writing and another challenge.

Third, you run the danger of becoming a perfectionist who is not willing to turn loose a piece of writing because he or she is still not satisfied with it. This kind of refusal to stop writing can become a form of protection. As long as you don't admit that the piece is finished and ready to be judged, you can shelter yourself from criticism. But finally you have to take your writing out of the drawer and make it public in order to find out if it works. That makes you vulnerable, but you cannot improve your writing until you are willing to expose yourself to criticism.

Finally it comes to this. Writers work at revising in order to make their finished product match, as far as possible, the ideal product they had in mind when they began to write or the ideal that they created as they wrote. They almost never succeed completely because they learn as they rewrite. As George Orwell said, "As soon as we perfect a style, we outgrow it."[4] In some ways, that is a discouraging comment, but in other ways it is optimistic because it suggests how much we can grow as writers.

---

4. George Orwell, "Why I Write," in *The Orwell Reader,* ed. Richard Rovere (New York: Harcourt Brace Jovanovich, 1956), 395.

10 ◇ Writing Research Papers

The task of writing a substantial research paper should hold no particular terror for people who can handle other kinds of writing assignments at school or on the job. The ways in which one chooses topics, gathers material, generates ideas, and works out a plan of organization are much the same for research papers as they are for term papers, grant proposals, or extensive case studies. In fact, all these kinds of working writing mingle and overlap; in important ways they are more alike than they are different.

There is, however, an approach especially suited to research papers, whether they are for a course, a magazine, a company, an agency, or an organization, and this approach includes the following steps:

◇ Topic selection
   formulating a research question
   identifying the audience
   defining the purpose
◇ Research
   setting up search strategies
   reading, collecting data, taking notes
◇ Writing
   organizing your material
   mastering the conventions of format and documentation

TOPIC SELECTION

FORMULATING A RESEARCH QUESTION

On-the-job research projects generally give very specific instructions about deadlines, the type of information needed, and sometimes even the uses to which that information will be put. If you are writing a research paper for a class, on the other hand, you may be assigned a specific topic, a general topic, or a selection of topics to choose from. Or you might be given free rein to decide for yourself what your topic will be. Regardless of the circumstances surrounding your research assignment, your first step must be to formulate a question (or questions) that you hope to be able to answer by consulting outside sources.

You are probably already familiar with this initial step if you have read or conducted empirical research studies in the sciences or social sciences. Such studies begin with a research question formulated as a *hypothesis*—a speculative statement of fact. For example:

⋄ Microwave radiation affects the reproductive behavior of rodents.
⋄ The absence of a father figure in the home adversely affects children's academic performance.
⋄ Radiation from visual display terminals is responsible for some human birth defects.

Although the hypotheses that initiate these types of research studies are phrased as statements of fact, they are actually *questions* in the mind of the researcher. The medical researcher, in other words, is not convinced that microwave radiation affects the reproductive behavior of rodents, but is actually conducting the study in order to answer the question, *Does* microwave radiation affect the reproductive behavior of rodents? Similarly, the psychologist or social studies researcher conducts an investigation to discover the answer to a question—*Does* a father's absence from the home adversely affect children's performance at school?

The research that you do in your college courses or on the job will follow the same principles, although the types of questions you ask and the methods you use to collect the appropriate data to answer them will differ according to the field for which you are writing. Strict scientific method demands that questions for scientific study be the kind with yes-or-no answers, even though the research that follows may reveal that the issues involved are not simply black or white. The answer resulting from research may in fact be a qualified yes or no. For example, "*In certain cases, under certain conditions*, vdt radiation is *probably* a contributing factor in producing human birth defects."

Outside of formal scientific/experimental research, however, you need not limit your questions to the yes-or-no variety. You may, for instance, want to find out the answers to questions such as "Why has the women's movement failed to gain the support of minority members and working class women?" "What means of financial assistance are available to college graduates wishing to continue an education in petroleum engineering?" or "How does the American public remember the Vietnam War twenty years after American troops were pulled out of Vietnam?"

Regardless of the particular discipline for which you are writing, however, you must avoid the temptation to begin your research with questions that are based on unproven assumptions or which lead to obvious or foregone conclusions. The question, "Why is it imperative for the United States to remain involved in the governmental affairs of Latin American countries?" for instance, is *not* an appropriate topic for academic research because it presupposes the validity of an arguable assumption—that it is imperative for the United States to remain involved in Latin American affairs. Similarly, the question, "Why has the women's movement failed to gain the support of minority members and working class women? would be inappropriate if it were not possible to demonstrate beyond a reasonable doubt that women in these two categories do not, in fact, support the women's movement.

Finally, questions with obvious answers do not make suitable research topics because they lead to papers that are uninformative—and therefore uninteresting—to both reader and writer. To a large extent the information- and interest-value of a research topic depends upon the audience for which it is intended. A question such as "How do vaccines work?" would not yield a very interesting paper for a group of immunologists, to whom the information, however complicated and thorough, would be old hat. The very same question, however, might produce a paper that was extremely interesting and worthwhile to a group of parents who wanted to know more about the vaccinations their children were receiving. It is therefore very important that you know who your audience is before you begin focusing your research.

IDENTIFYING THE AUDIENCE

The audience for a research paper that you write in college and the audience for a research paper that you write on the job are different, and you need to keep those differences in mind when you plan your paper. In both cases, however, you need to begin by considering what your readers want to get from the paper.

If you are writing a research report for a business or organization, you will probably have a very specific assignment. Your readers want answers to specific questions, and they assume that you know how to gather the information necessary for finding those answers. Furthermore, they expect you to be able to organize and document that information and present it in a clear, concise, and readable fashion. They are far more interested in what you have been able to find out than in how you went about your research. Nevertheless, they expect thorough documentation because it helps them judge the reliability of your sources and enables them to follow up on your research if they need to. Brevity and conciseness are usually important in research writing done for businesses and organizations. And because research projects of this sort are often expensive, you should not waste your time or your readers' with unnecessary comments or the detailed proofs and background information that you might feel a professor expects in academic research writing.

When you write research papers for your college courses, you are usually writing primarily for the professor who gave you the assignment. While most professors hope to learn something from their students' research papers, the research assignment in college courses usually has several other important purposes as well. In addition to reading for content, professors read in order to evaluate their students' knowledge of their subject matter, their ability to find and synthesize information from various sources and to present it in a clear and organized fashion, and their mastery of the formal conventions of research writing in their field. Often, research assignments in college courses are far less specific than those in businesses and agencies because they are meant to provide an opportunity for you to demonstrate your ability to independently pursue questions stemming from material you've studied in your courses. You must therefore consider yourself as a part of the audience for your research writing, since it must be your curiosity and interest that motivate this type of independent inquiry. Formulating your own research questions based on a combination of your own interests and the important issues introduced in class becomes a matter of finding your position within the readership of your discipline.

DEFINING THE PURPOSE

Research writing is by nature data-based; it presents answers to previously unanswered questions, and its overriding purpose is therefore informative. Because questions that motivate your research are ones to which you do not have answers at the outset of your investigation, the activity of conducting research is necessarily impartial. Your purpose is to discover the truth by objectively examining evidence and testimonies available to you and to present your findings as clearly and honestly as you are able.

Sometimes, however, your professor may want not only your findings, but the inferences you can draw from those findings as well. You might, for example, be expected to find out all you can about the recreational facilities in a certain area in order to make recommendations about how those facilities should be expanded or improved to meet the recreational needs of the area's inhabitants. Such an assignment requires more than the objective collection of data; it also demands that you interpret those data, make value judgments, and arrive at conclusions. In cases like this you could employ the inductive method (Chapter 5) by first describing the data you have found and then moving to a conclusion about it, or you could use the Toulmin method of reasoning (Chapter 5) by making your claim, giving your data, and explaining the warrant between them.

Finally, research can be used to persuade as well as inform. The research itself must still be an objective endeavor, of course, not a selective search for only those sources that support a predetermined conclusion. The very process of doing research on your topic, however, may convince you of the factual or moral superiority of one particular way of conceptualizing your topic. If this is the case, you may very well want to present your findings in such a way that your readers become similarly convinced.

In your investigations into the recreational facilities topic, for instance, your findings may lead you to believe that the area under study already offers adequate recreational opportunities to its inhabitants, and in fact, a great many residents are not taking advantage of the facilities currently available. You have come to believe that instead of spending money on additional playgrounds, picnic areas, and sports arenas, the area needs to advertise its present recreational facilities more effectively. In your paper, then, you would want to show your audience the evidence you have uncovered to support this position, and persuade them that your conclusions are financially sound, practically feasible, and supported by observable facts. Part of the persuasiveness of your paper would come from your objective and thorough examination and conscientious documentation of the available evidence.

If your conclusion is a controversial position, an inductive presentation is often more effective than one in which you make your claim first because it enables you to lead the readers to a position they do not hold initially. If the readers for your research report on recreational facilities initially favor a plan for creating new parks and playgrounds, you would probably want to present and document your research findings first, so that your readers, after being presented with the evidence, would be likely to arrive independently at the same conclusions you have.

Of course, persuasive discourse requires a closer relationship between writer and reader than do other types; you are addressing a specific set of readers and asking them to adopt a particular point of view or course of action. Consequently, although persuasive research papers are still data-based, they are usually characterized by a more personal tone than that of a strictly informative research paper.

RESEARCH

SETTING UP A SEARCH STRATEGY

Only when you have defined your research question and identified your audience and purpose are you ready to begin your research. You need to start it early because doing careful research is usually time consuming. Often the process of collecting data proves to be longer and more extensive than you originally think it will be, because some of the sources you consult may direct you to still other sources of information, which you were not previously aware of.

You may find it helpful to make a sort of research outline that lets you know what sources you need to consult and the order in which you need to work through those sources. If you need to send away for information or arrange to set up interviews or conduct surveys, you should take care of these time consuming research tasks first so that you will have time to think about your information before you write your paper. Another rule of thumb for scheduling your research tasks is to begin with those sources that you believe will provide the most direct and specific information. This way, if your research takes longer than you expected it to, you won't find yourself having to begin writing your paper without having consulted your most valuable sources.

Finally, it's a good idea to set a deadline when you must stop researching and begin writing. Once you are well into your research project, you may discover new leads on sources that you were not previously aware of. However tantalizing these leads are, you may not be able to follow up on them, simply because you are running out of time. If this is the case, you might plan to extend your research project further at a later date and mention in your conclusion or in an informational note the potential value of these sources for further study.

COLLECTING DATA: PRIMARY AND SECONDARY SOURCES

The researcher's next step, of course, is to collect data to either prove or disprove the validity of the hypothesis—or to answer the research question.

In much of the research you do for college classes or on the job, you will be concerned with two types of information sources—*primary* and *secondary* sources. Roughly speaking, the difference between them is the difference between first-hand and second-hand information. Primary sources are those that deal most directly and contemporaneously with your topic; often they are indistinguishable from your topic itself. Secondary sources, on the other hand, generally help you to interpret your primary sources.

In a research paper for a history course, for instance, your primary sources might be newspaper articles or government documents published during the historical period about which you are writing. Your secondary sources, on the other hand, might be books or articles written by historians who have also consulted those same primary sources in their analyses of the same historical period or event. In a research paper for a literature course, your primary sources would be the literary texts that you are interpreting or criticizing, or the letters and journals of the author whose works you are investigating. Secondary sources would include books, articles, lectures, and reviews by literary critics on the subject of your paper. In a scientific research paper, your own observations and experiments might be your primary sources, whereas the reports of other scientific investigators on a similar topic might constitute secondary sources.

If you are asked to do "original research," you must to some extent concern yourself with primary sources, since secondary sources are really someone else's research on the same or a related subject.

SEARCHING OUTSIDE THE LIBRARY

Although a great deal of academic research takes place in the library, this is by no means the only place where you can collect data for college research papers. In fact, there are times when non-library sources can provide more direct, specific, and up-to-date information.

Suppose, for instance, that you were trying to find out what the possible side effects might be of the feline leukemia vaccine. Because the vaccine is a very recent medical development, you might have a hard time finding published information about it in books or even journals and newspapers. You might, however, have access to some experts on the subject—namely veterinarians or faculty members from a school of veterinary medicine, who could answer some of your questions in personal interviews. These individuals would make a much better choice as first sources to consult than would library materials. In addition to the information they could provide in interviews, experts of this sort can often provide you with leads on other useful sources—for example, brochures from pharmaceutical companies or professional reports about the use of the vaccine.

Other potentially helpful non-library sources include television and radio broadcasts, pamphlets published by local community or special-interest organizations, and city and local government record offices. You might even have a topic that calls for you to perform your own empirical research, either by conducting polls and surveys or by scientific experimentation.

If you feel that collecting data through empirical research is in order for your research paper, you must be aware that there are certain ground rules to follow in designing questionnaires and conducting surveys. You will need to minimize the influence that the questions themselves might have on your subjects, and be aware of the extent to which you can generalize from your sample to a larger population. Your professor may be able to give you some guidelines on these and related matters or to direct you to other people or printed sources that can give you the information you need. Researchers in science and social-science disciplines should be familiar with this sort of research technique and may be willing to assist you.

USING THE LIBRARY

Another type of research—one which is important in all disciplines from the sciences to the fine arts—is library research. Scientists conducting experiments to determine the effects of microwave radiation on the reproductive behavior of rodents, for instance, will consult articles and research reports on the same and related subjects in order to decide how to set up their experiments so as not to duplicate what has already been done. They will also consult the literature in their specialized field to help them interpret their findings or to lend support to their conclusions. And finally, they will use this literature in order to place their own research within the broader range of radiation studies and thus demonstrate the contributions their particular study makes to a larger body of knowledge.

Similarly, a literary critic researching a question such as, "Is there a distinctly feminine form of the *Bildungsroman*?" might conduct an investigation by consulting novels categorized as *Bildungsromane* as well as by reading books, articles, and addresses in which other literary critics have responded to the same or a similar question.

Library research deals with printed or taped sources of information that you can locate by consulting various indexes, bibliographies, and catalogues in the library. Your topic, of course, will determine which kinds of library resources are most helpful to you. For topics that are very timely—for instance, legislation currently being enacted by Congress, or the latest developments in computer technology—newspapers, periodicals, and documents are more likely sources of information than books or reference works such as encyclopedias, which require considerable time for the publication process.

PERIODICALS

Usually the most recent issues of newspapers and periodicals are shelved unbound, while older issues are bound into individually indexed volumes. Finding articles in these sources requires that you consult special guides or indexes to periodical literature. The most general of these, and one that is apt to be found in even small libraries is the *Readers' Guide to Periodical Literature*. You probably learned to use this reference work in high school or as a college freshman; if you didn't, you can easily teach yourself to use it now by following the instructions printed at the beginning of each guide, or you can ask your reference librarian for assistance. Other useful and more specialized guides and indexes to periodicals usually also include instructions for use and are valuable sources of references to information contained in specialized academic journals. Some of the major indexes of this sort are the following:

Applied Science and Technology Index
Book Review Digest
Business Index
The Education Index
Engineering Index
Humanities Index
Index Medicus
MLA International Bibliography
Public Affairs Information Service
Social Sciences Index

If your library is fairly large, it probably has many more specialized indexes and bibliographies which can be located by consulting the subject cards in a special catalogue for reference works.

When you find a citation in an index or bibliography for an article that sounds helpful to you, copy down the full citation; this will not only help you locate the article itself, but will also save you time later on when you need to compile a bibliography for your paper. The same is true, of course, for citations to material from other sources as well—newspapers, documents, books, pamphlets, TV and radio broadcasts, interviews, and so forth.

While using bibliographies and indexes is an efficient way to locate periodical articles, you will find that current issues of most periodicals are usually not indexed. If up-to-date information is essential to your investigation, you can use the same indexes and bibliographies to identify those periodicals which are most likely to contain articles on your topic and check the most recent issues in the periodical display shelves.

NEWSPAPERS

The procedure for locating newspaper articles is similar to that for finding information in periodicals. The major index for newspaper articles on national and international topics is the *New York Times Index*. Other important reference works for locating newspaper articles are the *National Newspaper Index,* which lists articles from the *New York Times,* the *Christian Science Monitor* and the *Wall Street Journal;* and *The Newspaper Index,* which lists articles from four major U.S. newspapers: the *Chicago Tribune,* the *Los Angeles Times,* the *New Orleans Times-Picayune* and the *Washington Post.* In addition to national and international news, these four papers give regional news for their areas.

Some newspapers publish their own indexes, which you can use to find articles about your topic, but if this is not the case with the papers that are available to you, you can use one of the three major newspaper indexes listed above to identify the dates when your topic was being covered by the news media and check issues for those same dates in the newspapers you do find in your library.

GOVERNMENT DOCUMENTS

Most large libraries contain a special section for U.S. Government publications, a type of source that can be especially useful to you if you are writing a research paper for history, political science, law, or social science courses. Some government publications are indexed in the public catalogue and are shelved according to Library of Congress or Dewey Decimal numbers. Other, uncatalogued documents are kept in the government documents section of the library, arranged according to Superintendent of Documents numbers. Still others are kept on microform in collections called microform sets. These too are filed according to Superintendent of Documents numbers.

The following are a few of the major indexes you can use to locate government-document publications. In many libraries you will find a number of other indexes as well, and you should ask a librarian for assistance if you have difficulty using them.

U.S. Superintendent of Documents. *Monthly Catalogue of United States Government Publications*
   The Federal Index
   Index to U. S. Government Periodicals

C. I. S. U. S. Serial Set Index
Washington Information Directory

BOOKS

Books or sections of books can also be extremely valuable sources of information for research papers on a wide range of topics. Sometimes you will find entire books listed in the specialized indexes and bibliographies that you consult, but you can compile a more extensive list of potentially helpful books by consulting the card catalogue in your library. Books are indexed according to subject, title, and author cards, but generally speaking, the subject cards will be the most useful to you. To find out how your topic is likely to be indexed in the catalogue, you may want to consult the two volume *Library of Congress: Subject Headings,* which lists all the subject headings and their subdivisions that appear in the card catalogue. When you have identified the subject headings under which you are most likely to find useful information, begin searching for book titles first under the headings that most specifically describe your subject.

USING THE COMPUTER

Ask your reference librarian if your library has facilities for doing a computer search of the literature about your topic, and if it does, whether you can learn how to make the search yourself. Most libraries with such facilities run regular, short training sessions to show their patrons how to use the computer for research. You can learn the rudiments in an hour. If your institution has an extensive library that will enable you to follow up on the leads you get from the computer, you will have an abundance of material to work with.

There are some drawbacks to computer searches, however, and you should be aware of them before you decide to enlist the aid of a computer. First, computer searches are often quite expensive; once you find out how much it will cost, you will have to decide whether the price is worth the speed and thoroughness of a computer search. Secondly, the computer selects articles on the basis of *descriptors*—that is, key words that describe the contents of the article and which are entered into the data base along with the citation. Naturally, these can give only a general description of an article's content; therefore, even though the computer can generate a very long list of articles on the basis of these descriptors, only some of those articles are likely to be of use to you. The process of locating and then reading through all of the sources on the list in order to find the relevant entries can be time-consuming, and you may decide to dig in the library stacks instead.

FOLLOWING UP ON BIBLIOGRAPHY ENTRIES

A good way to expand your search for sources is to follow up on the citations you find in the bibliographies of articles and books that you have found to be relevant to your study. This method of conducting research has a number of distinct advantages that make it common practice among veteran scholars. First, the book or article where the citations appear will usually give you a fairly good idea of their content, so you may be spared some of the time you might otherwise have to spend deciding if a particular source would be helpful to you or not. Second, the frequency with which you find a work cited by others is often an indication of that work's reliability. If you find a particular book or article cited by more than one of your sources, you can be fairly sure that it is itself a credible source, even an important one for you to consult. And finally, following up on bibliographies of useful sources is a fast and efficient way of expanding your search. It is very possible that a single bibliography will yield numerous citations that are useful to you, and you will have been spared the trouble of poring over bibliographies and card catalogues to find them.

SERENDIPITY

However you do your search, remember to cultivate serendipity (Chapter 3). Because experienced researchers know the value of such lucky accidents, they stay alert for them, glancing at the titles of books shelved next to the ones they are seeking, or running their eyes over the table of contents in a periodical that has the article on their prepared list. Your best piece of information may be the one you stumble onto while you are looking for something else.

TAKING NOTES

Sometimes the chore of taking notes for a research paper looms so large that you are tempted to photocopy everything you find, then worry about making sense of it after you leave the library. That's not a good idea, however, unless for some reason you have only limited access to the library. Not only is it expensive, but it also delays the selective skimming you need to do in order to decide which material is usable. Moreover, if you use photocopies you will very likely be tempted to simply underline rather than take notes on what you have read. This practice encourages you to rely too heavily on the original words of your sources before you have digested their ideas and can articulate them in your own words. Photocopying, then, is often a shortcut that actually defeats the whole purpose of research, and in addition can result in inadvertent plagiarism.

Many people prefer to take notes on index cards because cards are easier to sort and reorganize than sheets of notebook paper. Others, however, prefer to keep all of their notes in a notebook because in this form they are easier to carry around and are less likely to get lost. Whichever method is most comfortable for you is the one you should use. In either case, you should be sure that you always include the source along with the substantive information you record in your notes. And get in the habit of writing down the page numbers for *all* the information you record, whether you directly quote that information or simply refer to it in a summary or paraphrase. If you don't keep track of page numbers at this stage of your research, you will find yourself spending a lot of time later going back to the library to hunt for page numbers.

In general, your notes will be of two kinds: summaries and quotations. For the most part, you should keep direct quotations to an absolute minimum. Overusing them means that you are letting your sources speak for you rather than synthesizing their information into a unified and coherent presentation of your own. Two questions to ask yourself when you are trying to decide whether to quote your source directly or summarize its content are:

○ Are the *words* themselves important to the development of my argument or to the clarity of my information?
○ Do the words or phrases of this source have a special rhetorical effect that will strengthen my presentation?

Only if you can answer yes to at least one of these questions should you consider quoting the material directly. In any other situation you should summarize the information in your own words. Usually it is best to summarize material when you have finished reading the source and can set it aside. In this way you avoid the temptation to slip into the author's own words or to change them so slightly that for all practical purposes you are quoting directly. There is an educational advantage to this kind of note taking as well; if you are able to summarize the important points from your source without having to look at the text, then you know that you have assimilated and understood the text's information and made it your own. You will therefore not run the risk of producing a research paper that is merely a patchwork quilt of other people's words and ideas with little of your own thinking to tie it all together.

When you write summaries in your notes, you might use the abbreviated form in which you take notes for your classes, but don't condense them so much that you will be puzzled when you try to read them a week later. The time you take to put your information into a sentence instead of a phrase might save you a trip to the library later on. When you want to use direct quotations, be sure to copy them down *exactly* as they appear in the original text, preserving all punctuation marks, spelling, and capitalization. Use quotation marks around them in your notes so that you'll know later on that they are someone else's words. It's also a good idea to indicate in your notes who is responsible for the quote and why, where, and when the words were spoken or written. This kind of contextual information will be helpful to have when you need to integrate the quotation into your own text. Remember also to put in the ellipsis points if you leave out any part of the quotation.

You will also need to set up a system for organizing your notes. At the very least, number them as you work so you will be able to arrange them in the same order in which you did your research. Or you may develop a system of classifying them according to subtopic, perhaps by using code words to remind you which part of the paper various notes will apply to. Having your notes arranged in such divisions will help you to see how the parts of your paper are going to develop and may be the first step you take toward deciding upon a plan of organization for your material.

WRITING

CHOOSING A PLAN OF ORGANIZATION

The best plan for organizing the material for your paper is the one that most directly answers the research question you set out to investigate. Usually you will begin to develop a sense of how this can be accomplished as you are collecting material from your outside sources. But regardless of how well you have your plan in mind at this point, it is probably best to make some sort of "road map" that reminds you where you are going as you write your paper. This in turn will help you keep your readers from getting lost or wondering what point you are trying to make.

Probably the best way to get all of your material under control is to make a rough outline based on the categories you have set up for your notes. If you do this, you will establish the broad classifications that you are going to cover in your paper and find a logical way to order them within the paper. Write those classifications down. Then make notes about subpoints you want to cover in each category. As you work, develop a series of general assertions that can serve as the framework for your paper. And as you outline, think about what subheadings you might use to keep your reader on the track.

You can also create a plan of organization by capsuling, summarizing, or writing an abstract for your paper. (See section on abstracts in Chapter 11). If well done, an abstract or summary can give you substantial guidance for organizing your paper and for beginning to articulate some of the points you want to make as a result of your research. Supplemented by a list of secondary or supporting points, a comprehensive abstract will serve you just about as well as an outline. And it gives an added advantage; after you finish, you can incorporate it wholly or in parts into your paper, or you can include it as a sort of preface to your paper to give your readers advance signals about what they will be reading. Do not, however, rely on an outline preface to do the work of a good introduction—that is, to inform your reader of your research question, your reasons for attempting to answer it, and your methods of searching for that answer.

MASTERING THE CONVENTIONS OF DOCUMENTATION

If you have used the bibliographies or endnotes provided in books and articles to expand your own search for information, you already know how helpful clear documentation can be to a fellow researcher. As you document your own paper you need to keep two main purposes in mind: first, you must let your readers know where you found your material, and second, you must make it possible for them to locate and use that material if they wish.

USES OF DOCUMENTATION

Documentation is not merely a matter of using the correct forms of footnotes and bibliography entries or the right form of citation in your text. The text of your paper itself can also contribute to the clear documentation of sources. When you do research you gather *ideas* from your sources as well as direct quotations and statistical information, and your readers should always be able to tell exactly which contributions are your own comments, interpretations, and evaluations, and which are reports of someone else's words and ideas. The text of your paper should enable a reader to make these distinctions easily.

In the case of direct quotations, where you use someone else's exact words, you supply this information partly by using quotation marks (for quotes that are shorter than four or five lines) or block indentation (for quotes of five lines or more). But you also need to supply an introduction to material gathered from outside sources, whether you are paraphrasing that material or quoting it directly. Introductory comments should precede the cited material even though the material itself may be enclosed in quotation marks or indented, and even though you provide a footnote or parenthetical citation. Such introductory comments not only make it clear exactly which information is being documented, they also help to integrate quotations smoothly and gracefully into the text of your paper.

The following example is flawed by a number of documentation errors:

> Until very recently it was thought that penguins were unique among the members of the animal kingdom, being the only birds to exhibit altruistic behavior. "In order to test the icy waters for seals, the penguin's deadliest enemy, one penguin risks her own life by plunging off the ice floe to where her predators possibly lie in wait."[1] If this penguin survived and the area thus appeared to be free of seals, the rest of the flock would follow her into the water. Later on, however, ornithologists came to believe that they had misinterpreted this particular aspect of penguin behavior.[2] "It appears now that the lead penguin is not willing to sacrifice herself for the survival of her group. Quite the contrary, our observations have led us to believe that she does not even jump into the water of her own accord, but rather that she is actually *pushed* into the water by the other members of her flock."[3]

The writer uses direct quotation where simple paraphrase or summary would easily suffice. In neither of the two direct quotations in this passage is it necessary to preserve the original wording of the sources cited and in fact, there are points at which the original wording is awkward when combined with the text of the paper—because of sense shifts, for example, or shifts in point of view. In addition, a reader cannot tell where the information in the paragraph comes from. The quotation marks around the second and the last sentences indicate that someone other than the writer of the paper is responsible for these sentences, but who is that someone? Is he or she a reliable source? Is the same source responsible for both of these quoted sentences? Or are there two different sources? Or are there three sources—one for each of the directly quoted sentences and one that is referred to by the superscript number 2? If more than one source is involved, how are they related, and why is the writer of the paper using them together in this paragraph? Who are the "we" referred to in the last sentence which relates "our" observations?

The reader might be able to find the answers to these questions by studying the footnotes at the bottom of the page or the endnotes which follow the paper, but such an interruption in the reading of the text is awkward, annoying, and unnecessary. The next example eliminates the unnecessary use of direct quotation and incorporates the missing information smoothly into the text. Citations are still needed, of course, because the writer of the paper is presenting information that originally appeared in another source, and because readers may need full citations in order to conduct follow-up research.

Until recently it was thought that penguins were unique among the members of the animal kingdom, being the only birds to exhibit altruistic behavior. Arctic explorers Nichole and Sam Thigpen reported in the log of their 1951 expedition that the lead penguin from a flock would apparently risk her own life for the survival of the flock by jumping off the ice floe into the water where arctic seals, the penguin's mortal enemy, were possibly lurking. If this penguin survived, the other birds in the flock would follow her into the water, assured that no predators were lurking there (Thigpen and Thigpen, 1951). Fifteen years later, however, when the Thigpens, accompanied by ornithologist Jordan Jones, made a second arctic voyage, they revised their earlier assessment of penguin behavior, claiming that the lead penguin was not at all willing to sacrifice herself but rather that the group seemed willing to sacrifice *her* to insure their survival. This conclusion resulted from the explorers' observation that the lead penguin apparently did not jump into the potentially seal-infested water but instead was actually pushed by her followers (Jones, Thigpen & Thigpen, 1966).

STYLES OF DOCUMENTATION

Styles of documentation vary considerably across disciplines, so you will need to find out which style is preferred in the field for which you are writing. If you are writing your research paper for a college course, your professor will probably indicate which type of documentation he or she wants you to use and which style manual you should consult if you have questions. Another way to find out this kind of information, particularly if you do not have a professor's guidance, is to check the form of notes and bibliography entries in articles published in scholarly journals in the field you are researching.

The two most common styles of documentation currently being used in academic writing are those endorsed by the MLA (Modern Language Association) and by the APA (American Psychological Association). Both of these organizations advocate the use of *internal documentation* with an accompanying bibliography. This means that brief citations appear in parentheses in the text immediately after the cited material. (See the citations that appear in the second example of the penguin text, above.) These parenthetical citations contain enough information to enable the reader to identify the cited sources from the bibliography, where full bibliographic information is given for all of the sources the writer has consulted in order to write the paper. According to this documentation method, footnotes, at the bottom of the page, or endnotes, at the end of the paper, are only used to give explanatory material that is somehow tangential to the text. For instance, a footnote to the penguin text might be something like this:

Until recently it was thought that penguins were unique among the members of the animal kingdom, being the only birds to exhibit altruistic behavior.[1] Arctic explorers . . .

1. The possibility that parrots might also demonstrate altruistic behavior by alerting their owners to potential dangers has often been put forward by parrot owners, but has been discounted (1982) as anthropomorphism on the owners' part by zoologist Soraya Mashat.

The information about parrots is included in the paper because the author feels that it may be of interest to readers who themselves might argue that parrots are altruistic birds or who have a more general interest in animal behavior than is addressed by the paper. Nevertheless, the parrot information does not appear in the text proper because the focus of the paper is penguins, not parrots or birds in general.

The major differences between APA and MLA styles are matters of punctuation, capitalization, and arrangement of material in bibliographic entries. The following examples demonstrate how the same source would be cited in a paper using APA style and one using MLA style:

APA   This approach corresponds to the frequently cited theory that scientific revolutions come about through paradigm shifts (Kuhn, 1970, p. 79).

MLA   This approach corresponds to the frequently cited theory that scientific revolutions come about through paradigm shifts. (Kuhn, p. 79).

Notice that the APA system uses the date of publication in the parenthetical citation, whereas the MLA usually does not. MLA style would cite the publication date only if it were necessary to distinguish this work by Kuhn from another included in the bibliography—let's say, one that was published in 1962. Regardless of which system you were using, you would need to provide a full citation to Kuhn's text in the bibliography at the end of your paper.

BIBLIOGRAPHIC ENTRIES

A bibliography is a list of all the sources that helped you formulate the content of your paper, whether or not you have cited them specifically in your text. Bibliography entries for both MLA and APA systems are arranged alphabetically according to the first word of the entry, which is usually, but not necessarily, the last name of the author. The following bibliography entries for Kuhn's book illustrate the major difference between APA and MLA styles:

APA   Kuhn, T. (1970). *The structure of scientific revolutions.* Chicago: Univ. of Chicago Press.

MLA   Kuhn, Thomas S. *The Structure of Scientific Revolutions.* Chicago: Univ. of Chicago Press, 1970.

Notice that MLA uses the author's full first name and middle initial, while APA uses the first initial only. Also, the placement of the publication date is different for each style; APA places it in parentheses immediately after the author's name, while in the MLA format the date is the final piece of information given, followed only, in some cases, by the page numbers of articles or chapters within the book being cited. Finally, MLA style uses the same capitalization conventions that you would use if you referred to a title in a prose passage, whereas APA style eliminates all capitalization in titles except for first words, words following a colon or period in the title, and proper nouns and adjectives. Similarly, titles of "short" works such as articles, poems, or short stories are enclosed in quotation marks in MLA style entries; in APA entries, the quotation marks are omitted.

Obviously, when internal documentation is used, there is no need for a separate set of endnotes containing bibliographic information. If you use a documentation system that uses superscript numbers in the text and provides bibliographic information in separate footnotes or endnotes, remember that there are a number of differences between notes and bibliographies. Most important is the fact that bibliographies are full listings of all sources consulted, whereas footnotes or endnotes contain citations for only those sources that are directly referred to in the text. Alphabetization provides the organization for bibliography entries, whereas superscript numbers provide the order by which notes are arranged. This means that bibliographies only list each source once, whereas the same source appears in footnotes or endnotes as often as it is cited in the text of the paper. Finally, depending upon the documentation style you are using, you will find various differences between the format and mechanical conventions of endnotes and bibliography entries. Because these distinctions are often minor and difficult to remember, you would be wise to use a handbook that gives you examples of note and bibliography-entry forms to follow.

The sample bibliography entries listed below illustrate the current MLA-endorsed form. For more unusual types of entries, you should consult the

1984 edition of the *MLA Handbook for Writers of Research Papers*. For APA-approved forms, consult the *APA Publication Manual*.

A BOOK WITH A SINGLE AUTHOR:
King, Martin Luther. *The Trumpet of Conscience*. New York: Harper and Row, 1968.

A BOOK WITH TWO AUTHORS:
Clark, Kenneth and Harold Howe. *Racism and American Education*. New York: Harper and Row, 1971.

A SIGNED PERIODICAL ARTICLE:
Walters, Samuel K. "Survival Tips for Third World Travelers." *Journal of the American Travel Association* 12 (1985): 32–40.

AN UNSIGNED MAGAZINE ARTICLE:
"The Saga of Boston." *Ebony,* Oct. 1974: 110–114.

AN ARTICLE IN AN ANTHOLOGY:
Britton, James. "The Composing Processes and the Functions of Writing." *Research in Composing*. Ed. Charles Cooper and Lee Odell. Urbana, Ill.: NCTE, 1978. 13–28.

A TRANSLATION:
Vygotsky, Lev. *Thought and Language*. Trans. Eugenia Hanfmann and Gertrude Vakar. Cambridge: MIT Press, 1962.

A PAMPHLET:
Subterranean Termite Control Proposal. Key no. 33020. Terminix International, 1985.

GOVERNMENT DOCUMENT:
United States. Congress. Joint Committee on the Investigation of Alternative Energy Resources. *Hearings*. 104th Cong., 1st sess. 11 vols. Washington: GPO, 1983.

MATERIAL FROM AN INFORMATION SOURCE SUCH AS ERIC:
Agha, Shahid Ali, ed. *Academic and Cultural Exchange Programs Between the U.S. and Asian Countries*. International Education Conference Proceedings, 1985. ERIC ED 247 6855.

LETTER TO THE EDITOR:
Pruitt, Oscar K. *Raleigh Gazette* 43 (1984): 11–12.

TELEVISION PROGRAM:

Ludwig von Beethoven: A Musical Biography and a Salute to Genius. Narr. Nancy Ratner. Writ. and Prod. Patricia Vivian. NBC. Famous Figures in the Arts. KCRG, Portland, Oregon. 27 May, 1984.

AN INTERVIEW:

Tepley, Peter. Telephone Interview. Aug. 30, 1984.

HELP WITH DOCUMENTATION

If you must write a complex and important research paper, you may want more help than you can find in this comparatively short section on the forms of documentation. If so, in almost any library you can get books that treat the topic comprehensively and will give you additional sources that you can consult. Perhaps the best complete and useful book is:

Jacques Barzun and Henry Graff. *The Modern Researcher.* 3d ed. New York: Harcourt Brace Jovanovich, 1977.

Other possible sources are the following:

Lester, James D. *Writing Research Papers: A Complete Guide.* 2d ed. Glenview, Ill.: Scott, Foresman, 1978.

Memering, Dean. *Research Writing: A Complete Guide to Research Papers.* Englewood Cliffs, NJ: Prentice Hall, 1981.

Spatt, Brenda. *Writing from Sources.* New York: St. Martin's Press, 1983.

Walker, Melissa. *Writing Research Papers: A Norton Guide.* New York: W. W. Norton, 1984.

11 ◇ Writing on the Job

Among the most common kinds of writing that you may have to do if you work for an agency, an institution, or a corporation are grant proposals, nontechnical reports, case studies, abstracts, and papers for oral presentations.

GRANT PROPOSALS

In recent years a kind of writing that must be both informative and persuasive has become increasingly important, the grant proposal. Most scientific researchers find that they must know how to write grant proposals if they expect to get their projects funded; so do educators who want to improve the teaching of writing, welfare workers who want to help their clients practice better nutrition, or librarians who want to encourage reading in their community. In fact, in many fields, almost any person who wants to start a project that involves more than routine activity will find that he or she can do so only by successfully applying for a grant.

A small industry has even grown up to help people master the art of "grantmanship." Self-styled experts contract to write grants for people, professional journals advertise expensive two- or three-day seminars on writing grants, and bookstores stock manuals with detailed instructions and indexes to a variety of funding agencies.

But you do not have to be an expert or a specialist to write a satisfactory grant proposal. The format is not mysterious, and the information you need is generally available from libraries or institutional offices. The agencies and foundations that give grants usually provide specific instructions about what you should include and provide a checklist and cover sheet to help you put the proposal together. So all the applicant really needs to have, besides patience and determination, is the ability to write clear, well-organized prose and some appreciation of the psychology of grant writing.

PURPOSE OF THE PROPOSAL

When you write a grant proposal, you have one overriding purpose: *to persuade someone to give you money.* In order to do that, you are going to have to convince the reviewers at the foundation or agency to which you are applying that you have a good idea for solving an important problem, that you have or can get the facilities and equipment for handling the task, and that significant benefits will result when you do solve the problem. In short, you have to do a major selling job, but you have to do it with rhetorical restraint and with an abundance of evidence and sound reasoning to support your request. Your task is made easier, however, because the conventions for grant proposals are well established and not difficult to follow.

PRELIMINARY PLANNING

Your first concern in writing a grant proposal should be to give yourself plenty of time. The research, legwork, writing, budget preparations, and so on will take longer than you think. Next, find out what kind of agency or foundation might be interested in funding it. If you are going to apply to a local organization, you need only get its application form and instruction booklet, but if you are unsure about where you should send the proposal, go to the library and ask for a directory of organizations that award grants. Not only the names are listed, but also the specific areas of interest and special requirements of the grant-awarding agencies. If you are connected with or close to a university or college, you can also get an abundance of information from its office for research.

Narrow the list of possibilities by noting the kind and size of grants that foundations make, and choose the funding organizations whose records show that they have been supporting projects similar to yours. Learn as much as you can about those organizations because their reviewing committees are going to make up the audience for which you will be writing.

Your next step should be to rough out a plan for your proposal. Although the sequence of items for the proposal is probably prescribed by the funding institution, write yourself some notes about how you are going to present that sequence. The key items you should think about are 1) the description of and rationale for the project. 2) the procedures to be followed in carrying out the project, 3) a description of facilities available for working on the project or research, 4) the credentials and experience of the people who will work on the project, and 5) the budget. You are not ready to start writing the proposal until you can draft a paragraph or two for each of those items, and until you can summarize what other people have already done in the specific area you plan to work in. And you should have done the research for such a summary before making your decision to apply for the grant. This planning is important because even though you will undoubtedly be doing some creative thinking and revision as you write the proposal, grant proposals must be carefully structured documents. One cannot depend on inspiration to guide their development.

THE BODY OF THE PROPOSAL

Although the forms provided by most grant-giving agencies specify that your proposal should begin with the title and an abstract, you will probably want to postpone writing those items until later. Begin your proposal with the description of your project, your reasons for proposing it, and a discussion of what you hope to accomplish with it. Obviously this introductory section of the proposal needs to make a good impression on your readers so as you write it keep in mind those cardinal virtues of good writing: significance, unity, clarity, economy, and vigor. Get to the point immediately by stating what you intend to do. Follow up with an explanation of why you think it is worth doing, what other people have done in similar work, and what you expect your project to accomplish that has not previously been done. You may need several paragraphs or several pages to cover all these points adequately, but try to write as succinctly as possible.

Suppose, for example, that you are an architect who has joined with a historian, an engineer, and a landscape architect to get funds to restore an old deteriorated market-area to its original condition. In the introductory section of your proposal you would identify and objectively describe the building you want to restore, describe the work that needs to be done and the approximate cost, give reasons for restoring the building—historic value, effect on surrounding area, attraction for tourists, and so on—describe and cite the effects of similar projects in other cities, and explain your belief that a restoration project that emphasizes the city's heritage can become the focus of an economic renaissance of the inner city. You should strive for a vigorous and confident tone in this section, and should include pertinent details and enough references to previous or similar projects to sound competent and knowledgeable.

If the first section of the proposal is important because it describes what you want to do and explains why you want to do it, the second section is equally important because it must explain *how* you plan to accomplish your goal. Now you need to prove that you are competent and knowledgeable by outlining practical procedures for carrying out your plan and giving a realistic timetable for the work. If your proposal involves research, specify how you are going to collect your data, how you will control variables, and what analytical methods you will use. Experienced reviewers will take a particularly close look at this part of the proposal because they do not want to waste money supporting a project that sounds worthy but is poorly designed.

When you describe the facilities available to you for working on the project or carrying out the research, and give the credentials and experience of your coworkers, you are also establishing your credibility as an applicant. This section needs to be written carefully and honestly to show that you have the qualifications to spend the foundation's money productively. It is a good idea to include a biographical data sheet for each person who will be working on the project.

How you conclude your proposal depends on the kind of format prescribed by the organization giving the grant. If it gives no specific guidelines use your best judgment. If the proposal runs to fifteen or twenty pages, you may need to help your reader by reiterating the key points in a summary section and stressing the innovative features of your proposal. Reviewers of such proposals tend to favor projects that explore new territory or suggest fresh approaches.

MAKING A BUDGET

The first time you estimate a budget for a grant proposal you should seek help if you can because such budgets must include hidden costs that are easily overlooked, items like contributions to retirement funds and to the operating expenses of the institution whose facilities you will be using. Almost every college has employees whose job it is to help applicants with their grant proposals; don't hesitate to use them. If you are drawing up a complicated budget and you do not have access to such people, try to find a professional consultant and pay for an expert opinion. At the very least, get a book on preparing grants and look at sample budgets.

But no one else can actually make a budget for you. Only you can estimate how long your project is going to take and consequently what the outlay for salaries will be; how much computer time you may need and how much should be allotted for travel expenses; what kind of equipment you will need and what it costs to operate it. And don't make vague estimates. Finding out what things cost takes leg work and lots of phone calls, but you need to figure all your expenditures as accurately as possible before you take your tentative budget to a consultant. Remember too that you should explain and justify any large item that does not seem self-explanatory.

Resist the temptation to underestimate your costs because you feel that an accurate statement seems so high that you would not have a chance of getting the grant. The people who review grants have a good idea what expenses on a project should run, and if you turn in a budget that is unrealistically low they will question your professional competence. If necessary, it would be better for you to scale down the scope of your proposal than to look financially naive.

WRITING THE ABSTRACT AND TITLE

When you have finished the budget and finished any other sections that the grant announcement may specify, you are ready to write your abstract and title. Since they will introduce your proposal to the reviewers, you need to write them very carefully so that they will succinctly and accurately state your case. The title should be as brief as you can make it and still be explicit. For example, "A Proposal to Make an Authentic Restoration of the Farmers' Market and Surrounding Square in Dayton, Ohio," or "A Study of the Effect of Syntactical Arrangement on the Readability of Nonfiction Prose."

The following excerpt from a 1977 grants announcement pamphlet from the National Institute of Education sums up the guidelines you should follow in writing your abstract.

Abstract: The narrative should be succinct, non-technical description of the research. It should not exceed 250 words, and should be so clearly written that the following questions could be answered by reading it.
Paragraph (a) What is the specific purpose of this study? What information is being sought?
Paragraph (b) Who needs it? Why is it desirable to do this?
Paragraph (c) How is the study to be conducted (a non-technical description of the general methodology)?
Paragraph (d) What difference might the results make?—to whom?

See pp. 223–27 for more detailed information about writing abstracts.

GETTING A SECOND OPINION

When you have finished writing the proposal and have revised it into a second draft, give a copy to a knowledgeable person whose judgement you trust. Ask that person to put himself or herself in the role of a reviewer and to read your proposal with a skeptical eye, looking particularly for omissions, oversimplifications, or unwarranted claims. Also ask that person to mark any places where the language is vague or confusing or where the writing is biased or inflated. If you can get two qualified and patient people to read the proposal, so much the better.

THE FINAL DRAFT

When you have the proposal in final form, have it professionally typed, leaving good margins, making sure to follow to the letter the instructions provided in the grant applications. Mark the internal divisions with headings and subheadings and make sure charts and diagrams are labeled. Proofread the final copy meticulously to be sure that it looks as good as it can, and get the necessary number of copies made by a reliable service so that they will not be streaked or dim. In other words, make sure that the packet of paper that is going off to represent you makes the best possible appearance.

EVALUATION CRITERIA

Reviewers for granting agencies and foundations judge proposals they receive on these criteria:

- Is the research or project relevant to the goals of the agency?
- Is the proposal innovative?
- Is the problem the proposal addresses important?
- Do the applicants show knowledge of previous work in this area?
- Is the proposal project adequately designed?
- Are the people who will work on the project competent?
- Can the project be carried out in the estimated time?
- Is the budget accurate and reasonable?
- Are the facilities and equipment for the project adequate?

If your grant proposal meets all these criteria and is clearly and carefully written, you stand a good chance of getting your money.

NONTECHNICAL REPORTS

Just as scientists, architects, or anthropologists who thought they were going into non-writing professions often find themselves spending a surprising amount of time writing grant proposals, so nurses, social workers, bankers, or psychiatrists—in fact, perhaps the majority of professional people—find that they spend an unexpected amount of time writing reports. The report is the essential document of the business and professional world, the instrument used to inform and instruct colleagues and customers and to furnish data on which people can make decisions. So important are business and technical reports that many specialists give courses and write textbooks on technical report writing; if you think you will do a great deal of that kind of writing, you will probably want to take such a course in college or after you go to work in your profession. But people who are called on to write occasional nontechnical reports, such as a summary of a public opinion survey or an analysis of customer complaints, can learn to write successful reports by following the ordinary procedures for writing good prose.

CHARACTERISTICS OF REPORTS

Reports are about facts. The person who reads the report you have written does not expect to find out what you feel, think, believe, fear, or hope; he or she expects to find out what you have investigated, observed, experienced, or read about. Meteorologists giving a weather report to a pilot do not say that it's a "nice day." Rather they say, "Clear skies, visibility unlimited, no turbulence in this area." From those facts they may draw an inference and add, "Should be a good day to fly," but strictly speaking, the inference is not part of the report.

Reports are based on data; we use them as we use reference books to find out information. Consequently the person who writes them should:

◦ Focus on the material under discussion.
◦ Not express personal emotions or opinions.
◦ Not argue or seek to persuade.
◦ Not use a literary style that calls attention to itself.[1]

Writing a good report becomes an exercise in restraint. It also becomes an exercise in practicing subtle communication skills, because although

1. Guidelines adapted from James Kinneavy, *A Theory of Disclosure* (Englewood Cliffs, N.J.: Prentice-Hall, 1971), 88.

writers must seem not to be thinking about their audiences, they must be acutely aware of the audience. Equally, though they must not draw attention to themselves directly, in an indirect way they must convince their readers that they are conscientious and reliable reporters.

THE AUDIENCE FOR REPORTS

People who write reports usually do so on assignment and for a specific audience. For example, a biologist might write a report on an environmental study for the state Fish and Game Commission; a nurse might write a report on her study of a pregnant diabetic woman for the instructor of her course in clinical practices; a navy officer might write a report on needed ship repairs for the head of the United States Bureau of Ships. Or a report might be as simple as a one-paragraph summary of snow conditions at Taos written for people who want to go skiing. The authors of any of these reports need to identify the intended audience as precisely as possible to decide just what it is they want to get from reading these reports. Because writers do not want to waste their audience's time by telling them more than they want to know, they need to assess carefully their audience's level of expertise. They also need to think about how much specialized vocabulary they can use; for the right audience it can act as a kind of shorthand, but for the wrong one it can impede communication.

Moreover, a writer needs to think about how many people will read the report and how much influence they have, how long it will last, and what actions might be taken on the basis of its contents. The snow report becomes useless after a day and is thrown away; the environmental study will reach readers at several levels of power, will serve as the basis for recommending action, and will almost certainly be filed and stored. For those reasons it should be comprehensive, documented, and written in a language nonspecialists can understand.

The language of the report should have an objective tone that puts considerable distance between reader and writer and avoids the pronoun *you* unless it seems required by the context. But writing this way should not mean writing stuffy, dull, or pedantic prose, nor should it mean writing an inflated and passive style loaded down with derived nouns and prepositional phrases.

The writer stays in the background with this kind of fact-centered, objective style. This effect is enhanced by using neutral language and by using few adjectives. But writers who try to sound objective simply by not using the pronoun *I* may create more problems than they solve. For one thing, they can wind up with a contrived and awkward style: for example, "This investigator visited Padre Island on June 25" or "The author of this report interviewed the patient." The writer trying to avoid *I* may also fall back on passive constructions and abstract subjects that can confuse the reader: for example, "The feasibility of the study was determined by the investigator" or "This material was decided to be relevant." Nearly any reader would prefer that an author write, "I interviewed the patient" or "I collected the data."

Moreover, using *I* in a report identifies you as a writer who deserves credit for having compiled and written a good report. And you can strengthen that impression by routinely citing and consistently documenting all your sources. You can furnish your documentation either with footnotes written according to the style prescribed by a reputable style sheet or by giving your references in parenthesis within the body of the text (see pp. 203–9).

THE STRUCTURE OF REPORTS

Reports usually function as documents that are meant to convey information to readers so that those readers can do a job. Therefore, the report should be organized to serve the reader.[2] How can you put it together so that the reader can grasp the contents as quickly and efficiently as possible? When you are writing reports on assignment, often the reader has already decided on a plan of organization and gives you specific instructions on how to carry it out. For example, the instructions for major term reports in one school of nursing stipulate that those reports must be organized as follows:

Abstract
Introduction, including statement of the problem
Review of the literature
Clinical application Conclusions
Recommendations

A business firm or government bureau might insist that writers reporting to them follow this kind of plan:

Abstract
Introduction
   a. Statement of the problem
   b. Purpose of the report
   c. Description of method used

---

2. Gordon H. Mills and John A. Walter, *Technical Writing*, 4th ed. (New York: Holt, Rinehart and Winston, 1978). 292.

Body of report
  a. Detailed description of procedures carried out
  b. Explanation of findings
Conclusions
  a. Detailed summary of results

Such formulas can simplify your task and serve as useful models for many kinds of report-writing assignments.

Sometimes, however, you must develop your own pattern of organization for a report. When you do, start with a comprehensive and accurate title that lets your reader know precisely what to expect from the report. (Remember also that the title controls how the report will be filed.) Immediately after the title page, many readers expect to find an abstract that summarizes the content of the report. Even if an abstract is not required, it is a good idea to include one for a long paper, as it helps to focus the reader's attention and makes it easier for him or her to follow your report. (See pp. 223–27 on writing abstracts.)

Begin the report itself with an introduction that states the issue or problem to be addressed, the purpose of the report, and the method used for carrying out that purpose. Such a businesslike opening may seem dull, but it is important nevertheless. Readers want to know from the start why they should read the report and where and how you got your evidence.

How you organize the body of the report will depend on your purpose for writing and the kind of material you are dealing with. If you are writing a research report about a diabetic pregnant woman, you would probably want to use a narrative form to recount the woman's case history, give the results of your interviews with her, and document the clinical symptoms as the pregnancy advanced. Then you would want to review the literature of what is known about the complications that diabetes causes for pregnant women, apply that information to the case you are writing about, and give your findings. In the conclusion of your paper, you would summarize what you learned.

In other kinds of reports writers usually begin by stating the most important information in the report. Although this kind of organization may not work well for persuasive or entertaining writing because it takes away the writer's chance to build to a climax, it does work well for factual explanatory writing. Readers for that kind of writing do not want to be intrigued and kept in suspense; they want to know results. If those results are important to them, they will probably read on to find out how they were obtained; if they are not, they do not have to spend any more time on the document.

After you have given the crucial information, you must then go on to discuss your procedures and findings in detail. Not everyone who is interested in the main content of your report will read the detailed discussion, but it should be written carefully nevertheless so it can be referred to if needed. Finally, most reports that run to more than a few pages should conclude with a summary that restates the main idea.

CASE STUDIES

Professionals in many fields must spend substantial time writing reports that deal not with impersonal data but with the behavior of people. Those reports are called *case studies* or *case histories,* and the methodology for education and research in a number of disciplines depends heavily on the case study method. Some of these fields are clinical and experimental psychology, social work, speech therapy, medicine, and the social sciences such as anthropology, sociology, and linguistics. People working in any of these fields of study need to know how to write case studies; so do nurses, policemen and emergency medical technicians.

Because most case studies are not highly technical, people who must write them usually do not have to take special training. They can manage quite well if they do their best to write clear, concise, economical, and unpretentious prose and keep in mind a few extra guidelines that apply particularly to case studies. The first is to learn to write objective, concrete descriptions of behavior without expressing personal opinions or biases and without judging; the second is to learn to write comprehensive reports that include all pertinent information; the third is to learn to anticipate the specific questions that the case study is expected to answer.

The first guideline is probably the most difficult to follow because most of us have trouble being neutral when we watch or talk to other people. We like or dislike them, approve or disapprove of their behavior even when we don't know them. Yet a linguistic researcher or social worker or clinical psychologist cannot afford to let emotion or bias appear in a case study that is supposed to be only a description. The professional responsibility of these people is to record what they observe, are told in an interview, or learn through a test. So a child-guidance counselor should write "Philip is below normal weight and height for his age and expresses fears about being attacked by larger boys in his grade," not "Philip is pathetically thin and intimidated by larger boys." And a cultural anthropologist should not describe an Indian tribe as "brave and proud," but should instead describe the behavior of the tribe. When a person is collecting and recording data, even data about human beings, that person must take great care not to prejudice the reader with connotative language.

Inexperienced report writers sometimes also have trouble deciding how much information they should include in their case studies. A writer does not want to waste the reader's time or mix irrelevant information with important data, but good case studies must include all *pertinent* facts. So the question becomes "What is pertinent?" and the answer must depend on the purpose of the case study.

In the case study of the diabetic pregnant woman, the nursing student needed to include information about the woman's weight, diet, economic circumstances, educational level, family hitory, marital status, and previous pregnancies, as all these matters affected her ability to control her diabetes. On the other hand, in behavioral psychologist Stanley Milgram's study of destructive obedience in a laboratory situation, the author gives only this much information about the subject:

> The subjects were 40 males between the ages of 20 and 50, drawn from New Haven and the surrounding communities. Subjects were obtained by a newspaper advertisement and direct mail solicitation. Those who responded to the appeal believed they were to participate in a study of memory and learning at Yale University. A wide range of occupations is represented in the sample. Typical subjects were postal clerks, high school teachers, salesmen, engineers, and laborers. Subjects ranged in educational level from one who had not finished elementary school, to those who had doctorate and other professional degrees. They were paid $4.50 for their participation in the experiment. However, subjects were told that payment was simply for coming to the laboratory, and that the money was theirs no matter what happened after they arrived.[3]

For the rest of the case study, Milgram reported only the subjects' actual behavior in the laboratory. Any other information about them was not relevant to the study.

Your ability to select data that are appropriate for your case study and to exclude information that is irrelevant or peripheral reveals a great deal about your competence in your field. If you cannot discriminate between useful and irrelevant data or judge how much evidence you need for a particular study, you signal to your reader that you probably don't know what you are doing. As one expert puts it:

> As to pertinence, the report writer should not collect data for its own sake, use it indiscriminately, or use it to pad or make the report appear to be more professional.[4]

Finally, people write case studies in order to answer questions that someone has asked or will ask about their work. You should be able to figure

---

3. Stanley Milgram, "A Behavioral Study of Obedience," *The Norton Reader,* revised, shorter edition, ed. Arthur Eastman et al. (New York: W. W. Norton, 1965), 195.
4. Jack Huber, *Report Writing in Psychology and Psychiatry* (New York: Harper and Row, 1961), 13.

out what those questions will be if you know *why* they are being asked. For example, the emergency medical technician who is writing a case history of a patient brought in from an automobile accident knows that the doctor wants information that will help in treating the patient, so the technician reports on blood type, location of injuries, temperature, blood pressure, treatment given, and so on. However, a rehabilitation counselor who is writing a case history in order to help that same person qualify for a state training program knows that the screening committee wants to know whether the person can be helped and why the state should subsidize rehabilitation. To answer those questions the counselor needs to include information on the person's injuries, educational level, financial status, and so on. The kind and amount of information the audience needs will vary with the task; thus people who write case studies may need to develop their sense of audience and purpose even more highly than other writers do.

ABSTRACTS

THE USES OF ABSTRACTS

People who write regularly in business, industry, technology, medicine, or the academic profession learn to write abstracts early in their careers because the abstract is an essential part of the communication system in their field. A good abstract summarizes an article or report so succinctly and accurately that readers can quickly infer from the abstract the essdential content of the longer work. Ideally, an abstract should have the same relationship to an article or report that an architect's model of a building has to the completed building. Just as one should be able to tell from an architect's model what a building is going to look like, one should be able to tell from an abstract what a report is going to say. And both the model and the abstract should be self-contained units, independent miniatures that make sense even when separated from the piece they represent.

PROMISSORY ABSTRACTS

Abstracts are important because they can serve both writers and readers in a number of different ways. First, a writer can draft a preliminary abstract of a paper as a way of beginning to think about the topic and as a device for organizing those ideas. This kind of abstract is preliminary and flexible, more like a working sketch for a building than like a model, and usually it will be substantially revised or discarded altogether when the paper is completed.

Second, a person may write an abstract that is a kind of promissory note to a program chairman or an editor. In this kind of abstract the writer sketches out the paper or report he or she plans to write and submits it for consideration. If the editor or chairman thinks the projected piece of writing is worth publishing or presenting, and if the person submitting the abstract has good credentials for writing such a piece, the abstract may be accepted, and the writer is then committed to produce the paper. People who submit abstracts of this kind must follow them faithfully when they write their final paper because they have made a contract on the basis of the abstract.

People who will be working in fields in which one earns rewards by publishing or presenting papers should master the art of writing these promisory abstracts as part of their professional training. For one thing, you can often meet a deadline for papers or program proposals if you can submit an abstract by the deadline rather than a completed paper. Second, once an editor or program chairman accepts your proposal on the basis of an abstract, you have made a commitment and established a deadline that will force you to write the paper. Many of us need that kind of motivation.

SUMMARY ABSTRACTS

Abstracts written after a report has been completed can also serve several purposes. First, they may appear at the beginning of a report and function as a kind of preview that lets the reader know what to expect; this is particularly useful for long reports. Second, they can serve as a summary that will give an administrator or executive necessary information in a capsule form. Third, the abstract can consult it quickly. It could also also appear in the program for a professional meeting to help participants decide if they want to hear the full paper, or it could be published in a journal or catalog of abstracts so that people searching for material on the topic could determine whether they want to read the full-length paper.

Since an abstract serves so many functions, you can see why it is so important that it be well written. One authority claims that it is the most important part of a paper:

> The first significant impression of your report is formed on the reader's mind by the abstract; and the sympathy with which it is read, if it is read at all, is often determined by this firs impression.[5]

5. Christian K. Arnold. "The Writing of Abstracts," in Sparrow and Cunningham, *Practical Craft,* 264.

WRITING THE ABSTRACT

Good abstracts are hard to write because they must accurately compress so much information into compact form, and because they should be written in easy-to-understand, nontechnical language. Moreover, your method of writing an abstract will differ when you are writing a promissory abstract and when you are writing a summary abstract. The first is creative, the second analytical.

WRITING THE PROMISSORY ABSTRACT

When you are writing a promissory abstract, you need to go through a process similar to the one you use at the preparatory stages of writing a paper. First write down the main idea or thesis that you want to present; then brainstorm and take notes on all the possible points you might want to make about that thesis. On a new page jot down souces and examples that you might use to illustrate your thesis. Finally you might write down why you think the paper you propose is worth presenting or why an audience would be interested in reading or listening to what you have to say.

Then, beginning either with a statement of your main idea or a listing of the main evidence on which you base your thesis, write a first draft that answers these questions: What are you going to say? Who needs to know it or what is the information good for?

Don't worry too much about length on this first draft. Get down as much information as you think the program chairman or editor needs in order to make a judgment about the paper. You can trim it to size later. In the second and third drafts cut if necessary, and simplify and polish your writing because this abstract will not only represent the content of your paper but will also be a sample of your prose style. You can present your credentials for giving the paper on a separate sheet or in a letter.

Here is a sample of a promissory abstract that I turned in for a conference:

ABSTRACT

By using interviews, questionnaires, the examination of drafts, and conference with editors and by drawing from work already done on the writing process, I plant to investigate the writing processes of ten professional writers of nonfiction. From this research, I hope to validate and expand tentative hypotheses that I have constructed about how such writers work and to gather a body of information about the craft of writing that will be available in itself and will also benefit other scholars working in this very new area. These data may also be useful to scholars interested in more general theories of creativity.

The program chairman accepted the paper, and four months later I wrote it.

WRITING THE SUMMARY ABSTRACT

In writing a summary abstract, you need to start by carefully rereading your paper and underlining the main points. Write brief summaries of each section in the margins as you would if you were studying for an exam on the paper; star the most important points you make. Then make a rough outline of the paper so that you see your plan of development at a glance; you may realize, for instance, that although you spent twice as long developing point one as you did in developing point two, the points are equally important and you do not need to give twice as much space to point one in the abstract. It is because of concerns of this kind that you should not try to write an abstract by stringing together sentences that summarize each paragraph.

One way to write an analytical abstract would be to put down the most important idea in your paper in the first sentence and in two or three more sentences develop that idea. Then decide how you arrived at your thesis, giving specific details if it seems useful. Finally, summarize the implications of your thesis or hypothesize about what its value might be. Another approach might be to begin by stating the problem you are writing about, then describe the approach you used to work on it, and finally give your results. And there are other ways to write an abstract. You do not have to organize abstracts in the same way that you organize your papers, but that method may be easier when you first start to write them.

As you write the abstract, think of the audience that may read it. Use terminology that an intelligent nonspecialist could understand and try to make your summary so complete that someone outside your field could understand what you are talking about. Keep reminding yourself that this abstract should be a self-contained piece of writing that can stand on its own when it is separated from the paper it represents. And when it is separated, it represents your thought, so you want it to be an intelligible, cohesive piece of writing.

For example, here is how a summary abstract of the proposal for the university day-care center mentioned in earlier chapters might look:

> The university needs to sponsor and subsidize an on-campus day-care center for the children of university faculty and students for several reasons. Such a center would help the university to attract more of the large number of women who are returning to school to finish their educations or improve their professional credentials. It would also help the university to attract and hold young men and women faculty who favor working for institutions who offer good family-related fringe benefits. In

addition, providing good on-campus child care would improve the performances of both students and faculty by reducing their anxiety about their children not being adequately cared for.

The university should provide funds for this facility on a prorated basis because doing so would help to compensate for its not providing paid maternity benefits or leaves of absence for faculty. Further, data from countries that provide this kind of care indicate that such facilities contribute to better infant health and to an increase in scholarly productivity among women faculty. The cost of such a center would be approximately $250,000 for the next year, and $120,000 a year after that. These costs would be met partially by tax money and partially by user fees.

LENGTH OF ABSTRACTS

Although one might think that the length of a finished paper would control the length of the abstract that represents it, such is not usually the case. More often, directions will say that abstracts should not exceed 250 words; that is, one double-spaced page typed in pica type. If the directions say "no more than one page" rather than giving the number of words, you can squeeze in another fifty words by using elite type. It is probably best not to single-space an abstract.

When you begin writing abstracts you will continually face a conflict between keeping the abstract short enough and putting in everything that you think should be included. Inevitably you compromise and your abstracts will never come as close to being perfect miniature reports as you would like. Neither do anyone else's. But as you continue to write them and to realize what a necessary professional tool they are, you will develop an instinct about what to include in an abstract, and your task will gradually become easier.

PAPERS FOR ORAL PRESENTATION

Many young professionals find early in their careers that they must often write papers for oral presentations. When they give such papers, they are not necessarily giving speeches; rather they are apt to be reading a paper to explain a concept or theory, offer a solution to a problem, or present the results of their research. They want to make a good impression, but too often they do not succeed because they have written their papers for a reading audience rather than for a listening audience. The needs of the two audiences are significantly different.

LENGTH OF PAPERS

The first concern of any person writing a paper to be given orally should be its length. How much time are you going to have? Ten minutes? Twenty-five minutes? You need to find out and take the limit very seriously. If you are asked to be on a ninety-minute panel with two other speakers, don't assume that you will have 30 minutes to read your paper. almost certainly the panel will start late, the moderator will need time to introduce the panelists, and time should be allowed for questions an discussions. You should really count on only twenty minutes to present your paper, and you should plan accordingly. And even if you are the only person who will be delivering a paper at a meeting, usually you should condense what you have to say into thirty minutes or less. Only the most charismatic speakers can hold their audience's attention much longer than that.

The best way to be sure your paper is not too long is to read it into a tape recorder, and time it as you play it back. That way you can judge the pace to decide whether you are reading too quickly. Probably you will be. Most of us tend to forget that the audience needs time to absorb our points as we make them. If you don't have a tape recorder, read your paper out loud and time it. Then start cutting if you have to. If, however, the paper doesn't quit fill up your allotted time you should probably resist the temptation to expand it.

When you are writing a paper for oral presentation, you should figure on at least two minutes to read one double-spaced, 250-word page in pica type. (For elite type, adjust accordingly.) If you can read 125 words in a minute—and that's a fairly brisk pace—you can plan on twenty minutes for a 2,500-word, ten-page paper. And if your finished paper runs 11½ pages, you should not plan to rush through it to meet your deadline. Better to cut it back to the proper length and read it effectively.

STRUCTURE FOR ORAL PRESENTATIONS

Once you know the time allotted for your paper, you can decide how to restrict your topic to one that you can treat adequately in the 2,500 or 3,000 words to which you are limited. You have to make your points clear the first time; therefore you should have fewer points. Because an oral presentation usually requires that you explain and illustrate your points more fully, you need to insert signal sentences to preview or summarize for your audience or to keep them headed in the direction you want to go. Remember that your audience cannot go back and reread earlier paragraphs.

Whether you choose to begin your oral presentation with a lead-in paragraph to catch your audience's attention, or with a direct statement announcing your thesis depends partially on the occasion and partially on your personal style. I usually prefer a direct opening statement that announces my thesis and starts my audience off in the right direction. For example:

> Students who are struggling to become writers can profit in several ways from learning about the behavior of professional writers.

I would then go on to list those ways in order to give my audience a preview of what they are about to hear. After the preview I would work my way through my points, being careful to use words such as *first, second,* and *next,* and strong signal words such as *therefore* and *consequently* to help my audience anticipate what is coming. And I would downshift frequently, particularly when I wanted to illustrate an abstract statement.

By using these obvious devices you help your listening audience move with you through your paper. You map it for them and provide directional signals. You can even reinforce your signals by writing your main points on a blackboard as you go. You can also punctuate your presentation with slides or charts shown with an overhead projector. These visual aids not only reinforce the content of your paper, but they give your listeners intermittent breaks in which to absorb the content.

ORAL STYLE

When you begin to work on the second or third version of a paper that you will be reading aloud, try to think in terms of an oral style. As one authority points out, that means several things:

> In other words, a style adapted to the ear instead of the eye means that the language will be simpler to grasp; unusual terms will be used more sparingly, and when they are used will be spoken more clearly and defined more fully; ideas will be paced more slowly; and the development will be less condensed than in writing.[6]

Three more strategies that will make your prose more listenable have already been discussed in earlier chapters as ways of making your writing more readable. The first is to construct sentences in which there is frequent closure. That is, try not to write long strung-out sentences whose meaning cannot be grasped until one reaches the end.

---

6. Roger P. Wilcox, *Communication at Work* (Boston: Houghton Mifflin, 1977), 454—55.

Second, when possible rearrange many of your sentences into the agent/action pattern. Since that pattern gives readers strong signals about what to anticipate, it should also help listeners. If your agent is a concrete or personal subject, so much the better.

Third, check your writing to see if it is overburdened with derived nouns—words ending in *ity, -ness, -tion,* and so on—or with a disproportionate number of prepositional phrases.

In addition, a listening audience will particularly appreciate a speaker who uses metaphors and analogies as explanatory devices. Probably nothing helps an audience grasp a vague or elusive concept as quickly as having a writer clarify it by a graphic comparison. In fact, listeners may remember the central point of a paper primarily because of the visual image triggered by an apt analogy. Thus if you were to form an image for your listeners by comparing the process of transmitting documents over telephone lines to someone transmitting braille impressions through the fingers you help them to understand a complex process.

Finally, it seems useful to point out that "reading a paper" should not mean that you stand before your audience with your eyes focused only on your paper. People do not like to feel that they are being read to. To counteract that impression, you should study your paper ahead of time so that you can look up from it frequently. Make eye contact with your audience to let them know that it is important to you that they understand what you are saying. And if you have written your paper specifically with that listening audience in mind, probably they will.

WHAT BUSINESS PEOPLE THINK ABOUT GRAMMAR AND USAGE

Early in the book, I included acceptable usage among the most important qualities of good writing. Indeed, some professionals seem to be bothered almost as much by shaky grammar as by shaky thinking. Benjamin De-Mott, not only a fine writer but an English teacher, recalls one rock-ribbed senior partner in a law firm who was obsessed with what he thought was the misuse of the comma. Obviously such quirks are impossible to predict. But are there any particular errors that most managers and professional people find especially troublesome? Oddly enough, there has been little research into this question.

In September of 1979, I sent a questionnaire to 101 professional people, asking them how they would respond to lapses from standard English usage and mechanics in each of sixty-three sentences if those sentences apeared in a business document that came across their desks. The eighty-four people who responded to the questionnaire represented a broad range of professionals: engineers, judges, bankers, attorneys, architects, public relations executives, corporation and college presidents, tax analysts, investment counselors, and a U.S. Congressman, to name just a few. They ranged in age from thirty to seventy, but most were in their late forties and early fifties. Twenty-two were women, and sixty-two were men. No English teachers were included in the survey.

Each of the sixty-three sentences on the questionnaire contained one error in usage or mechanics, and the respondents were asked to mark one of these responses for every sentence: Does Not Bother Me, Bothers Me a Little, Bothers Me a Lot. The last question asked for an open-ended comment about the most annoying feature they encountered in writing they had to read.

After tabulating all the responses to the sentences and reading all the comments, I came to these conclusions about how professional people react to writing that they encounter in the course of their work:

⋄ Women take a more conservative attitude about standard English usage than men do. On every item, the percentage of women marking "Bothers Me a Lot" was much higher than the percentage of men.

⋄ The defects in writing that professional people complained of most were lack of *clarity, wordiness*, and *failure to get to the point*. They also complained strongly about poor grammar, faulty punctuation, and bad spelling.

⋄ The middle-aged, educated, and successful men and women who occupy positions of responsibility in the business and professional world are sensitive to the way people write. Even allowing for the strong possibility that they were more than normally conservative in responding to a questionnaire from an English teacher, most professionals seem to believe that writers should observe the conventions of standard English usage.

Responses to the individual items on the survey indicate, however, that these professional people clearly consider some lapses in usage and mechanics much more serious than others. Here is the way they ranked items on the questionnaire:

⋄ Extremely serious lapses from the standard:
Incorrect verb forms ("he brung," "we was," "he don't").
Double negatives.
Sentence fragments.
Subjects in the objective case ("Him and Jones are going").
Fused sentences ("He loved his job he never took holidays").

Failure to capitalize proper names, especially those referring to people and places.

A comma between the verb and complement of the sentence. E.g., ("Cox cannot predict, that street crime will diminish").

◇ Serious lapses from the standard:

Faculty parallelism.

Subject-verb disagreement.

Adjectives used to modify verbs ("He treats his men bad").

Not marking interrputers such as "However" with commas.

Subjective pronouns used for objects ("The Army sent my husband and I to Japan").

Confusion of the verbs "sit" and "set."

◇ Moderately serious lapses:

Tense shifting.

Dangling modifiers.

Failure to use quotation marks around quoted material.

Plural modifier with a singular noun ("*These* kind").

Omitting commas in a series.

Faulty predication ("The policy intimidates applications").

Ambiguous use of "which."

Objective form of a pronoun used as a subjective complement ("That is her across the street").

Confusion of the verbs "affect" and "effect."

◇ Lapses that seem to matter very little:

Failure to distinguish between "whoever" and "whomever."

Omitting commas to set off interrupting phrases such as appositives.

Joining independent clauses with a comma; that is, a comma splice.

Confusion of "its" and it's."

Failure to use the possessive form before a gerund ("The company objects to *us* hiring new salespeople").

Failure to distinguish between "among" and "between."

◇ Lapses that do not seem to matter:

A qualifying word used before "unique" ("That is the *most* unique plan we have seen").

"They" used to refer to a singular pronoun ("Everyone knows *they* will have to go").

Omitting a comma after an introductory clause.

Singular verb form used with "data" ("The data *is* significant").

Linking verb followed by "when" ("The problem is when patients refuse to cooperate").

Using a pronoun "that" to refer to people.

Using a colon after a linking verb ("The causes of the decline are: inflation, apathy, and unemployment").

EXERCISES

1. In a paragraph of about 100 words, analyze the audience you would have for the following writing tasks. How knowledgeable would they probably be, and what would they want to get from reading your writing?
   A. A grant proposal is the National Endowment for the Arts to ask for $165,000 to support a project to give dancing lessons to children whose families cannot afford such lessons.
   B. A report to the commanding officer at the Air Force Academy on cadets' attitudes toward the honor code of the Academy.
   C. A case study to the probation officer about a thirteen-year-old child who is on probation from the juvenile court for stealing a car.
   D. A speech for the California Bar Association on the possible effects of legislation to limit liability in medical malpractice suits.
2. Choose articles from three magazines that vary widely in their focus, for instance, *National Geographic, Psychology Today,* and *U.S. News and World Report.* Read the articles carefully and take notes on points in each one that should be included by a person writing a summary abstract of the articles.
3. Analyze the purpose you would have in writing a promissory abstract for a paper you propose to give with one of the following titles:
   The Declining Use of Migrant Labor in the Food Processing Industry
   Existential Despair in the Novels of Joan Didion
   Using the Care of Pets to Raise Self-Confidence in the Mentally Retarded
4. In a paragraph of no more than 150 words, analyze the specific problems you would anticipate in giving an oral presentation under the following circumstances:
   A. Presenting a report on the effect of high interest rates on real-estate sales in your area.
   B. Presenting the results of a psychological experiment on factors found to produce writing anxiety in high-school students.
   C. Presenting to the directors of a corporation an oral report on new underwater oil drilling operations completed in the past year

SUGGESTED WRITING ASSIGNMENTS

For each paper, begin by defining and analyzing your audience and your purpose. Specify the characteristics of your audience that are important to keep in mind as you write, and state the specific points that your audience would want to get from reading your paper. Also state clearly and in some detail what you hope to accomplish by writing the paper. When appropriate, give your paper an accurate and descriptive title.

TOPIC 1:

Choose a foundation or government agency that gives money for research projects that will contribute to knowledge in a particular field or help to solve a serious problem. Some of the best-known foundations are these:

Ford Foundation
Rockefeller Foundation
Exxon Corporation
Sloan Foundation
National Institute for Education
National Endowment for the Humanities
National Endowment for the Arts
National Science Foundation

Write a grant proposal for one of these projects:

A. A film on nutrition for young mothers in poverty areas.
B. An expedition to New Mexico to record oral history of a tribe of Indians.
C. An educational film on the most effective methods of birth control. Specify a particular audience.
D. Outreach project to teach illiterate adults to read.
E. Research project to develop a chemical to eradicate mesquite from pasture land.
F. A film to teach high-school students how to establish and use credit.

TOPIC 2:

Write a report in response to one of these assignments:

A. A credit report on a family applying for a home loan. Give the wife's and husband's ages, employment, income, education, and whatever other features you think may be pertinent.
B. A report for an urban planning class showing how population patterns in your area have changed in the past ten years.
C. A report for the state legislature showing the comparative salaries and ranks of men and women in higher education in your state.

TOPIC 3:

Write a case study about one of these individuals. Specify the purpose of the study:

A. A twenty-one-year-old man who was blinded in an industrial accident on his summer job is applying for a tuition grant and financial assistance in order that he may return to college.

B. A family who wants to adopt a child from an ethnic group different from its own.

C. A forty-five-year-old displaced homemaker whose husband has died, leaving her with no insurance and only a small income. She has no marketable skills so she is applying for admission to a city retraining program offered for women who want to return to school. The program offers subsidies to ten such women each year.

TOPIC 4:

Choose an article from a magazine in which you are particularly interested and write a 250-word abstract that reflects the tone and emphasis of the article and functions as a miniature model of it. Attach a copy of the article to your paper.

TOPIC 5:

Write a promissory abstract to go with one of the oral presentations suggested under Topic 6.

TOPIC 6:

Write a talk on one of these topics, to be presented under the circumstances specified for each one:

A. A talk for a summer orientation meeting on campus. Try to get incoming students interested in working in campus organizations and politics.

B. A radio talk to persuade young people of the benefits of individual exercise programs and show why they are superior to team sports.

C. Prepare a talk for a local service club—Rotary, Optimists, Altrusa, or American Association of University Women—and outline your plan for increasing voter participation among eighteen to twenty-five-year-old people.

D. As education officer for your corporation, give a talk to a group of executive trainees on the value of learning to write clearly and effectively.

E. Present a ten-minute summary of the results of your research on how the typical middle-income family in your area spends its food budget.

INDEX